DATE			

And the Poor Get Children

And the Poor Get Children

Radical Perspectives
on Population Dynamics

Edited by Karen L. Michaelson

Monthly Review Press
New York and London

Library of Congress Cataloging in Publication Data

Main entry under title:
And the poor get children.
 Bibliography: p.
 Includes index.
  1. Population—Addresses, essays, lectures.
2. Family size—Addresses, essays, lectures.
3. Migration, Internal—Addresses, essays, lectures.
I. Michaelson, Karen L.
HB871.A5   304.6'01   81-38389
ISBN 0-85345-522X   AACR2
ISBN 0-85345-553-8 (pbk.)

Monthly Review Press
62 West 14th Street, New York, N.Y. 10011
47 Red Lion Street, London WC1R 4PF

Manufactured in the United States of America

10 9 8 7 6 5 4 3 2 1

Contents

6 Contents

Notes on the Contributors

Barbara C. Aswad is a professor of anthropology at Wayne State University in Detroit. She is the author of two books and several articles on Middle Eastern peasant organization and Arab communities in the United States.

Marianna Edmunds studied anthropology at the University of Connecticut at Storrs and spent two and a half years in Kenya and the Sudan. She now works as a journalist in New York and has an enduring interest in African affairs.

Eric H. Larson took his Ph.D. in anthropology at the University of Oregon and has done fieldwork in Columbia, the Solomon Islands, and Spain. He currently teaches anthropology at the Evergreen State College in Olympia, Washington.

Mahmood Mamdani took his Ph.D. at Harvard University and has taught at the University of Dar es Salaam, Tanzania, and at Makerere University in Kampala, Uganda. He is the author of *The Myth of Population Control* and *Politics and Class Formation in Uganda*, both published by Monthly Review Press.

Karen L. Michaelson took her Ph.D. in anthropology at the University of Wisconsin, Madison. She has conducted research in Bombay, India on the political, social, and economic life of the middle class; in Afghanistan on development processes; and in the United States on the social and economic impacts of planned change. She has taught anthropology at the University of Louisville and SUNY-Binghamton, and currently holds an administrative position at Eastern Washington University.

Rosalind Pollack Petchesky teaches political science and women's studies at Ramapo College, New Jersey, and is a fellow at the Center for the Study of Human Rights at Columbia University and a member of the Committee for Abortion Rights and

7

Against Sterilization Abuse (CARASA). She is the author of a forthcoming book, entitled *Reproductive Freedom: The Social and Political Dimensions of Birth Control*.

Elizabeth McLean Petras is Assistant Professor of Regional Science at the University of Pennsylvania. Her research and publications focus on Latin American and Caribbean labor migration and the theory of a global labor market.

Sari Tudiver is coordinator of an education and research project on Women and Development for the Manitoba Council for International Cooperation, a nongovernmental organization which funds development projects in Third World countries. In her spare time she teaches women's studies and is completing a dissertation on the political economy of eastern Kentucky.

James W. Wessman studied anthropology at the University of Minnesota and the University of Connecticut at Storrs. He did his dissertation research in Puerto Rico from 1972-1974 and has done fieldwork in Mexico, where he is currently studying on a Fulbright grant. He has taught anthropology at the University of North Carolina and Saint Olaf College in Minnesota, and is the author of numerous articles on the political economy of Puerto Rico. His book, entitled *Anthropology and Marxism*, is appearing this year.

Acknowledgments

The seeds of this book were sown in the summer of 1974, in long conversations with James Brow and David Rosen, fellow post-doctoral students at the Carolina Population Center. I am grateful to them for ideas and inspirations which emerge in numerous places in the text, and to the National Institute of Child Health and Development which gave me the grant to study population and demography at the center. I am also grateful to Alan Howard of the University of Hawaii and the late Steven Polgar of North Carolina for their continued encouragement. I would like to thank the contributors for their patience in the evolution of this volume, and Karen Judd and Susan Lowes of Monthly Review Press for their excellent editorial assistance and guiding hands in the process of producing it.

Introduction: Population Theory and the Political Economy of Population Processes

Karen L. Michaelson

It is a melancholly Object to those, who walk through this great Town, or travel in the Country; when they see the Streets, the Roads, and Cabbin-doors crowded with Beggars of the Female Sex, followed by three, four or six Children, all in Rags. . . . I think it is agreed . . . that this prodigious number of Children . . . is in the present deplorable State of the Kingdom, a very great additional Grievance. . . . I have been assurred by a very knowing American of my Acquaintance in London; that a young, healthy Child, well nursed, is, at a Year old, a most delicious, nourishing and wholesome Food, whether Stewed, Roasted, Baked or Boiled. . . . Children . . . may at a Year old be offered in Sale to the Persons of Quality and Fortune . . . I grant this Food will be somewhat dear, and therefore very proper for landlords; who, as they have already devoured most of the Parents, seem to have best Title to the Children.

—Jonathan Swift, *A Modest Proposal*

The laboring population . . . produces, along with the accumulation of capital produced by it, the means by which itself is made relatively superfluous, is turned into a relative surplus population; and it does this to an increasing extent. This is a law of population peculiar to the capitalist mode of production; and in fact every special historical mode of production has its own special laws of population historically valid within its limits alone. . . .

—Karl Marx, *Capital*

11

The "Population Problem"

Swift's "modest proposal" for reducing the surplus population of Ireland satirizes the exploitation of the Irish peasantry that led to widespread famine and suffering. Today the specter of famine, environmental destruction, and world catastrophe is the justification for equally "modest proposals" to deal with the problem of overpopulation: triage in foreign aid where only those countries deemed to have the greatest chance of survival are aided, the rest being abandoned to famine (Paddock and Paddock 1975), and control by the elite of reproductive processes, using force if necessary. Yet in Swift's day, famine in Ireland more likely resulted from increased cultivation of the potato than from "overbreeding": "Irish peasants under the British overlordship had little choice over their subsistence crops; this was determined not by population pressure but by the economic constraints to which peasants were subject" (Kleinman 1980: 78). When the potato crop failed, the peasantry suffered. The same is true with the "tragedy of the commons," which Hardin (1968) describes: the British peasants supposedly destroyed the common land by overuse; but the loss of the commons was a direct result of the seizure of land by those with power. "Wastes and fens were enclosed by commercial interests who obtained title with unlimited rights of ownership . . . the cost in human misery was high, due not so much to the growth of population . . . but to the manner in which social change was effected. . . . Excluded from access to the commons, the working people were proletarianized, their livings subject to the decisions of others, and those others were not kindly folk" (Kleinman 1980:269).

Today, during the devastating drought and famine in the African Sahel region, cited as a model of the consequences of overpopulation and land abuse, the export of crops from the stricken areas increased in some countries even as the local population starved (see the *New Internationalist* 1975:5). More generally, according to Bonnie Mass, the production of cereal crops has actually doubled and corn yields per acre have tripled over the past twenty years, while the world's population has increased by less than 50 percent (1976:113). Yet despite this increasing agricultural abundance, the catastrophic conditions forecast by many population theorists—hunger, lack of housing, premature death—have long been the fate of many in developing countries. What is excluded from the idea of "too many mouths to feed" is an analysis of the social classes who consume great quantites of the world's goods, and the historical circumstances that have led to the expropriation of surplus value in much of the world. Thus, while Mexico produces fresh strawberries and tomatoes for the tables of North America, its own supplies of beans, rice, and corn, the staples of poorer households, are in short supply. The point of view expressed by the contributors to this book is that overpopulation is not a matter of too many people, but of unequal distribution of resources. The fundamental issue is not population control, but control over resources, and the very circumstances of life itself.

As noted in the quotation from Marx cited above, capitalism itself encourages population growth. Contrary to much of classical economics, surplus population—that is, the number of people who are unemployed or underemployed—arises not because of natural increase outstripping resources but because the accumulation of capital, which this very population makes possible, allows investment in such things as automated machinery, which makes the people superfluous. Their superfluous numbers serve to drive down wages, thus increasing profit. And yet the laboring population continues, seemingly irrationally, to reproduce in great numbers. This is also a consequence of capitalist production, however, for as people are themselves divorced from the means of production, they are left with only their labor to sell. To increase their income, the poor must produce more laborers per household. Thus, while the rich can reinvest capital and get richer, the poor can only "get children." High birthrates are therefore not the *cause* of continued poverty; they are a *consequence* of it.

A Brief History of Population Theory

Malthus, the Eugenicists, and the Rising Tide of the Poor

Thomas Malthus, writing at the dawn of the industrial era, saw the unemployed and the poor as obstacles to the perfectability of society: through their promiscuous reproduction they brought increased misery and suffering, and their growth would soon outstrip the capacity of society's resources to support them. Rather than improve institutions that might alleviate the lot of the poor, as had been the suggestion of late-eighteenth-century thinkers like Godwin, Malthus felt that "systems of equality which try to alleviate economic distress are self-defeating" (Overbeek 1974:42). Malthus wished to abolish the Poor Laws, which provided some slight relief to the masses and which, in his view, simply encouraged them to reproduce. However, the theories of Malthus were disregarded as British productive capacities expanded, and the demand for cheap labor increased. In England, with the introduction of machinery and the extensive utilization of child labor, the poor were given a direct incentive to procreate in order to take advantage of the new opportunities for selling their labor power (Coontz 1957:63).

The next major period of concern with overpopulation occurred between World War I and World War II. This time, however, the emphasis was not on the potentially great increase in population that placed undo stress on the limited means of subsistence, but on the composition and character of those sectors of the population that were felt to be "over-reproducing." Like Malthus, the eugenicists focused on the birthrate of the poor, but they added the concept that this growing population was biologically inferior to the wealthy. Through a distortion of Darwin's theory of natural selection, supporters of the eugenics movement condoned sterilization of the poor on "scientific grounds" to prevent the overall deterioration of the human genetic stock. Many eugenicists joined forces with the growing numbers of supporters of birth control.

The issue of birth control should be distinguished, both conceptually and historically, from that of population control, which is the action of more powerful groups to control the reproduction of others (Gordon 1977). The movement for birth control in the United States was initially part of a radical movement in which women struggled to gain control of their reproductive processes. Margaret Sanger, for example, began preaching birth control as a working-class issue, and in the 1930s socialists were actively involved in the distribution of information and contraceptive technology as a means of furthering the liberation of working-class women. Rosalind Petchesky, in this book, points out that those concerned with population control coopted the use of the term "birth control" to soften their image. When Sanger turned to the wealthy to support her cause, she ultimately joined forces with those who sought to limit population growth among the poor on racially motivated grounds (Mass 1976:28).

The eugenicists' cause was also stimulated by the influx of immigrants between 1920 and 1930, which provided cheap labor for U.S. factories, but which also represented a potential source of social and political unrest. During the Depression, the population control movement prospered, as the growing ranks of the unemployed fed these fears. In 1942 the Birth Control Federation was established, becoming the International Planned Parenthood Federation in 1948. Tied closely to the eugenicists in the 1940s, this group later developed close alliances with population policymaking organs at both a national and an international level.

After World War II, the focus of those concerned with controlling population moved overseas, where unrest in some developing countries threatened U.S. access to resources and markets. As Mass argues: "Those nations which imperialists feared would be lost to communist control became known as the 'population powderkegs' of the 'underdeveloped' world. Population control and the ideology of 'overpopulation' fit neatly within the imperialist scheme of effecting a greater rate of exploitation in industrial development" (Mass 1976:36). While this may oversimplify the processes of domination and exploitation within the capitalist world order, there is no doubt that Western bourgeois "development" theorists perceive population growth as the major obstacle to economic progress (UN:FAO 1978). As Wessman points out in this volume, the leadership in many of these countries have adopted a similar view of population and unrest.

These arguments are no longer phrased in terms of biological inferiority, the eugenicists having been discredited by the abuses of Hitler's Germany, but rather in neo-Malthusian terms. In this view wages, and thus the standard of living, are determined by the relation of the population to demand for labor: the population has to be reduced in order to raise wages. Yet the limits to population growth perceived by neo-Malthusians are as much social as they are the physical pressure against the means of subsistence. As Tepperman (1979) notes, the fear that the world cannot meet demand is not simply a fear that we cannot feed the world, but that this increased population will desire "positional goods," which provide esteem and satisfaction, as well as the physical means of sustenance. These scarce goods—luxury items—gain value by their unavailability to the majority. If the demand for them were met, they would no longer define places of privilege and power.

Environmental Catastrophe Theorists

Concern over the growing population of the Third World and, to a lesser extent, of the domestic poor, led in the late 1960s and early 1970s to a burgeoning literature on the "population bomb" and the limits to growth. These neo-Malthusian analyses used mathematical models and computer simulations to show that the human race was outgrowing the capacity of the planet to support it (see Carter 1975:222). Looking at the relationship between population and resources, they saw the former as dynamic and the latter as static, and predicted a world of starvation and suffering as a result. For underdeveloped nations, however, the prospect of no growth itself spelled disaster. Analysts from the developed world, foreseeing a decline in their already comfortable standard of living, described in these models conditions that already existed for the overwhelming majority of Third World populations. Popularized through the "ecology movement," the picture of the world's hungry hoards have made population control appear acceptable and even imperative.

Yet famine has occurred in both sparsely populated and densely populated areas. By focusing on the most visible manifestations of famine, these analyses conceal the fundamental causes of the present-day food crisis (Mass 1976:110). The Sahelian drought and famine, for example, was not caused simply by overuse of the land but by historical circumstances that tied the area to world markets and the flow of profits to external investors. A 1979 editorial in the *New Internationalist* (published jointly by Oxfam and Christian Aid) noted some interesting points overlooked by the population planners. "In Haiti, peasants struggle to survive on the precarious mountain slopes whilst fertile valley lands below produce sugar, coffee, cocoa, and alfalfa to be fed to cattle owned by McDonald's hamburger chain" (1979:6). Just as English peasants lost their land when the commons were enclosed, so the peasantry of the Third World has been "marginalized" by interests external to their subsistence. In both cases, labor was released for industrialization and the commercialization of agriculture.

W. H. Pawney of the United Nations Food and Agriculture Organization (FAO) has commented that the world could probably afford to feed ten times its present population. Even now, the world produces more than enough grain to give every person the same caloric intake as the average North American (see the *New Internationalist* 1979:5). If population is out of balance with the environment, it is largely because of inequitable utilization of resources, not the explosion of a "population bomb." As the *New Internationalist* concluded: "The most salient factor of all about the food crisis is that only the poor starve. And they starve because they are poor—because they cannot afford to buy the food that is grown" (1979:5). In this volume, the articles by Edmunds and Mamdani describe situations where subsistence agriculture, which provided for the basic needs of a population, has been replaced by export-oriented agriculture controlled by factors outside the farming region and tied to the world capitalist system. This change has left the areas food-poor, usually with too little cash flowing to the laboring peasantry to enable them to purchase foodstuffs sufficient for their nutritional requirements. Apocalyptic visions of overpopulation and food crisis fail to take into account the ability of international capitalist enterprises to manipulate the food supply.

Political Economy and Population Processes

Analyses that weigh gross economic and demographic variables in the effort to understand the relationship of population to other socioeconomic factors ignore the international context in which population processes are played out, the relationships between and across societies, between the people of the poor nations and those of the industrialized nations, between those in power and those whose lives they control, and even between women and men. A political economy of population processes must take those relationships into account. Such an approach must consider the historical causes and processes that perpetuate those relationships and the impact of those relationships on population growth and movement. For it is the *social* character of human life and of human production that differentiates human societies from those of animals. With social production, humans allocate labor; it emerges as an objective category. With this consciousness, the relationships between different categories of labor, and between labor and the ownership and control of the means of production, become important.

In early societies, when producers controlled the means of production, the laws of population specific to that period required the survival of as many healthy productive members of society as possible. In those societies, births may have been spaced so that healthy infants might survive to productive adulthood. The goal of such "family planning" was not, as some have suggested, an attempt to control population with regard to resources (a justification for perceiving a contemporary, irrational population "explosion"), but to increase the productive population (Faris 1979:436). These population dynamics were justified when producers controlled decisions about their own production, for they could produce as required by their society's needs. However, "as producers no longer totally controlled decisions about their labor potential, they also became subject to modes of production whose dynamics introduced new and different population requirements over which they had no effective control" (Faris 1979:439).

Thus the perspective taken in this book is that population is not an independent variable, which "causes" poverty or underdevelopment, but a *dependent* variable—dependent upon the political economy of particular societies. The starting point for many of the articles is that under capitalism the law of population that is relevant is the law of a relative surplus population. That is, in order for profit to be extracted, there must be an abundance of cheap labor, for labor produces not only its subsistence (the minimum wages needed for the worker and his or her family to survive and reproduce), but surplus value, which is appropriated by capital. Of course, these processes vary with the particular historical conditions under which capitalism developed in various nations worldwide. The processes described here are necessarily general; the cases developed in this book make them more historically specific.

In the simplest terms, the pressure of the superfluous population (the reserve army of the unemployed) against wages lowers wages so that profit increases. But there are, in fact, two forms of capital that accumulate out of the surplus value created by labor over and above its subsistence needs. Constant capital, the outlay for the means of production such as factories, buildings, machines, and raw materials, is created by dead labor—labor previously expended—and does not create a demand for current labor. Variable capital, or wages for the purchase of labor power, creates surplus value (which can be accumulated as either constant or variable capital) and determines the demand for current labor. If population growth is smaller than the demand for labor, wages will rise. But labor itself has limits to its productivity, and if wages rise too high, the accumulation of capital is hindered. In this case, the state may step in with maximum wage laws, as occurred in some of the early stages of capitalism, or it may promulgate pronatalist policies such as family allowances to encourage workers to reproduce in greater numbers or introduce antiabortion laws to further restrict the context of reproductive choice. It is important to note that the state, at different points in time and under different historical conditions, may take a variety of actions, often seemingly contradictory, to achieve its ends. But the actions of states in controlling individual lives with regard to reproduction are not neutral. "The state is not an independent authority, an impartial arbiter between classes whose function is basically to ensure the continuity of society in general . . . [but] it is the supreme coercive power of the dominant class . . . an unfavorable ratio for employers between population and capital will lead to action by the State directed toward solving the problem" (Coontz 1957:112).

In later capitalism, it is constant capital that increases: investment in capital-intensive rather than labor-intensive machinery; variable capital decreases, decreasing the effective demand for labor. Thus labor, according to Marx, produces not just the accumulation of capital, but the very means by which it is made superfluous—the constant capital for "labor-saving" machines. "The process of accumulation now solves the problem of a cheap and abundant labor supply" (Coontz 1957:113). Wages are held in check by the pressure of this surplus population.

Industrialization in the West thus created a demand for fewer and higher quality workers. The family, no longer a productive unit but rather a reservoir for the labor needs of industry, bore the costs of upgrading the quality of labor. The cost of educating a child, the maintenance costs of feeding, clothing, and sheltering that child, and of keeping him or her out of the labor force for a prolonged period, fell heavily on the family and fertility declined.

Population and Uneven Development

While the demand for higher quality labor in the industrialized world resulted in a reduced fertility rate (known as the "demographic transition"), the penetration of industrial capitalism into the Third World had quite the opposite effect. A number of factors—taxation, land expropriation, the introduction of the plantation system, the destruction of handicrafts, and so forth—

all freed the peasantry for wage labor. At the same time, there was an increased demand for low-quality labor as the tertiary sector expanded, and the labor of children was increasingly valuable. As mortality declined with the introduction of immunization programs and rudimentary health care services, fertility rose to meet the new demands of labor; these processes worked to produce an increase in overall population in many Third World nations.

The penetration of capitalism in the Third World was wholly different from its development in the West. In areas of metropolitan capitalism, constant capital increased, was invested in machinery, and thus decreased the demand for labor. But in the Third World, the surplus value or profit was *not* reinvested at the site of labor; rather it was exported to the metropolitan countries. Thus, an increase in constant capital did not reduce demand for labor in the Third World, since the capital produced in the underdeveloped nations was invested in the developed nations to further reduce demand for labor there. The labor of the Third World population thus had a dual effect: increasing constant capital (and decreasing demand for labor) in the metropolitan countries, and at the same time providing a cheap, abundant supply of labor that depressed wages both in the dependent economy and for unskilled laborers in the metropole.

However, an abundance of cheap labor in the Third World, coupled with extensive unemployment and poverty, is also dangerous to capitalism. For while they are needed for capitalist expansion and accumulation, the masses of unemployed and underemployed may voice their discontent by trying to wrest control over their life circumstances from those in power. Rather than lose control of economic resources, the ruling elite proposes to control the numbers of the population of the poorer classes. It is an inherent contradiction of capitalism that the same system which proposes population control programs also, by its control over individual lives, sets the conditions for high fertility, extensive labor migration, and other distortions of capitalist development.

International Capitalism and Population Dynamics

Neo-Malthusian concerns have provided the basis for U.S. population policy in both domestic and international aid programs. Such policy holds the poor responsible for using up the developing nations' scant resources, thus preventing investment that would lead to an economic "take-off." Using the Western notion of children as dependents until age fifteen or more, development planners cite the high "dependency ratio" of underdeveloped countries as a factor inhibiting investment that could lead to economic growth. A reduced birthrate among the poor is seen as an essential prerequisite for economic and social development. But the notion that fewer children will lead to greater savings and more available capital is unproved (Carter 1975:228). Indeed, this way of approaching the problems of development ignores the realities of a world economic system, where profit flows out of Third World nations, rather than into the pockets of the workers.

The growth of the population of the poor is also viewed as a threat to the interests of the capitalist elites in controlling natural resources, raw materials, investments, and markets. Too many people with little work or hope might follow "power-hungry troublemakers"; younger age groups may be more prone to disruptive behavior (Overbeek 1976:42). In many countries, such as in Puerto Rico, the desire of a government for political stability is translated into a concern for eliminating the superfluous numbers of the unemployed who might threaten these interests. Population control became a means of preventing disruption cloaked in the guise of economic development policy.

The Population Establishment

A brief look at the personnel involved in the "population establishment" indicates the nature of ruling-class interest in population control. "The family planning establishment is a visible and respectable spin-off of the more general Eastern establishment, that influential and polished combination of 'old boys'; talented professionals and great wealth that operates in so many circuits of top U.S. power" (Demerath 1976:34). The names associated with the organizations that have been most active in this area—the Population Council, the Ford Foundation, the Rockefeller Foundation, the Population Crisis Committee, the International Planned Parenthood Federation (IPPF), the U.S. Agency for International Development (AID), as well as the Council on Foreign Relations—are the same names that appear as controlling interests of major U.S. and multinational corporations. These organizations have interlocking personnel and functions. Ford, Rockefeller, and AID all give money to IPPF. Their activities are legitimated by grants to sympathetic academics who conduct the research whose findings dominate the definition of current population issues and studies in the United States (Kleinman 1980:272).

Mass (1976) provides an excellent history of the development of these organizations and the nexus of influence in the link between population issues and development programs through the 1950s and 1960s. By 1969, President Nixon overtly expressed an interest in the "population problem," which would lead to misery, chaos, and strife; the World Bank encouraged Third World governments to view population control as beneficial in terms of increasing their gross national product, and the United Nations Fund for Population Activities provided a multilateral basis for population control programs. Indeed, since the mid-1960s, population control has been a priority issue in U.S. policy toward the Third World. Poor nations were to accept population programs, whether or not they felt that population was a problem, in order to qualify for food and other forms of aid. In the belief that the prolific numbers of the poor were responsible for the poverty of the Third World, the U.S. Congress authorized AID to withhold food and health allocations from "friendly" countries if they did not have a national population planning program. Between 1968 and 1972, AID's total health care outlay fell from $164 million to $60 million, while outlay for population control rose from $35 million to $123 million (Mass 1976; Clinton 1973).

The stock in trade of such population control efforts has been the technology of birth control and its ancillary techniques of communication and motivation. Rather than change the conditions under which the poor live or the power structure that creates these conditions, the population establishment has supported the development of more effective family planning techniques. Products not permitted in the United States have been exported to Third World countries. Surveys have been conducted with the idea that if only an acceptable contraceptive could be discovered, the poor of the Third World would rush to use it. R. T. Ravenholt, a leading, if controversial, figure who has held a variety of positions in U.S. government population programs, has pressed the idea that "availability of contraceptives" was all that was needed to lower Third World birthrates and stimulate economic development.

Not all population programs, however, are as simplistic. Various family planning campaigns use ideology to popularize a small family norm, raise the age at marriage, stimulate women's employment, stress child and maternal health benefits of longer birth intervals, and provide material incentives for those willing to accept contraceptives or undergo sterilization. By the 1970s, the Ford and Rockefeller foundations were already involved in disincentive programs, some of which took on a coercive character (Mass 1976:164). But coercion has not always been necessary, for women, who are the usual targets of population control actions, in many cases internalize the message put forth by those who have control over their lives, namely, male physicians, husbands, clergy. As Petchesky argues in this volume, women have thus not always been forced, but have accommodated to the interests of power by accepting even the most radical of efforts of others to control their reproductive processes, sterilization.

Yet population control programs have not had an outstanding record of success. Where they have been successful, the reduction in birthrates may be the result of other factors, or may occur in delimited areas such as Taiwan, where massive economic inputs have a magnified impact. Nonetheless, population money has remained available when other funds have been cut back. At least one AID official has said that the continued accent on population control is a cover-up for the failure of so many other economic assistance programs (Demerath 1976:48).

The search for a quick technological fix to solve population, and thus poverty, problems has overlooked the root cause of such inequality: differential control of the processes of production and reproduction. Even as contraceptive technology has developed, it has been applied not to give women greater control over their own reproductive lives, but to give others control over women's entire life circumstances. Thus the failure of advances in contraceptive methods to limit population is not a failure in technology but a reflection of the dynamics of the capitalist world system with its own particular laws of population and its social relations which give a powerful few control over so many individual lives.

Third World Responses to Population Programs

In 1974, the World Population Conference was held in Bucharest to sensitize the Third World to population problems and to develop a World Plan of Action to save diminishing resources— in truth, to save those resources for exploitation by the ruling class. However, as Mass points out, many Third World countries opposed demographic platforms that were intended to "stabilize" their population growth and treat birth control as a factor in isolation from the "health and well-being of the women, family and society" (1976:66-67). Emphatically, nation after nation declared that population was not the main source of the world's problems, and that population policy was not the primary means of solving those problems (Pajeska 1974:158). To the Third World participants at Bucharest, it was not clear that reduced fertility would make a decisive difference in income distribution or labor absorption without appropriate development strategies that affected the basic social and economic structure of the poor nations and their relationship to already developed countries. "Many experts are skeptical about the chances of achieving much success in inducing declines in fertility in poverty-ridden, ill-educated, traditionally-minded populations merely by making contraceptives, sterilization, etc., available, when their conditions of life are not favorable to the development of motivation for limiting births" (United Nations 1975:

20). The United Nations report on the conference noted that while overpopulation is usually phrased in terms of relationship of number of people to agricultural land, it is the distribution of that land, capital, and other resources among a given population that is more often a problem. As the conference concluded: "The consideration of population problems cannot be reduced to population trends only. It must also be borne in mind that the present situation of the developing countries originates in the unequal processes of socio-economic development, which have divided peoples since the beginning of the modern era. This inequity still exists and is intensified by the lack of equity in international economic relations, with consequent disparity in levels of living" (Pajeska 1974:155). The delegates to the conference did not denigrate efforts to develop safe, effective contraceptive techniques or to make them easily available. They stated that individuals and families should be able to decide to have all the children they desired, spaced as they desired, in a "free, informed, and responsible" way, but that efforts to provide contraceptive technology and information was not to substitute for the transformation of the inequities that were the root cause of poverty.

After Bucharest, there were, in fact, some changes in population policies. A World Bank report acknowledged that high fertility was part of a wider socioeconomic environment where "a high proportion of babies die in infancy or childhood, parents expect children to contribute to the family income rather than be educated, women remain illiterate, and support for the aged and disabled must be provided by the extended family (King 1974:3). The report noted that as income rises, fertility declines, but that more important than an overall rise in income is the *distribution* of income. Yet despite talking about income levels, the bulk of the report dealt with family planning services and delivery. While there has been more consciousness since 1974 on the causes and consequences of population growth, solutions that threaten the established order and the hold of the ruling classes are not given much more than lip service. Indeed, bureaucrats like Ravenholt still feel that social and economic development reduce fertility in a "haphazard, slow, uncertain way," and that the fastest way to stimulate development is to start equalizing the distribution of contraceptives. Despite the protest, Bucharest legitimized the idea of a "world population problem." In 1975, the U.S. Congress marked 67 percent of all the money for health care in the Foreign Aid Assistance Act for population planning. While population programs are now phrased in terms of a general development rubric to make them more acceptable ideologically, the interest in income distribution often becomes a smokescreen to hide the reality of the socioeconomic relations that underlie the unequal distribution of resources.

Issues in Population Processes

This theoretical overview has touched on a number of issues which are further expanded upon by the contributors to this book. The cost and value of children, the issue of women and reproductive freedom, and the causes and consequences of migration are topics that emerge from the concern with relations between classes and between nations in the capitalist world system.

The Value of Children

The uneven development which occurred as capitalism penetrated differentially into different countries led to an emphasis on the production of different "qualities" of labor by the various classes and by the populations of different nations. The notion that the quality of children produced for the future labor force varies, and that the production of children can be measured in terms of costs and values to the family unit has gained credibility since 1957 when Liebenstein noted that as income rose, the birthrate dropped, and that parents can make a rough calculation of the costs and benefits of children in deciding to have a child. There are certainly noneconomic values to having children: achievement of adult status as a parent, ties to immortality, affection, creativity and accomplishment, social competition, and other forms of fulfillment. There are also noneconomic costs, such as anxiety over the child's well-being (Espanshade 1977:4-5). But because such costs and values are difficult to quantify, economic demographers concentrated on the more easily measurable value of children as productive agents who might earn income, as security in old age or in emergencies. The economic costs are counted as direct maintenance costs: food, clothing, education, and so on, and indirect costs, such as loss of the woman's labor, the foregoing of other consumption items or savings, the restrictions on other investments. Because in most Western industrial societies children do not produce income, they are economic burdens: their utility, or value, is in "personal satisfaction." But in the developed nations, the wealthy have fewer children than do the poor. Demographers explained this phenomenon by stating that greater satisfaction accrued from producing a higher "quality" child—better educated, clothed, etc. In the West, because of the increased investment in constant capital noted earlier, even those with less wealth "chose" higher quality children, thus reducing the overall birthrate.

However, as Petchesky notes in this book, the concept of choice and calculation in reproductive decisions presumes that such decisions are necessarily made by "couples," a cooperating unit that acts harmoniously in deciding whether or not to have a baby or buy a car. But reproductive decisions are not always made in "families," and even when they are, there can be substantial disagreement over whether a birth is in the man's or the women's overall interest, or who, in fact, controls the women's reproductive life. Moreover, there are real limitations to equating the decision to have a child with the decision to buy a new car or refrigerator (if your child is a "lemon," you can't trade it in). The costs and values are based on Western, middle-class notions of childrearing and children's labor-force participation. Most of these models presume an industrial, capital-intensive economy where the skills and training needed by the future laborers prevent children from entering the labor force until they are quite mature. Even in the household, the labor of children is not essential, being restricted to minor chores, which are a convenience rather than a necessity in the household's survival.

In Third World nations, and in pockets in the West which have been unevenly developed, the labor of children has value from a very early age. The result of this in human terms is noted by a number of contributors to this volume. Michaelson, Mamdani, and Larson note the short-run strategies of individual families in meeting their subsistence needs in situations of low wages and relative unemployment: the production of large numbers of children whose cumulative wages can support the wider family.

Very young children are set to work in agriculture or in the household in ways which directly benefit the well-being of the household. Even in urban areas, which, because they are more modern, were thought to be conducive to reduced fertility, the tertiary sector is swelled by the labor of children, who shine shoes, empty bottles, and hustle for income on the city streets. Because there is a high demand for low-quality labor, the investment per child is low for any given household, while the potential for benefit is high. "The smaller the chances of employment for young men, the greater the incentive for individual parents to produce more sons, so as to increase their own chance of insuring that at least one of their sons earns a regular income" (Epstein and Jackson 1977:10). With few social services or old age pensions available in underdeveloped economies, children are also an insurance against starvation in old age or infirmity.

The cost for children under these circumstances is low. Little is expended by the poor for education, clothing, toys, private rooms, and other middle-class childhood amenities, not because such niceties are not valued, but because the poor know that they are not necessary to their child's present or future productivity. Moreover, up to age seven or so, when a child might be largely (though not completely), unproductive, the cost of its maintenance may be shared by an extended family, which makes childcare and other necessities less burdensome. Once a child, particularly a female child, is old enough to look after younger siblings, the cost of future children drops even further, for the productive labor time of adults is released from child care. Only among the upper and middle classes has the birthrate dropped, because the costs of children outweigh the economic benefits.

But to say that the poor "choose" large families is somewhat misleading. While it is often true that the poor express a desire for large families—a rational desire given their economic circumstances—their freedom to choose, even if contraception is readily available, is illusory.

Women, Reproduction, and Power

The issue of choice and control of the circumstances in which choices are made is also the critical issue in any discussion of women, population, and reproduction. Control of fertility is conceived by population planners to be a "women's issue," and they are the targets of population control campaigns. But such campaigns do not necessarily increase the individual woman's control over her own reproductive processes, which are in fact increasingly controlled by others.

The notion that birthrates can be reduced by providing women with income-earning opportunities denies the reality that women are oppressed both as wage earners and at home. In order for income-producing activities to have an impact on birthrates, a woman's wages must be high enough to substitute for the loss of wage earners in the decreased number of children. She must have work that provides not only income but sources of prestige and status to substitute for the esteem she receives as a mother— work which gives her greater control of her own life. Yet women's work is frequently poorly compensated, and less regarded than the labor of men. The labor-force participation of women in such jobs has not yet significantly reduced fertility, for the structural conditions that make many children a benefit have not changed.

Working women, in fact, have a dual role in capitalist society, both as producers and reproducers of the social order. They must limit one job if they are to do the other adequately and they usually have little choice as to which job they will limit. Most become second-class workers, subject to protective legislation that supports their reproductive role. The penetration of capitalism into the Third World, therefore, has not necessarily improved women's position. As Boserup has amply demonstrated (1965), development has often meant a reduction of jobs for women, and the disruption of traditional societies, rather than "liberating" them, has sometimes made them more dependent on men. Capitalist development pitted male against female workers, and often resulted in an ideology of women's place being in the home. The women took over the activities of maintaining and reproducing the labor force, but their productive activity was not compensated. Thus, those controlling the means of production got the labor of two adults in the overall productive process for the wages of one.

Development has also affected women in other ways that have led to increased fertility. The disruption of traditional societies has meant that customs requiring long postpartum abstinence—a means of spacing births—have broken down. As women have become more dependent on men for economic support in many areas of the world, they fear losing their mates during a prolonged period of abstinence. Additionally, breast-feeding has declined in many Third World countries as a result of the promotion of packaged infant formula. The nutritional horror stories of diluted formula, malnutrition, and the like have become fairly well known in the West, but the fertility consequences of the decline in breast-feeding are not yet clear; however, one result may be closer births and a consequent decline in maternal and child health (Nag 1980:571).

While delivery of family planning services is an essential right for all women, single issue discussions are often misleading, masking real issues of inequity.

The issue of abortion is a particularly sensitive one in this context. While few countries have had a substantial decline in the birthrate without recourse to abortion, whether legal or not, it is far from an ideal means of birth control. Yet those who argue against abortion under the guise of being "pro-family" conceal the reality that such policies are not in reality pro-natalist. The same medicaid programs that do not pay for abortion and contraception, pay 90 percent of the costs of sterilization. Petchesky argues in this book that the antiabortion campaign in fact harkens back to the eugeneticist movement, for its results are skewed by race and class.

Migration and the Flow of Labor

Labor migration is an essential feature of the uneven development wrought by the expansion of capitalism. Conventional approaches to population migration assume that people move in response to such factors as available land, drought, and so on, which are distributed "naturally" and not a part of the changes which have occurred with development (Amin 1974:88). Indeed, there has recently been a growth in the idea that migration is a normal, natural response to conditions, an "adaptive strategy," which is part of the rational choices available to people to gain their subsistence. These choices, supposedly freely made, are seen outside of the historical development of particular modes of production and of the workings of a world system.

Under capitalism, however, the causes of migration (which is not simply the movement of people but of labor power) are quite specific. People base their decisions on the advantages or costs of migration, taking into account the reality of the limited alternatives they believe this system offers them. These "choices," however, like reproductive choices, are structured by the social and economic context in which they are made. One factor in this decision is the transformation of the rural areas as a result of their integration into the world capitalist system. In some cases, colonial rulers have imposed taxes which have forced the local population to earn money for cash payments. Capitalist investments in cash crops push peasants out of agriculture to earn their subsistence; they cannot grow cash crops without capital. At other times, lands are directly expropriated for plantations. Larson notes a case where seemingly positive efforts on the part of a multinational corporation to develop a reliable, cheap labor force have resulted in both migration and increased fertility. But despite the fact that peasants often choose to migrate, these choices are rarely completely free or voluntary, as the articles by Petras and Edmunds clearly demonstrate. Just as people "choose" to have large families in a system which leaves them little alternative, so they also "choose" to migrate. Indeed, there is a direct link between fertility and migration; labor migration out of the rural areas may create a desire for large families to take advantage of new options for rural and urban labor-force partici-

come law, increasingly restricting women's choices in matters of family planning.

At the same time, welfare, educational assistance, and other programs which enable low-income families to remain outside the labor force while they gain the needed work skills to improve their economic lot, are being cut. As the middle class increasingly feels the impact of inflation and bears the cost of larger families, they, too, will demand cuts in programs for the poor: already, in the early 1980s, the demand that the poor be "made to work" even at below a living wage can be heard.

As the decade proceeds, the implications of policy changes taking place in this period should become increasingly clear. Cloaked in the guise of a return to "traditional values," this legislation is in reality an excellent example of the interaction of political and economic forces on demographic processes. If these forces continue to structure the climate in which reproductive decisions are made, the rich will certainly get richer, and the poor—and middle class—will indeed get children.

Part I

Reproduction and Mode of Production

The Ideology of Population Control

Mahmood Mamdani

Population theories—particularly neo-Malthusian versions—have become widespread in the last decade. In essence, neo-Malthusian theories use *existing* rates of development to project *future* national resources and population. Shorn of their individual trappings, these theories argue that the rate of population growth is outstripping the rate of resource development: the result is imminent catastrophe—hunger, starvation, and social conflict—on both a national and an international level.

The left critique of neo-Malthusian theory has stressed that the very presentation of the problem is ideological, obscuring the class nature of appropriation in national societies. National societies are class societies, in which appropriation has a dual aspect—it is appropriation both of nature and of producers, national appropriation as well as social appropriation. The so-called national resources should thus best be conceptualized as the economic surplus, which is controlled not by the nation as a whole but by a particular class or classes. The objective interests of that class or classes dictate the way in which the economic surplus will be used and hence its future growth and composition. Moreover, the appropriation of the economic surplus is not confined within a national context, but occurs primarily in an international context. Thus, any analysis of population growth must be made within this context, that is, the international capitalist system.

A critique at the level of ideology, however, is only a first step, albeit a necessary one. It must be followed by a *scientific* explanation of the rising rate of population growth in most underdeveloped capitalist countries. Such an explanation is possible

An earlier version of this essay was presented at the World Population Conference, Bucharest, Rumania, on August 22, 1974.

only if the phenomenon is viewed in its social and historical context. Birth rates are not so much territorially specific as specific to particular social groups. Anybody familiar with the demography of a particular town or village knows that the reproductive practice of land laborers is different from that of landlords, and that of the petit bourgeois is different from that of the proletariat or the unemployed. Reproductive behavior is, therefore, a social phenomenon. National or regional birth rates are statistical abstractions that do not advance our understanding so much as mystify it. In addition, this same behavior is neither idiosyncratic nor accidental but is substantially *reproduced* over time. My concern with reproductive practice is not with its individuality—a subjective phenomenon—but as a phenomenon that is both social and objective. Thus the real question is: What are the social relations that underlie these practices?

Since the social relations themselves did not always exist, but were historically created, they must be understood in their historical specificity. This essay analyzes the reproductive practices of two social groups that form the bulk of the population in most underdeveloped capitalist countries: the working peasantry and the urbanized unemployed.[1]

The Working Peasantry

The countries today referred to as underdeveloped were incorporated into the world capitalist system over the last four centuries. The incorporation, although universal, was uneven. The capitalist mode of production developed only in those territories that capitalism populated. In the territories that it dominated, however, capitalism did not simply appropriate the peasants and turn them into wage laborers. The tendency here, as Charles Bettelheim (1971) points out, was toward both the dissolution and the conservation of the precapitalist mode: the precolonial modes of production were partially destroyed, restructured, and then incorporated into the world capitalist mode of production in a subordinate position. Precapitalist modes

were henceforth not autonomous but derived from their dependent relationship to the dominant mode in the international
capitalist system. Within the colonies the capitalist mode itself
was confined to small pockets, but it dominated the precapitalist
mode through the agency of the state, at first colonial and later
neocolonial. Outside of these pockets, whatever the relations of
production on the land—whether it be the hacienda community,
the plantation–small-holding relation of Latin America, the
landlord-tenant relation that predominates in large parts of
Asia, or the domination of peasant commodity production by
merchant capital characteristic of large parts of Africa—the unit
of production remained the family.

This phenomenon has very important implications. It means
that socialization for productive labor is also carried out within
the family. The relations of work are reflected in the relations
within the family, and the discipline of work becomes the discipline of the family. Family relations among the working peasantry remain rigid and hierarchical. The parent, generally the
father, is the head of the family and exercises absolute control.
The parent-child relationship is simple: the parent commands,
the child obeys. Age and experience are the yardsticks of merit
and claim to authority. Parental chauvinism flourishes, but it is
not simply an attitudinal phenomenon. The point here is that
these family relations, sustained by the nature and relations of
work, make it possible for adults to control the time and labor of
children, including the fruits of that labor.

The situation is qualitatively different under developed capitalism, where the unit of production is no longer the family but the
capitalist enterprise. Similarly, socialization for work is carried
out not so much within the family as within the school or the
prison. The primary producer is not so much a family member as
a wage laborer, a salaried worker, or a capitalist; the family here
remains a unit of consumption and procreation rather than a unit
of production. Thus emerges the bourgeois family, its relations
being part of the material basis of the ideology of individualism
and individual freedom. The ideology of the underdeveloped
family, on the other hand, is that of loyalty and unity; these values
form the ideological basis of parental authority over children.[2]

Control over children's labor, however, can be of material consequence only if the structure of production allows for the productive use of the child's labor. In other words, what use can the family make of the child's time? Another characteristic of underdeveloped agriculture is that, outside of small pockets of capitalist production, the forces of production remain backward. The technology of production in agriculture remains low. In fact, throughout the colonial period there has been little change here. Unlike developed capitalism, underdeveloped capitalism does not revolutionize the forces of production: most of the African peasantry still uses the hoe as the basic tool for cultivation, and the Asian peasantry the plow. Given its low technological base, the process of production is characterized by activity that includes numerous tasks that are both simple and repetitive—from grazing, cleaning, and feeding of farm animals to the laborious tasks of weeding and, to some extent, sowing and harvesting. Outside of productive labor, the presence of children can also assure a certain ease in life. The youngest may massage the parent when the latter returns from a day's toil in the field, or simply bring water for a bath or make a drink for relaxation. The smallest children perform a variety of tasks that the adults regard as tedious, time-consuming, and tiresome. The youngest children, who are too small to do any work, will be cared for by older children, who include them in their play or carry them on their hips when they tend to their work. In the words of a north Indian Jat (farmer): "A forest is not made of one tree; a Jat is not made of one son."

It is precisely because children's activity can be a source of considerable gain to the family that their time and lives are closely regulated by the family, more so as they become older. The very nature of childhood is affected: there is no adolescence—a category specific to advanced capitalism—only childhood and adulthood. When they grow up, children become not youths but young adults.

It might be pointed out that the extremely high levels of unemployment and underemployment in the agricultural sector limit the access of children to productive labor. Unemployment, however, is far more characteristic of entire families than of individuals. In the agricultural sector, adult and child unemployment go hand in hand as family unemployment, for almost all members of a family are, in fact, available for work. Without access to the means of production, the family moves. The movement of the pauperized and appropriated peasantry is characteristic of under-developed capitalism.

Nonetheless, in the case of the working peasantry—the petty commodity producer on the land—it is necessary to keep two factors in mind. First, given the low level of technology, the rhythm of work corresponds to the rhythm of nature and is highly uneven. Periods of intense work alternate with periods of low employment. Harvesting, weeding, and sowing times—over half the year—are the peaks of productive activity and correspond with an acute need for labor. For example, in Ludhiana in the Punjab region of India, it takes only three people with a tractor and all the necessary implements to work fifty acres of land. Without a tractor, the same land requires at least fourteen people year-round, and twenty at sowing, weeding, and harvesting times. In these periods of high employment, the entire family works and earns, but the parents control the earnings.

Second, the social relations of production, however reminiscent of precapitalist relations, derive their motion from their subordination to the international capitalist mode of production. Peasant production, formerly petty commodity production for use, is now petty commodity production for the international capitalist market. The domination of this market is expressed at the level of the national economy as the subordination of peasant production to monopoly-based merchant capital. The result is the appropriation of the peasant producers, which leaves them with no more than their bare subsistence needs and certainly no surplus to expand the technical basis of their production. There is neither a movement from manual to mechanized labor nor a rise in the productivity of labor, since agricultural surpluses are siphoned off into the commercial sector rather than reinvested in agriculture. When there is the added oppression of a landlord, the result is competition for tenancies among producing families. Whatever the form of appropriation of producers—by landlords, merchant capital, or international monopolies—whatever the form of competition between producers, the only means by which the individual producing unit, the family, can increase the physical product at its disposal is by increasing its labor power, that is, its rate of reproduction. High birthrates are not the cause of present impoverishment; they are the response of an impoverished peasantry. Furthermore, because of the hierarchical relations within the family and adult control over children's labor, the cost to the producing family of having additional children declines and the benefit rises. In the absence of a class organization of the exploited, the only possible (though not necessarily effective) form of security for peasant producers is the family. As a middle peasant in northern India put it: "A rich man invests in his machines. We must invest in our children. It's that simple."

The ideology in peasant societies incessantly emphasizes the virtue of childbearing. In India, it is considered one's *dharma* (religious and social obligation) to have children. To desire as many children as possible is not only in the natural order of things but also an indication of virtue. Marriage vows and blessings put emphasis on the good fortune of having many children. Folk songs, usually sung on occasions such as marriage, childbirth, or the harvest, sing praises of the prolific mother and the fertile soil. A popular theme running through many stories is the love of the mother for the son: it is considered the purest form of love. Sanctions against childless women further underline the necessity of children. In other words, ideology reinforces the demands of reality.

The Appropriated Masses

One important characteristic of an underdeveloped economy is that "unproductive capital" dominates agricultural production: agricultural surpluses are not plowed back into agriculture to expand its technical base. Rather, they are siphoned off into the commercial sector, where they take the form of merchants' profit or landlords' rent, or they are externalized as the profits of metropolitan export-import firms. Commerce takes primacy over agricultural production, with the twofold result that there is only a limited class differentiation in the countryside, coupled with an increasing pauperization of the lower sections of the peasantry. The poor peasantry is appropriated, and a rural bourgeoisie that could potentially employ the appropriated peasantry fails to emerge. In countries that lack an agricultural landlord class, the *social* consequence of the underdeveloped economy is that the rich peasant does not develop into a capitalist farmer, but instead branches off into trade. The rural unemployed, unable to work in the countryside, flock to the cities. The high figures of rural-to-urban migration in underdeveloped capitalist formations is testimony to the existence of this process.

The ranks of these appropriated masses are swelled by another social group: the precapitalist artisans, whose material base was undermined by the expansion of metropolitan imports during the colonial era. The artisans formerly provided not only consumer goods for the cities but also the basic tools for agricultural production, such as hoes in Africa. Metropolitan imports of both consumer goods and tools made these skilled laborers redundant. In fact, the first phase of colonialism reduced all labor to the lowest common denominator: unskilled agricultural workers engaged in the production of cash crops for export to metropolitan markets. All that remains are a few skilled artisans who make souvenirs for tourists. The bulk of these skilled workers join the ranks of the unemployed, a process of varying significance from one underdeveloped economy to another.

While this same process—the appropriation of the poor peasantry and the redundance of skilled workers—also occurred in early Western capitalism, there was one critical difference: this process was followed by another—proletarianization. By contrast, what we find in underdeveloped capitalism is appropriation without proletarianization. In order to understand this, we must turn to both the nature of industrialization and the structure of urban employment in the underdeveloped economy.

With the creation of an export-import economy comes the formation of those social groups that act as "conveyor belts," to use Samir Amin's phrase, in the economy. These are the unproductive intermediate classes that manage and service the export-import economy. These social groups—the landlords, merchants, and bureaucrats—exercise dominant control over that part of the national economic surplus that is retained in the underdeveloped countries. Their lifestyle, revolving around the consumption of luxury goods of metropolitan origin, puts a firm stamp on the structure of consumption in the underdeveloped economy. As Fanon pointed out, the "national middle class" finds its point of unity with the metropolitan bourgeoisie at the level of consumption, not at the level of production.

This structure of consumption determines the choice of the product for industrialization when the first phase of import substitution begins. Import substitution is the production within the internal market of those commodities that were formerly imported, namely, consumer durable goods. Samir Amin's (1974) four-sector model shows the qualitative difference between the structure of an underdeveloped economy and that of a developed economy.

Whereas the determining relationship in a developed economy is between capital-goods production and mass consumption (2 and 3), in an underdeveloped economy it is between export production and luxury consumption (1 and 4). Even when the capital-goods sector does develop in such economies as India, Brazil, and Mexico, it does so in relation to the sector producing luxury consumption goods, *not* in relation to the sector producing mass consumption goods. Finally, production for luxury consumption, durable consumer goods, forms the objective basis for the collaboration of the national ruling classes with multinational corporations to provide the necessary technology. In return, the independent neocolony provides the multinational corporations with anything from tax holidays to high tariff protection to freedom from workers' strikes. Important for our purposes is an understanding of the consequences of this kind of industrialization, which utilizes the capital-intensive technology of the multinational corporations for the structure of employment in the urban economies.

Factories and machines multiply, but not the workers in them. The real meaning of industrialization—the creation of a skilled proletariat, which is the social embodiment of technical advance—evades the underdeveloped economy. The development of the working class is but a trickle compared to that of industry; in some cases there is even a reverse trend. In India, according to official statistics, the percentage of working population living by modern industry *fell* from 5.5 percent in 1911 to 4.3 percent in 1931 and registered an increase only in the 1950s. Correspondingly, the percentage of population dependent on agriculture for its living was *higher* in 1950 by 10.9 percent than in 1891! The 1960 International Labor Organization report on India remarked that "during the period of the first five-year plan, urban unemployment increased in spite of the rise in industrial production . . . from [an index of] 117 in 1951 to 161 in 1956." Villareal (1973) estimates that between 1965 and 1975 Mexico had a net *loss* of industrial employment of 1,861,000 workers, "part of this resulting from a decline of employment in labor-intensive industries . . . but most of it resulting from increasing productivity in a manufacturing sector that has not been matched by a commensurate growth in demand." An ILO case study of Brazil concluded: "Such scanty data as are available on employment in manufacturing industry indicate a surprisingly slow growth throughout the period 1945–57 of the number of employees in industry, despite an annual average rise of about ten percent in the value of industrial output" (Campos 1962: appendix).

In fact, in Latin America as a whole, whereas the share of industrial production in the regional gross domestic product increased from 11 percent in 1925 to 19 percent in 1950, 22 percent in 1960, and 23 percent in 1967, the proportion of the total labor force employed by industry remained constant at about 14 percent over the whole period (United Nations 1972).

The dominant process in the underdeveloped economy undergoing dependent industrialization is not proletarianization but appropriation without proletarianization. An entirely new social group emerges in the urban areas, the appropriated masses, living on the fringes of respectable society and marginally employed at best. It would be a mistake to see them as a lumpen proletariat, or even as Marx's relative surplus population necessary to the smooth functioning of a capitalist labor market. Quite the contrary, this is a new historical formation, specific to underdeveloped capitalism, which Utsa Patnaik (1972) calls a "chronic surplus population" in the case of India, and Hussein (1973) calls "the proletarianized masses" in the case of Egypt. In Brazil, "unable to find employment in manufacture, the migrant workers swelled the ranks of the urban population engaged in petty trades and services or remained as casual laborers, part-time construction workers, and unemployed, living usually in shanty towns on the fringes of the big cities" (Campos 1962:145).

The slums of São Paolo and Santiago, of Bombay and Calcutta, of Dakar and Nairobi are all testimony to the rise of this social group—the appropriated masses—in the urban centers of underdeveloped capitalism. Some of the highest rates of population increase are registered in this social group. Why, then, do marginal employment and high population growth go hand in hand?

The marginal employment available to the appropriated masses is daily casual labor: in construction, in hawking, as restaurant waiters or cleaners—in what are euphemistically called the "service industries." But, most important, this employment is skewed in favor of child labor. Children shine shoes, open car doors or clean cars, and most of all they beg. In fact, begging becomes a regular occupation: it is organized. Denied productive employment by underdeveloped capitalism, the poor make demands on the "conscience" of the local ruling class and their metropolitan tourist friends. For a member of the affluent classes it is difficult to walk a hundred yards in any of the urban centers of underdeveloped capitalism without hearing a call for *baksheesh*. The younger and more innocent-looking the caller, the better the chances of being rewarded. Here, unlike in agricultural work, the female child is as much an asset as, if not more so than, the male child. Once they grow up, these children may desert their families, but as long as they are young and physically unable to leave, these "innocent ones" in fact support the adults. In slum populations it is not unusual to find whole families who are supported by the children.

The Ideology of Population Control

The decision to have a number of children by a family located within the working peasantry or the appropriated masses is essentially a rational decision, a judgment of their social environment. That decision does not exist in the abstract: it is a product of a particular social context. The pitfall of neo-Malthusian liberalism is percisely its "rationalism," its assumption that there is a universal rationality, which exists apart from a class society and a *class* rationality. The demand for population control may be rational in one class situation but not necessarily in another. The "rationalism" of the neo-Malthusian universalizes this situation and thus the rationality of a particular class: what is good for the propertied classes is good for all.

Ideological thought is not simply false. It is thought that presents a single aspect of reality as reality and obscures the relation between that aspect and the totality. The specific historical relation between high rates of population growth and social oppression is obscured. When the phenomenon is defined as the "population problem," its core assertion is that people are poor because they are too many. Exploitation is viewed merely as poverty, and the explanation of poverty becomes the poor themselves.

Notes

1. The term "working peasantry" here refers only to the petty commodity producers on the land, not the proletarianized peasantry. I am aware of the need to analyze the relations between these two sectors, however. In Africa, for example, large sections of the proletarianized peasantry are migrant laborers who return to their families after a period of wage labor. The wife may become the petty commodity producer, and the structure of the peasant family is altered. Observation leads me to think that this alters the relationship of husband to wife, but not the parent-child relationship. Only an analysis of concrete social conditions can clarify the laws of population growth.
2. Certainly the bourgeois family can be found in underdeveloped social formations. Its existence, however, is class specific, located within the bourgeoisie or the petite bourgeoisie.

"Reproductive Choice" in the Contemporary United States: A Social Analysis of Female Sterilization

Rosalind Pollack Petchesky

The Sterilization Phenomenon

Early in 1979, national newspapers reported the story of four women workers at an American Cyanamid chemical plant in West Virginia who had chosen to be sterilized rather than give up their jobs—jobs that exposed them to dangerous teratogenic and mutagenic substances (*New York Times*, January 5, 1979). This case, and the growing number of cases like it, raises a number of issues for women, not the least of which is the trend of major companies to adopt sexist exclusionary policies instead of eliminating reproductive hazards that infest workplaces and affect both women and men (see Petchesky 1979a; Wright 1979; Chavkin 1979). On a broader level, the dilemma of the American Cyanamid women brings into dramatic focus the question of so-called family planning choices in advanced capitalist society and the importance of understanding these choices in relation to their social, economic, and cultural contexts. While the women's decision was "voluntary" in a narrow sense, it was made under a number of material and political constraints: women's need to work outside the home and the difficulty working-class women face in securing relatively well-paid jobs; the danger of miscarriage or pregnancies that might issue in deformed children; the refusal of the company, later backed up by the courts, to take responsibility for either transferring the women to safe jobs with equal pay or cleaning up the toxic substances; the unwillingness of many labor unions to fight around such issues. Given these

---

This essay is a revised version of a chapter from the author's forthcoming book, *Reproductive Freedom: The Social and Political Dimensions of Birth Control*, to be published by Longman.

conditions, it seems accurate to argue that these women "chose" sterilization under circumstances that left them little choice.

While this example is not necessarily typical of the conditions facing most American women, it is certainly symptomatic of the larger forces that determine reproductive choice in American society. In varying degrees and ways, women of different occupations, classes, racial and ethnic groups, ages, and sexual orientations find that their reproductive decisions are structured by a set of conditions over which they as individuals have very little control. This article will demonstrate the historical and material nature of "reproductive choices" by focusing on the recent rise in female sterilizations relative to other forms of contraception in the United States. Sterilization patterns vary among different groups of women, thus illustrating that broad social conditions and structured inequalities, rather than "individual preferences" or "technology," determine women's birth control experience.

The rapid and large-scale growth of sterilization in the United States and throughout the world became a common theme among family planners and demographers in the late 1970s (see Newman and Klein 1978; Westoff and McCarthy 1979). It is a remarkable phenomenon, not only for its scale—sterilizations have increased *threefold* in the United States since 1970, the largest increase of any method of contraception—but also because it remains practically irreversible. Not long ago sterilization was associated mainly with the eugenics movement, used mostly in involuntary institutions or otherwise blatantly coercive situations to control the propagation of immigrants, the poor, the mentally disabled, and those considered "unfit." As recently as 1970, an article in a family planning journal remarked, "sterilization is not commonly part of family planning services offered . . . is not encouraged by the medical profession, and must be actively sought out" (Scrimshaw and Pasquariella 1970:40). Today the opposite is true.

According to one study, based on data from the National Survey of Family Growth, sterilization in the United States is now "the most popular method of contraception for all married couples" and has surpassed the pill as the most prevalent form

Figure 1
Trends in Surgical Sterilization Among Married Couples,
United States, 1955–1976

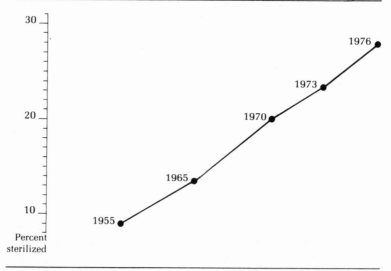

Source: Presser and Bumpass in Westoff and Park 1972:533; Ford 1978a:Table 1.

of contraception among divorced, widowed, and separated women. Among both groups, rates of surgical sterilization had reached around 30 percent by 1976 and were close to 40 percent for persons over thirty-five (Westoff and McCarthy 1979:147; Ford 1978:268; U.S. DHEW 1978: No. 36 and No. 40).[1] When the data are examined carefully, however, important social differences emerge. First, *class divisions* have a major bearing on sterilization: rates are significantly higher among low-income women and women of little education than they are among middle-income and college-educated women. Second, there are differences in *sex and ethnic patterns* of sterilization. Among most minority groups in the United States, women rather than men are sterilized, whereas among white, middle-class, married couples there is a high proportion of vasectomies. Indeed, vasectomy is performed primarily on white middle-class and upper

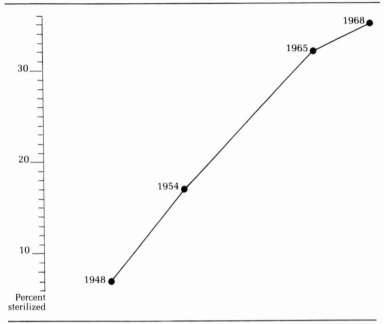

Figure 2
Trends in Surgical Sterilization Among Married Women,
Puerto Rico, 1948–1968

Source: Presser in Newman and Klein 1978:26-27; Mass 1976:95

middle-class men. Moreover, it would seem that black, Hispanic, and Native American women are more likely than white women to be the victims of involuntary sterilization or hysterectomy for contraceptive purposes (Pratt 1975:45). Thus, the rise in sterilizations represents very different realities for different groups, reflecting the major divisions of class, race, and sex in American society.

To appreciate these differences fully, we need to analyze not merely their statistical dimensions but their deeper social, economic, and cultural roots. Following a critique of some prevailing theoretical approaches I will present my own analysis of sterilization trends and the social reality of "reproductive choice."

Table 1
Percent Surgical Sterilizations Among Married Couples
by Age and Sex
(United States, 1976)

Ages 15-44			Ages 25-34			Ages 35-44		
female	male	total	female	male	total	female	male	total
17.8	10.5	28.3	16.1	10.0	26.1	31.0	17.1	48.1

Source: Ford 1978a: 264–69.

Theoretical Explanations of Sterilization Trends

Like birthrates, rates of sterilization among different social groups cannot be compared apart from their social context. For example, statistically comparable rates for black and white women in certain age and income categories tell us nothing about the different conditions under which each group was sterilized, particularly whether those conditions were "voluntary." Sterilization is also a different phenomenon for men than for women, involving a much greater risk to life and health for

Table 2
Percent Surgical Sterilizations Among Married Couples
by Age, Sex, and Race
(United States, 1976)

	Ages 15-44			Ages 25-34		Ages 35-44	
	female	male	total	female	male	female	male
Black	19.7	1.9	21.6	16.2	.4	34.3	4.9
White	17.8	11.3	29.1	16.4	10.9	29.4	18.3

Source: Ford 1978a: 264–69.

Table 3
Percent Surgical Sterilizations Among Married Couples
by Age, Sex, and Income Category
(United States, 1976)

	Ages 15-44			Ages 25-34		Ages 35-44	
	female	male	total	female	male	female	male
Low-income	21.7	4.6	26.3	26.5	8.4	34.0	3.3
Middle-income	16.7	12.0	28.7	14.7	11.0	28.3	20.2

Source: Ford 1978a: 264–69.

the latter. Finally, a 30 to 40 percent sterilization rate has very different consequences for middle-class whites in American society than it does for minority groups and poor whites, who suffer much higher rates of infant mortality, morbidity, and early death, and therefore require a higher birthrate simply to replenish themselves (U.S. DHEW 1978:78-1232). Yet demographic approaches tend to explain the upsurge in sterilization purely in

Table 4
Educational Characteristics of White Married Couples
Who Became Contraceptively Sterilized
(United States, 1975)

Wife's education (yrs.)	Percent sterilized		
	female	male	total
<H.S. 4	25.2	15.2	40.4
H.S. 4	20.0	17.3	37.3
College 1-3	16.2	20.7	36.9
≥College 4	12.9	16.5	29.4

Source: Westoff and McCarthy 1979: 149.

terms of either "technological advances" or "popular demand" in a presumably "free" contraceptive market.

Arguments attributing the rise in sterilizations since 1970 to technological developments—in particular the availability of relatively safe techniques for cauterizing or clipping the fallopian tubes—are especially pronounced in the medical literature (see Porter and Hulka 1975).[2] This technological determinist approach assumes that a method's reliability, or "efficacy," has an irresistible influence on the individual's choice. But the state of birth control technology at any given time is at best a condition, never a cause, of changes in fertility rates or contraceptive practices. We have to understand the social, political, and cultural mediations that give a particular technology salience at a given time. The ovulation-suppressing effects of estrogen and progesterone were known for many years before the widespread commercial distribution of the pill, which became the dominant method of contraception in the early 1960s. Likewise, both vasectomy and tubal ligation have been established procedures for decades; "technology" cannot explain their growing use in the last ten years, much less the class, race, and sex differences in their occurrence. In this respect sterilization rates are no different from fertility rates, which fluctuate independently of existing techniques. In fact, some effective methods of fertility control have been known in most societies, in most historical periods (Gordon 1977:47; Devereux 1967:98; Polgar 1972, 1975). Shifts in fertility rates during the twentieth century suggest that it is not the state of birth control technology but the prevailing social conditions (including the dominant medical and family planning ideologies and how they are perceived) that determine family planning practices and their effect on birth rates.[3]

A somewhat different interpretative framework may be called the "market model," since it transposes the assumptions and vocabulary of bourgeois economics to the field of family planning.[4] References to "consumer choices," "most popular method," couples who "opt for sterilization," and so on, reflect bourgeois liberal assumptions about privatism, voluntarism, and "choice." This model assumes that decisions about childbearing and contraception are normally "personal" decisions made in the privacy of the bedroom or physician's office, impelled strictly by individual concerns, not by larger social contexts. A second, related assumption is that the "consumers" of family planning "products" are invariably "couples," usually married, and that they decide things as a unit—rationally, harmoniously, and without any conflict between the partners or with the outside world. Hence the bureaucratic-clinical euphemism, "family planning," which long ago replaced the more radical political term, "birth control" (see Gordon 1977). Moreover, these "couples" (or "families") remain undifferentiated. Like the bourgeois economist looking at buyers of soap and automobiles, the demographer or family planner may see birth control consumers as having different "budgetary constraints," but the class and racial divisions that affect these families' choices are usually left out of the picture.

The core of the market model, however, is a marginal-utility theory of "reproductive choice": the notion that family planning services and products, like any other commodity, circulate freely in a market subject to the laws of supply and demand; that they are purchased "voluntarily" by consumers who act on the basis of their personal "preferences" (limited by their economic resources); and that the ultimate choices made by consumers are always a true expression of their desires (see Simmons, in Newman and Klein 1978:187-88). Whatever method is most cost-effective and technologically efficient—currently, surgical sterilization—is taken to be most desirable, and the statistical prevalence of a given method is taken as evidence that it is "the method of choice." Thus, for example, in a recent major article on sterilization in the United States, Westoff and McCarthy (1979:148, 150) erroneously infer from the fact that it is irreversible that "sterilization is only elected by couples who have had all the children they wish." Evidence that it is just as frequently women acting on their own in opposition to husbands, or against their own wishes to *placate* husbands, who become sterilized; that unknown numbers of women are *not* informed of the operation's irreversibility; or that like the women at American Cyanamid who feel constrained by external pressures to be sterilized even though they *do* wish to have more children—this is conveniently overlooked by mainstream demography.

In sum, the market approach to sterilization disregards any element of social conflict underlying "family planning choices"; people's reproductive and contraceptive behavior is assimilated to a false model of consumer behavior generally; and the *specificity* of their conditions—as women or men, as sexual beings who seek birth control for sexual as well as reproductive reasons, as members of different kinds of families, households, and sexual arrangements, and as members of different classes and racial and ethnic groups—is completely ignored. Insofar as it ignores these social realities, the model is circular: increasing numbers of people "choose" sterilization because that is the choice they make. Hidden behind its circularity, however, is also an ideology of national chauvinism, for implicit in the assumptions of these demographers is the view that family planning is by definition "free" and "voluntary," unlike what may exist in the Third World.

An example of this approach is the work of Harriet Presser (1978:25-48), who explains the rapid rise of sterilization in the United States and Puerto Rico as largely a "grass-roots response," or the product of "public demand." Yet this explanation runs counter to her own analysis of "structural" influences that have shaped the "demand" for sterilization in Puerto Rico: the pro-sterilization policy of the medical establishment; the construction of sterilization clinics and their failure to provide alternative contraceptive methods; the rising labor-force participation of women, with no public provision of child-care services; the Catholic church's condemnation of abortion and birth control devices and its comparatively weak opposition to sterilization.[5] Presser is able to maintain her view of "freedom" in the midst of massive social constraints because she accepts the classical liberal ideology of a split between the "public" sphere of state intervention (legal coercion) and the "private" domain where medical practices, sexual relations, the labor market, and religious sanctions operate.

By contrast, Bonnie Mass views the rise of sterilization in

Puerto Rico as part of a systematic imperialist campaign of population control, conducted first through private hospitals and later directly through the Ministry of Health's population and family planning department, aided by the U.S. government and international population control organizations. Mass (1976: 101-03) locates the sterilization program, first launched in 1937, within the broader framework of U.S. colonial domination over the island's economy, documenting the policy that emerged in the early 1970s to reduce the volume of unemployment (in an increasingly capital-intensive economy) by reducing the number of potential workers.

A deliberate campaign to limit the Puerto Rican population, and thus to "solve" the problems of unemployment and emigration, seems undeniable. At the same time, Mass's analysis treats the political economy of sterilization in Puerto Rico in isolation from an array of cultural, social, and sexual conditions, which politicians and imperialists did not create but which have mediated the sterilization experience in ways that they were able to exploit. On the one hand, the rise in Puerto Rican women's labor-force participation reinforced their need for effective means to control fertility. On the other hand, as Presser and Stycos document, women's own consciousness about birth control possibilities was strongly influenced by the patriarchal authority of physicians, husbands, and priests (Stycos 1968; Presser 1978; Ad Hoc Women's Studies Committee 1978). In the context of traditional culture, sterilization was less stigmatized and less offensive to the moral and patriarchal sensibilities of all three than any other form of contraception. In a Catholic culture largely antagonistic to birth control, sterilization is not a sin, and it can also be kept secret, unlike other methods. Moreover, given the complex interaction of these cultural, sexual, economic, and political forces, Puerto Rican women have now developed three generations of sterilization experience. Most women know kin or friends who have undergone *l'operacion:* it is spoken about, ingrained in the culture, a way of life, which no longer rests upon the apparatus of coercion and propaganda.

Mass's analysis ignores such elements of consciousness and culture, the ways that power is internalized and accommodated;

Third World women are depicted as the helpless victims of imperialist population controllers, and the dialectical reality of sterilization in Puerto Rico remains obscure. Like the "market model," the "repression model" of reproductive activity cannot explain the sterilization phenomenon in its totality. Material forces (labor market dynamics, technology, state policies, medical practices) and cultural or subjective influences (religious norms, sexual values, personal aspirations for upward mobility) are *both* important to such an explanation, and interact in complicated ways. Direct economic, political, and social constraints on the reproductive options available to different groups of women affect, and are affected by, a range of cultural and sexual conditions: women's own consciousness and perceptions of their medical and sexual needs, the kinds of sexual and family relations they have to rely on, and the strategies they adopt to negotiate sexual and familial conflicts about birth control and childbearing.

Fundamental to this analysis is the view that in most instances individuals make choices "freely," that is, as conscious moral agents, but that they do so always within a particular social framework that is not of their own making and which they, as individuals, are powerless to change. Most sterilizations, including those among poor and Third World women, do not result from outright manipulations and lies. Their sources are larger, more pervasive, embedded in the structure of capitalist medicine and society itself. I shall thus look at some of the main influences that account for the rise in female sterilization in the United States in the last ten years.

Social Bases of Sterilization

Although a wide range of factors is involved in determining which women are likely to be sterilized, four social determinants seem to me critical: women's changing position in the family and the labor force, patriarchal culture and sexual relations, medical policy and the health care system, and state policy on reproduction and population.

Women's Position in the Family and the Labor Force

The continued primary responsibility of mothers for children, along with the steadily increasing labor-force participation of women, especially mothers, is the major contradiction for women under late capitalism, and defines the outer limit of the social conditions determining decisions about fertility and its control.

As a consequence of the prevailing sexual division of labor around childrearing, the main responsibility for contraception and pregnancy lies not with "couples" but with women alone. Whether or not she is part of a couple, the woman finds that she is still the one who is expected—by her husband or partner, by her family, by society, even by herself—to undertake contraception and to deal with the consequences if she does not. The high ratio of female to male sterilizations, despite substantial differences in safety and risk, reflects this disproportionate burden. This is true not only for the vastly growing number of women who head families—one out of seven white women and one out of three black women today is supporting children on her own—but also for married working women (who make up the largest proportion of working women as well as being the fastest growing cohort in the labor force as a whole). These women retain their primary responsibility for household maintenance and child care, despite working hard and long hours outside the home—a situation commonly known as the "double day." It is thus not surprising that a much higher—and growing—proportion of women than men are concentrated in part-time and irregular employment. (One quarter of all working women, as compared with only one-tenth of all working men, held part-time jobs in 1978.)[6]

Meanwhile, the participation rate of women in both full-time and part-time work continues to rise steadily. The increased demand for women workers, especially in the low-paid clerical and service sectors, is experienced by individual women in the context of mounting inflation and economic crisis and the inability of families to maintain a decent standard of living on a single wage.[6] This situation would inevitably affect decisions about childbearing and contraception, but women's reproductive choices are even more constrained by a series of related economic, political, and social realities: for example, severe cutbacks in government-funded social services, especially child care and health care; the low pay of jobs generally available to women (women still earn one-half to two-thirds of what men earn in comparable jobs); and the rise of wife battering and child abuse within the male-dominated family, which raises serious questions about that institution's capacity to protect women and children. Public policy manifests different contradictions with regard to lesbians. Lesbian mothers encounter severe difficulties in securing custody of their children or the right to participate in mothering at all. The legal and social attack on lesbian mother-hood suggests that although women remain primarily respon-sible for children, their responsibility must be exercised within traditionally accepted frameworks of kinship and sexuality— that is, within heterosexual coupling and marriage.

These are conditions that affect women differently, depending on their class, race, age, sexual orientation, and occupation. The five women workers at American Cyanamid were facing condi-tions common to working women today. But their position was anomalous in certain ways, for they belong to an elite among women workers, those few who have been admitted to the skilled industrial jobs that are organized, secure, decently paid, and thus traditionally reserved for men. Their "privileged" position was something they could not afford to give up, especially as that privilege (female intrusion into male enclaves in produc-tion) is now under systematic attack. Other groups of women don't have the luxury of a choice between their fertility and better-paying jobs. Whether as black, Hispanic, and Asian women employed in hospitals, laundries, and sweatshops, where the worst kinds of reproductive hazards exist unnoticed; as clerical workers, black and white, mostly unorganized and working without pregnancy or maternity benefits; as welfare mothers confronted with the virtual abolition of medicaid funds for abortion and cuts in child health and other benefits; or as lesbian mothers fighting for child custody and against patriarchal norms of childrearing, different groups of women experience different forms of reproductive oppression. But for most women, economic crisis and the loss of the possibility of the family as a safe refuge must be understood as an important structural determinant of the decision to undergo an irreversible surgical procedure to control pregnancy. Faced with the consequences of pregnancy and childbirth, without publicly funded social supports, and under living conditions that are harder and harder, many women no doubt *choose*—rationally, without coercion—the surest available birth control solution.

Yet the desire for effective birth control, which forms an important backdrop to the rise in sterilizations, cannot be reduced to economic conditions alone. Birth control of any sort also involves issues of women's autonomy and self-determination. In commenting on the drop in the birthrate during the 1930s, Linda Gordon observes that the conscious adoption of contraception characterized not only women employed outside the home but also working-class housewives:

> As letters and interviews showed, women wanted control over pregnancies to improve and make easier their traditional home work, not to escape it. . . . [T]he desire for birth control came overwhelmingly from women, not men, and was not quite identical with . . . so-called economic motives. . . . For working-class as opposed to more prosperous women, reducing family size and extending the gaps between children was not just a matter of the budget but also of working a little less hard and in a less alienated fashion: having more control over the conditions of housework and child care. (1977:323).

Moreover, while it is true that women still bear the primary consequences of birth control and childrearing, it is also true that the conditions of motherhood have changed significantly in developed countries. While more women than ever before are engaged in motherhood at some time during their lives, they have fewer births within a vastly compressed time frame relative to their grandmothers. Indeed, the great majority of women born after 1940 face some thirty to forty years of "post-motherhood" life, a social condition that undoubtedly influences sterilization trends in ways that are semi-independent of class divisions and economic pressures (Sullerot 1971; Moore and Hofferth 1979:126-32).

Patriarchal Culture and Sexuality

To these social and economic factors influencing the nature of women's fertility, particularly among poor and minority women, must be added deliberate policies of population control. But while clinical pressures and abuses undoubtedly shape the "choice" of sterilization for many women (and with increasing menace as the right wing gains power), we can assume that most cases of sterilization result from a rational choice by the women themselves, albeit one structured by conditions of oppression. Those conditions are cultural and sexual as well as material, demonstrating the problems involved in characterizing sterilization trends within a strictly coercive framework.

One agency reinforcing the sterilization trend, at least among the middle class, is popular culture—the media, popular magazines and books, even songs. In the late 1960s and early 1970s, as the medical profession and family planners began to promote the idea of sterilization, male and female, as a normal means of birth control for ordinary (i.e., middle-class) people, that idea became merged with the dominant ideology of "sexual liberation" borrowed from the feminist and gay movements. Seizing on the media version of the "sexual revolution," sterilization advocates conveyed the notion that sterilization could provide a "quick technological fix," not only for the "population explosion" but for individuals' own sexual hangups:

> Take away tension. Take away conflict. Eliminate fear, resentment, frustration, worry and anger. Replace them with a sense of security and an ability to relax. The result is a new sexual freedom. (Wylie 1977:74)

Sterilization, particularly of the mini-lap variety, becomes one among numerous techniques guaranteed to transform the experience of sexuality for a middle-class market of sexual consumers.[7]

The reality of sex for most women, however, particularly those women who undergo sterilization, may be quite different from the myth of sexual freedom projected in sterilization marketing rhetoric. There is evidence that sterilization may be a means of avoiding birth control for those women who are most influenced by traditional sexual relations and ideologies. In the United States, the Roman Catholic church has actively participated in the vehement campaign against abortion and in the right-to-life movement but has remained virtually silent on the subject of sterilization abuse. As mentioned, unlike other methods of birth control—particularly abortion—sterilization involves no sin. But there may be another reason for this silence: it is the method of birth control most removed from the sexual act and carries no particular implications with regard to a woman's sexuality.[8] She may be sterilized and never have sex again, whereas abortion is a remedy after the fact; it *implies* a sexual act having been committed. Likewise, other forms of birth control are by definition articulated with sexual planning and practices, therefore with sexual awareness and volition.

Sometimes women may seek sterilization to comply with husbands' demands or to save a floundering marriage, only to regret it later.[9] Interviews with Puerto Rican women suggest that husbands and male partners manifest less opposition to sterilization than to other forms of birth control. In one study men complained actively about the inconvenience of other methods of birth control, whereas only 12 percent were dissatisfied with their wives' sterilization (Ad Hoc Women's Studies Committee 1978:31-32). Whereas Stycos (1978) found an extreme aversion among men to condoms or other mechanical methods, which they associated with immorality, ill health, prostitution, and "filth," sterilization could be simply "forgotten"; unlike diaphragms, condoms, or pills, there is no awkward reminder of the volitional nature of the sexual act and, above all, of the possibility for women of removing it from procreation and enjoying it for its own sake. These attitudes no doubt influenced women as well, particularly those women who felt dependent on husbands materially and psychologically and anxious not to arouse their anger or annoyance. Thus Stycos quotes one woman as saying,

"It is only once, sure, and then you forget about it and don't have to use those dirty things" (Stycos 1968:78). For women defined by traditional modesty about their bodies, deference to sexual norms of female passivity and nonassertiveness, and fears of being stigmatized as "loose," sterilization does not carry the same burden of sexual initiative and responsibility as do forms of birth control that require self-consciousness about sex.

The correlation between nonresponsibility in contraception and greater susceptibility to sterilization suggests that the level of consciousness about sexuality involved in regular use of contraception is very different from the idea of being "done with it" that appears connected to a sterilization decision. But it is also true that the sexual and material context in which a woman finds herself may make sterilization seem the method most conducive to maximizing her own control over her life. Where male partners are hostile to birth control or unwilling to take any responsibility themselves, women may prefer the method that seems least conspicuous, surest, and least dependent on male cooperation. In working-class and poor families where women are saddled with most of the responsibility for children as well as, perhaps, an exhausting job outside the home, this may be especially true. As one working-class wife interviewed by Lee Rainwater in the 1950s put it:

> He doesn't care how many times I get that way; he'd never do anything. The wife [should be responsible] because after the first pleasure the man has no more to do. It's the woman who carries the baby and goes through all the suffering at birth. He goes off to work or gets out of the house and that's all he cares about. He wouldn't use anything at all, he just lets fly. He says that's the only way to get enjoyment; he's selfish enough not to want to miss a second of the pleasure. (1974:127)

Medical Policy

While the conditions just described are important for understanding the general social and economic context encouraging female sterilization, they do not explain the distorted allocation of today's "contraceptive market," monopolized by just two methods: the pill (which involves serious health hazards) and sterilization (which involves major surgery and is usually irreversible). In the mid-twentieth century, birth control has become a major industry controlled by highly concentrated economic interests—the medical profession, pharmaceutical companies, insurance companies, and private and public population control agencies. The commoditization of birth control takes a form that reflects the common ideological perspectives and material interests of these groups: their acceptance of population control as a major political priority and family planning as a means to deal with poverty and social instability; a definition of "efficacy" in terms of control by physicians and technicians rather than the health and safety of users; and a preference for those methods that are the most technologically sophisticated, the most cost-effective, and therefore the most profitable and efficient. Hence the predominance of the so-called medically effective methods.

But the producers and providers of birth control commodities do not impose their preferred methods without having to accomodate the self-perceived needs and organized demands of women themselves. The politics of reproduction proceed through a subtle process of negotiation and struggle. When we try to analyze why medical professionals and population experts favor any one fertility control method over another at a given time, the reasons often have as much to do with strategies for securing control, political legitimacy, and the absence of vocal resistance to a method as with technological sophistication and profitability.

A pertinent illustration is the recent history of the pill and its relation to sterilization. From women's point of view, sterilization may become a preference, not because it is desirable in itself, but because the available alternatives appear less desirable or more dangerous. The tremendous rise in sterilizations since 1970, particularly among older women, is directly related to growing disillusionment with the pill. Alarming studies in British journals, Senate hearings, press reports, and some pressure from the Food and Drug Administration have all produced a public atmosphere of caution and unease. While physicians and population controllers frequently dismiss this concern, the clinical evidence of risks associated with pill use—most of all for women over thirty-five and women who smoke, but for other women as well—became public around 1970 and has continued to accumulate. The morbidity now associated with synthetic hormones extends beyond the early connection with thrombo-embolisms, to myocardial infarction, cardiovascular disease, gall bladder complications, liver tumors, and possibly breast and cervical cancers. This evidence has resulted in a significant drop in demand for the pill, particularly among women over thirty and black women of all ages (Westoff and Ryder 1977).[10] Moreover, it is interesting to note that opposition to the pill was growing among users for several years prior to the news-paper stories and the Senate hearings, since the drop-out rate began to rise in the mid-1960s. This indicates that women were responding not merely to adverse publicity but to the pill's less dangerous but uncomfortable side effects, such as weight gain, nausea, headaches, and so on (Westoff and Ryder 1977:46-48; Hoover et al. 1978:335-41).

With the growing informed popular opposition to the pill, in 1970 the American Medical Association, the American College of Obstetricians and Gynecologists, and the American Public Health Association abruptly changed their traditional restric-tive policy regarding sterilization. Sterilization had already been the subject of an active campaign by the Agency for International Development and the International Planned Parenthood Foun-dation in their international population programs, particularly in Puerto Rico and Latin America. Now, under the influence of organizations like Planned Parenthood Association of America, the Population Council, and the Association for Voluntary Sterilization, the ideology of zero population growth, and sterili-zation as the means to achieve it, were promoted domestically as well.[11] The shift to advocacy of voluntary sterilization as a pre-ferred form of birth control for women of all classes and ages reversed years of hospital practice, which had allowed steriliza-tions of women only under specified conditions based on age, parity, and "medical indications." Within a period of six months during 1970, the AMA and the ACOG issued statements recom-mending that sterilizations be provided as a normal part of "family planning services," without regard to age, marital status, or "medical reasons."[12] Thus surgical sterilization as a routinely recommended means of contraception for women resulted from a conscious shift in family planning and medical policy.

Private physicians control health care distribution in the United States and therefore women's access to reproductive health care and birth control. This is particularly true of sterilization, which, unlike abortion or mechanical methods of contraception, is available almost entirely through private doctors and hospitals rather than through family planning clinics.

Since there are no public agencies to enforce standards of medical care in the United States, private physicians—who are predominantly white, upper-middle-class, and male—control access to reproductive services. Historically, this has resulted in class and race divisions in reproductive health care to women. For example, an unpublished analysis of the 1973 National Survey of Family Growth reveals that "black and Spanish women have markedly higher proportions of hysterectomies for contraceptive purposes compared with white women" (Pratt 1975:5). Moreover, there is evidence that so-called package deals, requiring sterilization as a condition for an abortion, are imposed especially on low-income and minority women patients in large urban teaching hospitals. Doctors tend to assume that poor, poorly educated, or non–English-speaking women are unable to "manage" nonpermanent forms of contraception, and that postpartum sterilization or hysterectomy is "the most feasible solution to the problem."[13]

These assumptions and practices, however, result not merely from physicians' race and class bias but from the dual system of care that has long characterized medicine in the United States. The careful and sensitive counseling that would be necessary for poor and uneducated women to use nonpermanent birth control successfully is reserved for private offices and clinics that cater mainly to middle-class women; in truth, there is little possibility of such care in the hurried, overcrowded conditions of large hospital outpatient clinics, on which poor women rely.[14] More generally, the tendency among medical professionals—instilled by everything in their training and professional culture—to maximize their control over patients reinforces an emphasis on techniques that involve surgery and hospitalization rather than self-administered or ambulatory procedures. According to Victor Fuchs:

> Many physicians have a built-in bias in favor of hospitalization. . . . Their training is heavily oriented toward the hospitalized patient. When in doubt they feel more comfortable if the patient is in the hospital. It is more convenient for the physician, there is more control and supervision of the patient's condition, it is easier to carry on diagnostic work, and emergency care is more readily available if needed. (1974:96-97)

Physicians have an economic interest in sterilization as well. With the declining United States birthrate of the 1960s and 1970s, transformed fertility practices have totally changed the nature of obstetrics and gynecology, resulting in an emphasis on high-technology and high-cost procedures: Caesarean sections, amniocentesis, and fetal monitoring in obstetrics; increasing use of hysterectomies, tubal sterilizations, and routine D&Cs; and pathology (Muller, personal communication). Rather than suggesting a conspiracy by the ob-gyn profession, these patterns indicate *structural* incentives to perform unnecessarily complicated and risky gynecological procedures. These incentives help to explain why physicians have actively promoted sterilization and even hysterectomy as a preferred form of contraception.[15]

The Health Care System

An important aspect of the health care structure in the United States is the system of third-party payments. Public and private health insurance is overwhelmingly biased toward surgical sterilization, both reflecting and reinforcing the shift in medical practice. In the public sector, while medicaid funding for abortion is now virtually nonexistent (except in a few states such as New York), medicaid pays 90 percent of the costs of sterilization. Furthermore, it appears that most commercial and group carriers reimburse abortion only restrictively: they deny coverage to single dependents or to students; they tie abortion coverage to larger and more expensive maternity plans; or they deny coverage for abortions performed in freestanding clinics (where 60 percent of all abortions are performed) (Muller 1978; Forrest et al. 1978). Moreover, nonsurgical forms of contraception are rarely covered by prepayment plans; surgical sterilization, on the other hand—particularly female sterilization—is covered by nearly all commercial carriers and reimbursed according to regular surgical fee schedules (Muller 1978).

This emphasis on female sterilization in all major health insurance plans and medicaid payments reflects a much more general feature of American medicine: the tendency to downgrade ambulatory, primary, and preventive care in favor of hospitalization and, above all, surgery. Hospital care has increasingly taken the form of specialized, capital-intensive modes of treatment—particularly surgery—which are central to its escalating costs (Klarman 1977). What is disturbing is the evidence concerning unnecessary surgery and its particular relevance to sterilization. In its 1978 report, a subcommittee of the House of Representatives Committee on Interstate and Foreign Commerce found that some 2 million "unnecessary" surgical procedures had been performed in 1977, at a cost to the public of $4 billion and approximately 10,000 lives.[16] But the major focus of the report is hysterectomies, and particularly hysterectomies for sterilization purposes. Indeed, the data indicate that a significant part of escalating surgical incidents (and therefore of runaway hospital costs) is gynecological surgery, most of all female sterilization.

The political economy of sterilization, and of surgically prone U.S. medicine, is not gender neutral. It is based on a pronounced sexual division of labor both among practitioners and "consumers." In 1975, in the United States as a whole, operations were performed on women (by a virtually all-male surgical profession) at almost twice the rate they were performed on men; the rate and number of gynecological operations relative to any other procedures was disproportionately high. Indeed, gynecological operations performed in that year were almost *three times as frequent* as the next highest category of surgery and constituted nearly *20 percent of all operations*. Sterilization procedures, in turn, constituted 45 percent of gynecological

Table 5
Estimated Annual Mortality Rates by Method of Contraception
(United States)

Method	Rates per 100,000 users
Diaphragm, condom, foam	0
Vasectomy	—
Induced abortion, 1st trimester	2.5–3
Oral contraception	3–5
Vaginal delivery, full-term pregnancy	20
Induced abortion, 2d trimester	27
Tubal ligation	25–30
Hysterectomy	300–500

Source: Adapted from Arnold 1978 in Newman and Klein, Table 2-1.

operations and nearly 25 percent of the *increase* in all types of surgery between 1970 and 1975 (U.S. DHEW 1978: No. 78-1785). Moreover, sterilizations (including hysterectomies) were performed on women 3.5 times more frequently than on men.[17]

The disproportion between male and female sterilization rates seems "natural," because contraception has been culturally and historically viewed as part of fertility control rather than of sexuality, and fertility remains the responsibility of women— their risk. But the assignment of contraceptive risk to women is not necessarily rational, particularly in the case of sterilization. By every public health measure, vasectomy would appear to be a more rational alternative than tubal ligation or cauterization, to say nothing of hysterectomy, as a means of birth control. First, while the *mortality rate* for vasectomy is virtually zero, for tubal ligation it is around 30 per 100,000, and higher for women over thirty-five—a rate that, in fact, compares quite unfavorably with other methods of contraception (see Table 5) (Arnold 1978:10-12; Porter and Hulka 1974:31). As one researcher conservatively concludes, "the risk of death is sufficiently greater with tubal ligation to warrant consideration of strategies of contraception other than surgery" (Arnold 1978:13).

Figure 3
Annual Rate of Top Twelve Operations for Inpatients Discharged
from Nonfederal Short-Stay Hospitals, Excluding Newborn Infants,
United States, 1975

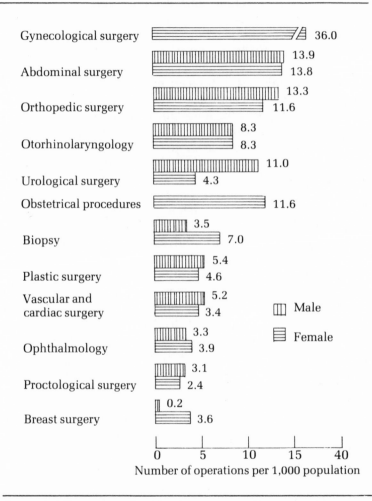

Number of operations per 1,000 population

Source: U.S. Department of Health, Education and Welfare, Surgical Operations in Short-Stay Hospitals, United States, 1975 (Washington, D.C.: Government Printing Office, 1978), p. 8.

Second, morbidity and complication rates are also higher for most female procedures than for vasectomies, particularly when combined with abortion or Caesarean section, when there is an increased risk of infection. Other complications include ectopic pregnancies (which may be fatal to women). For hysterectomies, morbidity rates are some 15 to 20 times higher than for tubal ligation (Arnold 1978; Porter and Hulka 1974; Poma 1980). More generally, whereas vasectomy is a minor outpatient procedure, all types of female sterilization are major surgery requiring considerable skill and technical competence. The older types of female operation involve hospitalization of up to a week and general anesthesia, which always increases surgical risk (Arnold 1978). Newer outpatient methods involving laparoscopy and electrocoagulation have been hailed by Planned Parenthood and other promoters as easy and safe—"Band-Aid surgery." Yet reports accumulate of adverse consequences such as "extraordinary" destruction of tissue and burns to the abdominal wall and bowel. In at least two known cases in the United States, women (one of them twenty-two years old) have died protracted, painful deaths from such burns.[18]

Despite the substantial mortality and morbidity risks, American physicians increasingly recommend hysterectomies strictly as a means of birth control. According to a Center for Disease Control survey, the number of hysterectomies in the United States rose between 1970 and 1975 by an astonishing 40 percent, an increase that is attributed mostly to white women under the age of thirty-five.[19] The major reasons for this alarming increase are sterilization and cancer prevention, with the two often linked: "Proponents of 'hysterilization' argue that the major function of the uterus is to serve as a 'baby carriage,' and that, when a woman desires no more pregnancies, the 'useless' uterus remains a potential site of future cancer" (Porter and Hulka 1974:35).

In other words, the risk of cancer—often predicated on uterine pathology that is not specifically precancerous or even on a complete absence of pathology—is used to rationalize routine sterilization by means of hysterectomy. According to a study in Los Angeles, 20 percent of hysterectomies performed there in 1969–1970 were done for sterilization purposes. Further, "over a third of the patients receiving a hysterectomy had originally requested tubal sterilization," but instead many of these "had been persuaded to accept hysterectomy either because of the enthusiasm of the attending physician or because of coexisting minor degrees of pelvic relaxation or a stress incontinence."[20] Note that these were not women with cancer or any serious diagnosed pathology, but women who were persuaded that a hysterectomy would be a "convenient" way of "managing" birth control while at the same time preventing (a nonexistent) cancer. The trend toward "hysterilization" persists, even though the House subcommittee report on surgicial performance (p. 16) found such a practice to be "arbitrary, capricious, and out of synchronization with the appropriate and conventional practice of medicine"; even though the federal government, in its sterilization regulations, has prohibited the practice altogether, declaring it "a risky, painful, and expensive procedure" and not "appropriate" for sterilization (Federal Register 1978:52163); and even though the ACOG itself has opposed the practice in its official pronouncements.

How do we understand the contradiction between these official statements and the clinical realities of sterilization? What accounts for the failure of medical practice to adhere to the most minimal canons of public health rationality? While hostility toward women no doubt plays a role here, the two fundamental characteristics of U.S. reproductive medicine are reflected: its economic compulsion toward ever more costly forms of intervention, particularly surgery, as sources of profit; and its ideological and practical focus on women's bodies as the appropriate, and accessible, terrain of intervention. Most insidious of all is the apparent practice of some doctors to use women's fear of cancer, along with their desire to be free from worry about pregnancy, to persuade them to undergo hysterectomy. Women who lack education, English-language facility, or the wherewithal to get a second opinion are more vulnerable to this sort of persuasion and to the influence of medical authority than are educated, middle-class women; and, as the evidence suggests, they are more frequently its targets. It is in such situations that the line between "coercion" and "choice" in clinical reality becomes hopelessly faded, and the role of clinicians in defining women's "choices" appears decisive.

Population Control, Capitalist Production, and State Policy

Both directly and indirectly, the state reinforces the official medical and family planning policy of sterilization. However, unlike the situation in Third World countries, the role of the state in this sphere tends to be somewhat opaque. Indeed, the dominant presence of private medicine conveys the *appearance* of freedom of choice in reproductive matters and thus serves important ideological, legitimating, and economic functions. Even where state intervention is most blatant—as in the sweeping legal restrictions on abortion since 1977—it is in the name of deference to both "private" morality (of individuals, religious groups, etc.) and formal "liberty." (Thus the abolition of funds to pay for abortions is said not to interfere with poor women's abstract "right" to an abortion.) But, as with other aspects of production and reproduction, actual state policies affect the reproductive health market in ways that benefit owners more than consumers and that often enlist the forces of repression in the service of capitalist (or private medical) control.

The role of the capitalist state in articulating reproductive functions with the needs of production takes particular forms in the case of biological reproduction and population control. This role is intricate and sometimes ambiguous, however, because of the complex relationship between changes in fertility and in gender relations and the needs of production and the labor market. The main reason for this complexity is the contradiction between capitalism's persistent need to maintain the sexual division of labor in production and reproduction, and its need to hire more women, especially in the clerical, service, and public sectors.[21] Women's labor-force participation has mixed consequences for patriarchal reproductive dimensions of capitalist society (and, indeed, of socialist society). One such consequence is the recent decline in the U.S. birthrate. The political and economic significance of this decline for the advanced capitalist state and economy is uncertain. On the one hand, demographers and policymakers agree with the neo-Malthusian view that if birthrates in the United States and Western countries generally fall below replacement level, their economic and strategic position might be jeopardized vis-à-vis the developing and socialist countries. Thus, after two decades of propaganda about the dangers of population growth, we now hear that fertility in the United States should be increased. However, it is not numbers alone that worry mainstream demographers and capitalists, but numbers in relation to class and race and to the supply of skilled workers and technicians. In fact, U.S. population growth has remained steady, despite the falling birthrate, largely because of immigration, but there are definite limits on the capitalist economy's capacity to absorb even skilled workers and to maintain and pacify the "relative surplus population" that racism bars from acquiring skills and training. Thus, what seems to be re-emerging is a dominant population politics in which fertility and immigration are encouraged among certain groups and discouraged among others, namely, the poorest and those least readily assimilated into production.[22]

The most immediate state policy that is likely to contribute to the rise of sterilization, particularly among poor women, is the curtailment of abortion funding. After the passage of the Hyde amendment, and similar restrictions on the use of medicaid funding for abortions in most states, publicly funded abortions declined by an estimated 98 percent (Trussell et al. 1980). Moreover, the impact of the antiabortion campaign has gone beyond the medicaid-dependent sector, affecting military dependents, women dependent on work-related health insurance plans, women who are either refused abortions or charged exorbitant fees by hospitals or private physicians (Nathanson and Becker 1977, 1980). To the extent that the state refuses to enforce women's presumed "right" to an abortion by providing either funding or public health practitioners to perform abortions, it thereby puts into effect a deliberate antiabortion policy that particularly affects low-income women. The practical unavailability of abortion services to growing numbers of women, especially those dependent on medicaid, that results from this state and medically supported policy will have the unavoidable impact not so much of increasing the birthrate but of increasing the pressure on poor women to become sterilized. This is so because of the prevailing social conditions described earlier, and because of the generous reimbursement for sterilization through medicaid and other health insurance plans. When this compelling fact is added to the virtual absence of any state-sponsored supports for children or child care and the present need of capital to employ most women outside the home, it becomes clear that the antiabortion campaign does not represent a "pronatalist" population policy in the United States, any more than the legalization of abortion was primarily a policy to limit births. In fact, the coexistence of restrictions on abortion and support for sterilization illustrates the important point that the politics of population and reproduction are not only about numbers but about control over women and their relationship to work and to childrearing. To limit the analysis of those politics to the "law of a relative surplus population" overlooks this crucial dimension of fertility control—its relation to gender divisions.

The antiabortion campaign is not primarily pronatalist but rather *antifeminist*, part of a concerted right-wing offensive in the United States and other advanced capitalist countries to seize control of the state apparatus, using the ideological legitimacy of conservative religious and sexual values (Petchesky 1981). This campaign is also related to the racist politics of eugenics, for if there is a pronatalist thrust to the antiabortion campaign, it is clearly directed at white middle-class women. The coincidence of antiabortion and prosterilization policies is not contradictory but, rather, *class- and race-specific*.

Existing policies and practices of involuntary sterilization and sterilization abuse in the United States seem, on the basis of court suits and anecdotal evidence, to be aimed systematically at poor and minority women—particularly welfare recipients in the South, Native American and Latin women, and poor women who are institutionalized or mentally disabled. The only conceivable purpose of such practices is to limit the populations of these groups, in an advanced capitalist economy where the need for a "relative surplus" of unskilled workers is steadily shrinking and where migration from the Latin and Caribbean periphery over-supplies that need in any case. Many of the incidents of sterilization abuse publicized in the last decade have occurred in federally funded facilities which serve largely poor and minority patients. Thus, whether officially mandated or not, through recurrent sterilization abuse affecting these women, the state has been practicing a de facto program of population control.

Many cases of such abuse have come to light since the early 1970s, reminiscent of the hundreds of thousands of involuntary sterilizations that distinguished the early twentieth-century eugenics movement (Rodriguez-Trias 1978; Petchesky 1979b). The most famous involved the Relf sisters and other poor black teenagers in a federally funded clinic in Alabama. In adjudicating that case, the federal district court in 1974 found:

> Over the past few years, an estimated 100,000 to 150,000 low-income persons have been sterilized annually under federally funded programs. . . . There is uncontroverted evidence in the record that minors and other incompetents have been sterilized with federal funds and that an indefinite number of poor people have been improperly coerced into accepting a sterilization operation under the threat that various federally supported welfare benefits would be withdrawn unless they submitted to irreversible sterilization. (*Relf v. Weinberger*, C.A. Nos. 73-1557, 74-243 [D.C. Cir. 1974])

The publicity given to the Relf case generated a chain of complaints and lawsuits about sterilization abuse, most of them involving poor, minority, or institutionalized women. In addition to threats of suspending welfare benefits or health care, abuses by clinicians included the obtaining of consent while women were undergoing labor or under anesthesia; making sterilization the condition for performing abortion; failure to inform the patient clearly, in her own language, that the procedure is virtually irreversible; and in some cases failure to obtain written consent at all.[23]

In response to the publicity and organized protests surrounding these cases the federal government in early 1978 passed a set of new regulations to prevent involuntary sterilization in federally funded programs (*Federal Register* 1978).[24] These very

thorough regulations—a victory for activists against sterilization abuse—were from the beginning opposed vehemently by
organized medicine and by the population policy establishment.
The latter have coopted the idea of "reproductive freedom" from
the feminist movement for reproductive rights, arguing that the
sterilization regulations restrict women's (and doctors') "right
to choose" and disregarding the blatant abuses that limit the
choices of poor and minority women. For its part, the federal
government has provided little in the way of funds or resources
to secure the *enforcement* of the regulations; as with other state
measures presumably designed to protect the interests of consumers or workers against the excesses of capital, it would
appear that the burden of enforcement will fall on those who are
meant to be protected. Indeed, federal auditors from the Department of Health and Human Services report that many abuses
continue with impunity in hospitals throughout the country.
Federal officials complain that they are unable to secure compliance "because they cannot impose any penalties other than
asking doctors and hospitals to repay the federal money."[25] In
other words, when it comes to effectively regulating the rights
and well-being of patients against the abuses of organized medicine, the capitalist state claims impotence. With the ideology of
"deregulation" and privatism that has gained a new hegemony
under the Reagan administration, this impotence becomes official state policy. Economic conservatism and reproductive repression are linked together through the mediation of the conservative state.

Conclusion

Involuntary sterilization of poor and minority women in
the United States grows out of and is nourished by the larger
context of economic, cultural, medical, and political conditions
that encourage sterilization as a voluntary method of birth control. "Voluntary" and "involuntary" sterilization, "choice" and
"coercion" in women's reproductivity, are two poles of a con-

tinuum, with most instances of sterilization falling somewhere in the complex area in between. In most cases it is not individual choices themselves that are irrational or unfree, in the sense of unknowing or forced, but rather the very narrow social constraints in which those choices are made.[26]

For feminists, socialists, and health activists concerned with universalizing genuine reproductive choice, the strategic implications of this analysis are both clear and ponderous. No less than the equality of women and the elimination of reproductive hazards at work; the extension of childrearing and birth control responsibilities to men as well as women; the complete socialization of medical care; and the establishment of a state that provides decent child care and health services are the minimal social changes that reproductive freedom would require. The changes in male-supremacist culture, sexual relations, and motherhood would go deeper still—stretching the radical imagination.

Notes

1. Figures for sterilization rates are so high in part because I have combined the categories of "contraceptive" and "noncontraceptive" sterilization, which the National Center for Health Statistics keeps separate. While collapsing this distinction means that we are including an undetermined number of sterilizations performed for exclusively medical reasons (precancerous conditions, uterine cancers, diabetes, severe hypertension, or cardiac conditions contraindicating childbirth), it gives a more accurate picture of the increase. Even family planning experts agree that the distinction is ambiguous in practice, since surgical sterilizations reported as noncontraceptive in intent are often performed for a combination of reasons, which include terminating childbearing. This is true for hysterectomies (which constituted nearly half of all sterilizing operations in 1973) as well as for tubal ligations and other less drastic procedures. The Department of Health, Education, and Welfare (now Health and Human Services) abolished the distinction in its regulations governing sterilization services in federally funded programs, arguing that whenever sterilization is performed in a situation where "other medical options exist" it is necessarily "contraceptive."

The distinction is further complicated by the system of third-party payments (both medicaid and commercial). Many women may declare "health reasons" in order to claim medical reimbursement, or because they fear the health consequences of other forms of contraception such as the pill or the IUD, or because, in the case of hysterectomies, physicians persuade them to undergo this drastic surgery as a preventative to cancer (see Pratt 1975:6-7; Ford 1978b: 24; *Federal Register* 1978).

2. Other sources include Samuel M. Atkinson and Seaborn M. Chappell, "Vaginal Hysterectomy for Sterilization," *Obstetrics and Gynecology* 39 (May 1972):759-66; and T. W. McElin, J. C. Buckingham, and R. E. Johnson, "Tubal Sterilization," *American Journal of Obstetrics and Gynecology* 97 (1967):479.

3. During the Depression, the United States experienced a sharp decline in the birthrate among all classes and ethnic groups. Although this was the era before the so-called medically effective methods of contraception, there is evidence that the decline was nevertheless related to deliberate efforts by individuals to control births. Thus, for example, over 96 percent of the clients of family planning clinics in New York City in the 1930s were estimated to have used some method of birth control (usually withdrawal or the condom) before visiting the clinic (Himes 1963:336). In contrast, during the 1950s when the more effective methods did become widely available, birth rates rose sharply, in the famous "baby boom."

4. Representatives of this approach include Hyman Joseph, "A Stock Adjustment Model of Child-Spacing and Desired Family Size," in Bahr (1980); George Simmons, "Economic Aspects of Sterilization," in Newman and Klein (1978); see also the critique of this literature by Judith Blake, "Are Babies Consumer Durables?" *Population Studies* 22 (March 1968):5-25.

5. See also Stycos (1968:78) who suggests that in the late 1940s and early 1950s some "one out of five" hospital deliveries in Puerto Rico was followed by sterilization.

6. For this and preceding data on women in the United States, see U.S. Department of Commerce, Bureau of the Census, "Marital Status and Living Arrangements: March 1978," *Current Population Reports* Series P-20, no. 338 (May 1979), pp. 3-6; Heather L. Ross and Isabel V. Sawhill, *Time of Transition: The Growth of Families Headed by Women* (Washington, D.C.: The Urban Institute, 1975); U.S. Department of Labor, Bureau of Labor Statistics, *U.S. Working Women: A Databook* (Washington, D.C.: U.S. Government Printing Office,

1977), Charts 3-4 and Tables 18-22; Gabriel Kolko, "Working Wives: Their Effects on the Structure of the Working Class," *Science and Society* 42 (Fall 1978):257-77; *A Statistical Portrait of Women in the U.S., 1978,* Current Population Reports, Series P-23, no. 100 (Washington, D.C.: U.S. Government Printing Office, 1980), pp. 42-50; Howard Hayghe, "Families and the Rise of Working Wives—an Overview," *Monthly Labor Review* 101 (February 1978):12-19.

7. See the advertisements which appear regularly in the *New York Times* for the "Creative Surgery Center" on New York City's east side ("What God did not give you, we can," the center promises).

8. In fact, the sexual connotations of female sterilization are so strong that it has on occasion been used deliberately—if illogically—as a means of sexual repression and punishment: from *Buck* v. *Bell* on, the unavoidable implication of eugenic sterilizations of countless mentally disabled (or so judged) women was that their allegedly promiscuous sexual behavior would thereby be curtailed. See, for example, *Stump* v. *Sparkman,* 435 U.S. 349 (1978).

9. A British study of women at one London hospital who requested sterilization reversal in 1975 and 1976 found that "an extremely high proportion emphasized bad marital relations before sterilization" as the reason for getting sterilized; some of these women "had been sterilized in an attempt to save their marriage, and nine patients said that their husband threatened to leave them unless they were sterilized—in each case the marriage dissolved after sterilization, often within months." The study also emphasizes that "many of the patients were very bitter," and that "most patients were remarkably young . . . when sterilized," the great majority under thirty. R. M. L. Winston, "Why 103 Women Asked for Reversal of Sterilization," *British Medical Journal* 2 (July 1977):305-07.

10. See also Barbara Seaman and Gideon Seaman, *Women and the Crisis in Sex Hormones* (New York: Bantam Books, 1977); Philip E. Sartwell, "Oral Contraceptives: Another Look," *American Journal of Public Health* 68, no. 4 (April 1978):323-24; and Judith Blake, "The Pill and the Rising Costs of Fertility Control," *Social Biology* 24, no. 4 (Winter 1977). Blake's study, based on Gallup polls and a sample of women in the greater Boston area, reveals that in 1970, just after publication of studies in British medical journals, publicity in the U.S. press, and the Nelson Committee hearings in the Senate, women were discontinuing pill use at the rate of around 66 percent. Moreover, this "dropout" trend has continued through the 1970s, affecting women under thirty as well as older women, so that

by July 1977, Blake found that 48 percent of men and 62 percent of women claimed that the pill is unsafe. The difference in men's perceptions and women's in this respect—given who bears the risks of the pill and who, some argue, has reaped the benefits of the "sexual revolution"—is noteworthy.

11. The Association for Voluntary Sterilization assumed that name in 1965, when it also began to campaign widely for "voluntary sterilization" as a means to foolproof birth control and sexual happiness. Prior to that, AVS had a long history of association with the eugenics movement, whose major goal was involuntary sterilization of the mentally retarded and the allegedly "unfit"; from the 1920s to the early 1960s, it underwent various name changes (including "Human Betterment Association" in the 1950s, and before that, ironically, "Birthright"—connoting, apparently, the "right" of an "unfit" person not to be born).

12. See "Official Statement of the American College of Obstetricians and Gynecologists," and "New Guidelines of the American College of Obstetrics and Gynecology on Voluntary Sterilization," appendices in Wylie (1977:193, 201) and editorial, *Journal of the American Medical Association* 204:9. In the late 1960s a number of articles appeared in obstetrics journals advocating female sterilization as a simple, medically sound procedure which could be performed on an "interval" as well as a postpartum basis (Wheeless 1970; Cohen et al. 1970; Bopp and Hall 1970).

13. According to Stycos (quoted in Presser 1978:28), "Many physicians [in Puerto Rico] thought, and still think, that contraceptive methods are too difficult for lower class Puerto Ricans and regarded postpartum sterilization as the most feasible solution to the problem." Another observer's review of the ob-gyn literature on surgical sterilization in the late 1960s and early 1970s led him to conclude that arguments "for the use of hysterectomy solely for sterilization purposes . . . are often accompanied by faintly concealed derogation of the lower socioeconomic class, minority-group women who are frequently lost to follow-up post-partum counseling on contraception." The medical authors cited (C. J. Roach et al., "Vaginal Hysterectomy for Sterilization," *American Journal of Obstetrics and Gynecology* 114 [1972]) "urged hysterectomy especially for those who usually fail to comply with medical and contraceptive management"—a likely reference to poor and uneducated women. Charles B. Arnold, "Public Health Aspects of Contraceptive Sterilization," in Newman and Klein (1978:15).

14. Thanks to Dick Glendon for reminding me of this important point. See also Frederick S. Jaffe, Barbara L. Lindheim, and Philip R. Lee, *Abortion Politics: Private Morality and Public Policy* (New York: McGraw-Hill, 1981), pp. 38 and 64 for a nice summary of the dual system of medical care as it affects reproductive health; and Barbara L. Lindheim, "Services, Policies and Costs in U.S. Abortion Facilities," *Family Planning Perspectives* 11 (1979).

15. Some excellent critical historical studies of changes in the organization of U.S. obstetrical care include Richard W. Wertz and Dorothy C. Wertz, "Epilogue," *Lying-In: A History of Childbirth in America* (New York: Schocken, 1979); and Nancy Stoller Shaw, *Forced Labor: Maternity Care in the United States* (New York: Pergamon Press, 1974). See also Helen Wolfers, "The Incidence of Psychological Complications After Contraceptive Sterilization," in Newman and Klein (1978) who suggests that evidence for such "active promotion" may be found in clinical literature (which she cites) that not only advocates contraceptive sterilization but minimizes the risks and complications. Presser (1978:28-29) points out that "physicians in Puerto Rico seem to have played a key role in making surgery a viable option for women interested in family planning," even implying that without the active initiative of physicians, Puerto Rican women "would have relied essentially on the traditional methods of withdrawal and (illegal) induced abortion." Westoff and McCarthy (1979), whose attempts to use statistical measures to estimate who among a sample of women would become sterilized between 1970 and 1975 failed, concluded that factors which their study had "not taken into account" must be responsible for the sterilizations—listing, particularly, *"exposure to medical opinion,"* dislike of other birth control methods, and the promotional publicity given to sterilization.

16. United States, House of Representatives, Subcommittee on Oversight and Investigations of the Committee on Interstate and Foreign Commerce, 95th Cong. 2nd sess. (December 1978), "Surgical Performance: Necessity and Quality" (Washington, D.C.: U.S. Government Printing Office, 1978), p. 2. The committee defines "unnecessary surgery" as "surgery performed without appropriate medical treatment having been tried first; two separate operations performed within days of each other on the same patient when it appeared that there was no medical justification for not performing the second procedure during the first operation; or an excessive number of surgical procedures performed on one patient." It asserts in its

findings that "contentions by organized medicine that unnecessary surgery cannot be defined are diversions and obfuscations which serve to be counterproductive."

17. I have compared the figures given in U.S. DHEW 1978: No. 78-1785, Tables K and L, with those provided by AVS estimating the number of vasectomies among U.S. males in 1975. Since vasectomies are done almost entirely on an outpatient basis, usually in a private physician's office, they are not included in the hospital survey.

18. Herbert B. Peterson et al., "Deaths Associated with Laparoscopic Sterilization by Unipolar Electrocoagulating Devices, 1978 and 1979," *American Journal of Obstetrics and Gynecology* 139 (1981). The authors, researchers at the Center for Disease Control in Atlanta, were prompted by these tragic deaths to conclude: "We question the need for continuing [the] use [of electrocoagulation methods] in female sterilization." See also, "Female Sterilisation—No More Tubal Coagulation," *British Medical Journal*, April 12, 1980.

19. In the Congressional hearings on surgical performance, cited above, one physician testified that some "40 percent of [U.S.] women will have had a hysterectomy by age 65"; and the chairman of the Department of Obstetrics and Gynecology at Harvard remarked "that the number of hysterectomies done in this country at the rate of 647 per 100,000 females of all ages is 'staggering'" (p. 14).

20. Lester T. Hibbard, "Sexual Sterilization by Elective Hysterectomy," *American Journal of Obstetrics and Gynecology* 112 (1972):1077. This study found a 293 percent increase in the utilization of hysterectomy for sterilization over a thirty-month period, in the Los Angeles County-University of Southern California Medical Center, and a 722 percent increase in "elective hysterectomies not associated with a pregnancy."

21. For a much more developed presentation of this analysis, see Zillah Eisenstein, *The Radical Future of Liberal Feminism* (New York: Longman, 1980), Ch. 9.

22. See, for example, Charles F. Westoff, "Some Speculations on the Future of Marriage and Fertility," *Family Planning Perspectives* 10 (March-April 1979):79-83. Westoff's "speculations" offer a novel proposal for "solving" the problem of U.S. population decline. He suggests that all U.S. women of childbearing age be divided into two groups: (1) a class of "professional breeders," who would specialize in reproduction and who, prodded by "maternal incentives" (state subsidies, child-care centers, etc.) would be required "to reproduce at an average rate of 3 births per woman"; and (2) a

class of women involved primarily in productive labor who "would never have any children." That Westoff's concern is not simply numbers of births but *kinds of people* becomes clear when he discusses immigration, recommending that current restrictions be tightened rather than lifted: to "set [qualifications] fairly high to bring in persons with training in skills in short supply in our economy." A similar neo-eugenicist purpose obviously inspires Westoff's "pronatalist" proposal: "maternal disincentives," and sterilization as a highly recommended "choice," would no doubt continue to be offered to poor women and women of color especially.

23. In 1976 the General Accounting Office found "that 3,000 female sterilizations had been performed in a four-year period in the federally funded facilities of the Indian Health Service" using consent forms which were "not in compliance with [federal] regulations" (Ad Hoc Women's Studies Committee 1978:20). Teaching hospitals acknowledged the common practice of performing elective hysterectomies on poor black and Hispanic women as part of standard ob-gyn training. Court cases revealed instances of abuse by private physicians, such as the South Carolina rural doctor who for years had refused medical treatment to his financially indigent female patients when they declined sterilization after three children (*Walker v. Pierce*, 560 F. 2d 609, 1977). In California, ten Chicana women in 1978 brought a suit against interns and residents at the Los Angeles County Women's Hospital, a facility meant to serve the poor, charging that they had all been sterilized involuntarily in the early 1970s. This case is still on appeal at this writing.

24. The regulations provide, among other things, that full voluntary consent be obtained and all information be provided orally as well as in writing, and in the patient's own language; that no valid consent may be obtained during labor or before or after an abortion; that patients may not be coerced by overt or veiled threats of being denied their welfare or medical benefits if they refuse; that patients must be given complete information—in their own language—about the irreversibility of sterilization, its risks and side effects, and the contraceptive alternatives; that no sterilizations may be performed on persons under twenty-one, legally incompetent, or involuntarily institutionalized; that there must be a thirty-day waiting period between the time of consent and the time of the operation; and that *no hysterectomies may be performed for sterilization purposes.*

25. Howie Kurtz, "Sterilization Abuses Discovered in Nine States, Including Kansas," *The Wichita Eagle-Beacon*, February 8, 1981. See

also Richard D. Lyons, "Virginia Is Sued by Victims of Involuntary Sterilization," *New York Times*, December 30, 1980, p. A6. It should be noted that even the relatively mild sanction of withdrawing federal monies does not affect providers directly, since in practice federal auditors do not require that providers return misspent funds but simply deduct funds from their next medicaid payments to the state. Thus, in effect, there is no real sanction or penalty imposed on providers, who have no incentive to stop committing abuses.

26. Cf. Agnes Heller, *The Theory of Need in Marx* (New York: St. Martin's, 1976), p. 52: "The individual chooses the object of his needs and molds his personal needs in a way that conforms not with his personality, but with [his/her] position in the division of labor." The implication is clearly that it is the division of labor itself—the social relations of production (and, we should add, of reproduction) —that must be transformed.

Rural Family Size and Economic Change: A Middle Eastern Case

Barbara C. Aswad

Discussions of population and family size once looked at ideological factors to explain the apparent failure of rural families in developing areas to correlate economic variables and decisions about family size. While not ignoring the role of ideology in family size decisions, critics have pointed out that the size of a rural family must be regarded primarily as a means of manipulating and attempting to adapt to economic processes and access to resources (Mamdani 1972; Gross and Underwood 1971; Mass 1976; White 1973). This perspective, which I share, allows us to understand the relationship between family size and access to resources in a rural area of Turkey.

Household studies from the Amouk Plain in the Hatay region indicate that the penetration of capitalism in that area has created multiple reasons for an increase in the number of children and only a few for a decrease. The Plain, which comprises 250,000 acres, is adjacent to the city of Antioch and located in the southwest part of the country. The Hatay region was part of Syria until 1939, when it was ceded to Turkey by the French mandate government. In essence, this was a political maneuver, aimed at keeping Germany from using the Dardanelles (Sanjian 1957). Hence many of the area's inhabitants, particularly the lower classes and petite bourgeoisie, are ethnically Arab and bilingual in varying degrees. The soil of the plain is rich black alluvial at its center and terra rosa around the peripheral high ground, conditions which permit high agricultural yields with adequate rainfalls, and also lend themselves to agricultural intensification. Wheat has been the major subsistence crop, and cotton the major cash crop.

Until recently, land and labor relations in the region resembled a form of feudalism, or semifeudalism. A century ago, the Otto-

man authorities forcibly settled a nomadic Turkish confedera-
tion on the land, giving title to the chiefs. Eventually an estate
system developed, in which lower-ranking members of the con-
federation as well as members of various Arabic and Kurdish
tribes became sharecroppers for noble landowning Turkish families, who constituted a class of latifundists.

Around the edge of the estates, patrilineal kin groups (primarily Arabic speakers) settled in villages and held their land
jointly as corporate kin groups. The dominant kin groups or
lineages expanded into the villages of weaker kin groups on
their borders by offering protection to noble chieftains in exchange for land. These dominant tribal lineages became the rich
peasants, while those whose land was taken became middle
peasants, poor peasants, and sometimes even sharecroppers.

From approximately 1920 to 1950 urban notables, both Arab
and Turkish, further expanded their land holdings by extending
credit to poorer peasants and foreclosing if crop failure or bad
weather occurred. The rich peasants, who served as the agents of
the urban elite, also furthered their holdings, since they could
obtain credit easily; but they managed their lands and economy
corporately, so that any debt incurred by an individual was
payed off immediately by the kin group.

The process of agricultural mechanization and increased capitalization began in the early 1950s with heavy investment in
cotton production. Initially the process involved primarily the
use of tractors, ditch irrigation, and fertilizers. Later, other elements were introduced such as aerial spraying of pesticides and
aerial irrigation. The agrocapitalists formed a marketing cooperative and received technical and economic assistance from the
U.S. Agency for International Development and Turkey's Department of Agriculture. It was difficult for poorer farmers and
peasants to compete because of their limited capital and the
power of the larger landowners and rich peasants. Mechanization was also accompanied by the release of thousands of sharecroppers from their jobs, the destruction of hundreds of villages,
and the impoverishment of former sharecroppers. The increase
in economic stratification is witnessed by the disparity in in-

comes. In 1965 an agrocapitalist could earn $250,000 annually while sharecroppers made $50 a year as members of a rural subproletariat of harvest laborers.

A limited land distribution program initiated in the early 1950s aided some former sharecroppers, but most were forced to live in nearby urban slums. The land distribution plan gave ex-sharecroppers ten acres of land, primarily land expropriated from Syrian landlords or drained from a nearby swamp. The program was designed to serve a number of political purposes: to undermine the economically powerful Syrians by taking their lands and to quell the growing land demands of the impoverished sharecroppers. It was not part of a nationwide program for socio-economic change; nor was it accompanied by supportive measures to enable these peasants to keep their land or act collectively. No further lands were provided for their children. Because land distribution is a popular political strategy, often undertaken without further economic reorganization, the results of the increase in family size reported here have critical implications for development schemes based around this policy.

In addition to the data from the estates and the villages involved in the land distribution areas, I also examined the effects of increased capitalism on the villages at the edge of these estates, those of the rich, middle, and poor peasant owners. A limited number of sharecroppers also live in these villages to serve the rich peasants, but as the owners mechanize production, the sharecroppers are being released.

These changes are taking place within a state economy that has been characterized by the import of luxury goods, machinery for capital-intensive industry and agriculture, and military equipment, and by the export of resources. Such a process has resulted in an increased demand for foreign capital and has caused heavy debts. Turkey's debt was $14 billion in 1979 (Benhabib 1979). Part of the capital is locally owned in the Hatay and there is a low return to labor; this strengthens certain internal social classes: latifundists or agrocapitalists, rich peasants, and state bourgeoisie. Production for the internal market suffers. In the area under discussion, the state has begun to share in industrial investment with the agrocapitalists. Most of the important products are for export, such as cotton, but some, such as fertilizer are also consumed within the country.

One of the most important effects of increasing capitalization of the countryside is the separation of sharecroppers and other peasants from their means of subsistence, which results from the profitability of cash cropping over subsistence cropping and the ability of those with capital to control the markets through monopolistic means. Thus peasants must often buy food they once grew or else eat less. However, since land, which is scarce, is also a factor of production, capital alone does not dominate the area, and noncapitalist relations continue to be important. One cannot be a member of the landed aristocracy just because one has capital, for access to land is still heavily determined by inheritance and is important in determining control of capital and market relations (Rodinson 1973). Thus we must consider the forms of landholding to understand the development of one form at the expense of another and to understand the social reactions of various strata of rural peasants and workers.

Rural Socioeconomic Categories and Family Patterns

In order to examine the responses of family size to resource control more thoroughly in the Amouk plains area rural population, I broke households down into the following categories:

Rich peasants. Those are peasant landowners who own their land corporately as a kin group based on patrilineal principles. They do no agricultural labor themselves, but hired sharecroppers in the past and are now increasingly using machinery. They have a surplus and, today as in the past, serve as middlemen in the flow of trade and capital to poorer rural populations. They also have political and religious functions.

Middle peasants. There are two forms of middle peasants in this region. There is a poor version of the rich peasant, living in villages surrounding rich peasant villages. They do little labor but have less surplus and smaller landholdings, and thus must occasionally work. There are also former sharecroppers, given small amounts of land by the government in areas of land distribution, who use family members to perform agricultural work.

Poor peasants. The poor peasants have very little land and must cultivate their own small plots as well as the lands of the middle and rich peasants or that of an absentee landlord. The entire family works. There are few poor peasants in this area, because of the extensive use of sharecroppers and machinery.

Sharecroppers. These have no land of their own and work one share for a portion of the crop on latifundist estates or in rich peasant villages. From the latifundists, sharecroppers receive 25 percent of the crops cultivated, after taxes, and from the rich peasants 25 percent or 50 percent depending on whether or not they own their own animals. This category is extremely oppressed; all members of the family work, although not necessarily as a single family group.

In general I found that some rich peasants who formerly had very large families, high rates of polygyny, and early marriages are now beginning to form a middle bourgeoisie. Although most still have fairly large families, they are discussing limiting their families. Some find that the children are becoming a burden. At the other end of the economic scale, sharecroppers on estates who, under conditions of semifeudalism before the 1950s, had small families, virtually no polygyny, and later marriages, *doubled* the number of children when they were given land through land distribution. Marriages are earlier, but there remains little polygyny. I also found a change in family size among the second generation of this latter group, since further lands were not made available to them, and they had to resort to wage labor in which children could participate or take to the risky business of renting lands. Despite unemployment resulting from mechanization, seasonal cotton picking remains manual labor, and thus children can add significantly to family income from about the age of six.

My data include samples from four villages, providing representatives of each category of peasant and workers. Village A consists of rich peasants who form a patrilineal landholding corporation. Village B is an estate where sharecropping is still practiced by the older generation while their children are primarily seasonal laborers. Village C consists of persons who had been sharecroppers and were given ten acres of land in the early 1950s (middle peasants of the second type). This village also includes some who continue primarily as sharecroppers and a younger generation who have been forced to work for wages or rent lands, since no additional parcels were allocated for the children of the original owners. Village D borders the rich peasant village A, and provides a sample of the first type of middle peasant, as well as a sample of poor peasants.

The largest group represented in the sample are the landless sharecroppers. In 1961, 60 percent of the 40,000 people in sixty villages of the plain were represented as landless (Planlama 1961). Thus the rates of population increase in villages A and B should be most significant for overall population trends in that region.[1] The effects of a governmental policy that undertakes limited land distribution without supporting measures to secure peasant land tenure and does not incorporate land reform into a nationwide program for social change is seen in this group.

The unit of analysis in this study is the family household, which is the major arena for decisions concerning family size, as well as the specific controlling unit for consumption, production, and allocation of resources. Among rich peasants there are primarily extended family and lineage networks, while among sharecroppers there are mainly nuclear families. The families have been divided for analytic purposes into two main age groups according to the age of the head of the household: one category is thirty-two years of age and over, the other under thirty-two years. This division corresponds generally to households formed before and after the period of land distribution and increased mechanization in the region, and these reflect changing economic conditions. It was intended to measure the effect of these changes on family size among formerly landless sharecroppers, the group that has experienced the most dramatic change (Table 1). As a control, in the same village we examined those who did not receive land and remained primarily sharecroppers. The age division and its relation to family patterns

Table 1
Mean Number of Children by Economic Structure of Family

Occupation	Age category	Average number of children	Number of households	Average age of head of household
Village A: Rich peasants				
Rich peasants	1	6.3	23	50
	2	3.9	8	29
Village B: Estate sharecroppers and laborers				
Mainly sharecropping	1	3.1	12	46
Mainly labor	2	3.6	6	29
Village C: Land reform village: former estate sharecroppers, now middle peasants, sharecroppers and laborers				
New landowning middle peasants	1	6.4	20	48
	2	3.7	10	27
Mainly sharecropping, some renting	1	3.0	12	45
Mainly renting	2	3.6	6	29
Mainly sharecropping, some labor	1	3.0	8	46
Mainly labor	2	3.8	7	28
Village D: Middle and poor peasants				
Middle peasants	1	4.6	18	47
	2	3.4	9	28
Poor peasants	1	4.5	9	45
	2	3.9	5	28

Age category 1: head of household 32 years and over
Age category 2: head of household under 32 years

among rich, middle, and poor peasant families reflects to a greater extent the effects of mechanization rather than land distribution.

Changes in Household Strategies and Family Size

Rich Peasants: A National Middle Bourgeoisie

The reasons for the large families among the rich households reflect economic and political considerations dating from conditions of semifeudalism. They controlled land as corporate kin groups (the larger the family, the more land) and achieved economic and political power through marriage alliances, which were accompanied by large economic transfers in the form of brideprice. In addition, leaders of the rich family kin groups had economic and political connections with the landed elite, the latifundists, which they used to expand their control of land, by offering protection and credit to weaker groups in exchange for land.

Thus continuing their local brokerage position, the surplus accumulated by rich peasants allowed early and numerous marriages. Also women did no fieldwork, allowing more time for child care. Persons at the edge of kin group control had fewer wives and smaller families than the leaders, but the average number of children for the kin group was high (6.3 for those household heads thirty-two years of age and over). Rich families traditionally used sharecropper labor, but where one latifundist family on an estate may have employed 200 sharecropping families, each rich peasant family had one sharecropping family, normally living next to the main family house. Rich peasants occasionally took sharecroppers' daughters as one of their wives; no such marriage was possible on the estates.

Historically, these rich peasant villages had been settled by nomads, and the leaders of the kin groups served as intermediaries in trade and arbitration between the chieftains of the plain and those of the surrounding mountains, for their villages lay between the two. When the latifundists moved into the urban areas in the 1920s, the rich peasant lineage leaders retained their intermediary positions by acting as rural agents (wakils) for the absentee landlords as well as for other newly emerging urban-based landowners, overseeing the sharecroppers and managing production.

The lineage I resided with during my year on the Amouk Plain were of saintly status; they served not only as agents and traders, but as arbiters and religious leaders, interpreting the Sharia and the Koran. They were also healers and functioned as local "psychiatrists." It is among this group that we find the strongest forms of patrilineal organization, together with corporate lineage control of major resources and means of production. Even today, despite the attempts of various governments to divide their lands and give individual titles, the land is collectively owned by the families of the village. Inheritance rules within the lineage allocate division of produce to nuclear families (Aswad 1971).

By acting as their political patrons the latifundists, in turn, had protected the rights of corporate ownership for the rich peasants against the regulations of various governments. In addition, the latifundists gave the lineage leaders credit, which they used for several purposes. They expanded their land and acquired more wives; their families were large and polygamy rates were high. The rich peasants, however, valued their children for their potential alliances rather than for their labor, and the average number of children for the leaders over four generations was 15.0.

Since leadership passes to the sons of the most successful leader of the former generation, there is a buildup of population at the center of the lineage. In Islam, sons are guaranteed equal shares, while a daughter's share is half of a son's.[2] One would imagine that the buildup of population at the core of a lineage would decrease the power of succeeding generations through inheritance. However, the leaders used their alliances with patrons to obtain additional land from surrounding villages on which to place some of their sons. In the villages today (Village A), those older rich-peasant families average 6.3 children, while the younger ones average 3.9 children; 42 percent of the first group is polygynous, none of the second group is.

I examined three rich-peasant lineages, one in the center village owning its property corporately, the other two in neighboring villages. The three are related by a fictive ancestor, share the same last name, and form a highly (80 percent) endogamous unit. The older generation has high polygamy rates compared to other peasants, and there is a direct relationship between the amount of land owned and polygamy rates (Aswad 1971:67). Residence is patrilocal. Although endogamy is high, polygamy allows simultaneous marriage both inside and outside the clan section with the same name, thereby controlling property and extending political alliances to the outside. Marriages were planned either at birth or by nine years of age. Brideprice payments begin after betrothal and are paid in full by the time of marriage: for girls at about age fourteen, for boys, about age seventeen.

The children of this group did little physical labor, although the girls aided their mothers. No children worked in the fields. Children were important for the economic and political transactions of their fathers: the more children one had, the more transactions one engaged in through the use of brideprice. The size of the unit of males is also important for reasons of vengeance and as a fighting unit, since force sometimes entered into land disputes. Women processed food, did domestic chores, and raised children. They did not engage in work in the fields, and thus had more time for children and for personal care during periods of pregnancy, a factor they boast about when comparing themselves to women of poorer families.

Chayanov and Shanin have argued that the increased amounts of land held by rich peasants does not give them additional power because their large family size dilutes the person/land ratio. They failed to recognize the power relations which such peasants have with the upper classes, relations which allowed credit, expansion of marriage alliances, and political control, contingent on large family size (see Littlejohn 1973).

In the recent market period, however, especially since 1950, the role of the rich peasant as an intermediary or agent for a landlord has diminished as landlords no longer need them. Landlords either personally oversee their estates or hire overseers who live on the estate year round. They are even attempting to buy the lands of their former agents instead of protecting them as they once did. This means that rich peasants no longer have access to additional land and now take loans from merchants rather than latifundists. Rich peasants use a variety of methods to maintain their standard of living. They have retained the corporate land ownership which operates to reduce risks; they have released their sharecroppers; and they have slowly increased production through mechanization. Their average income in 1965 was $1700 annually. Most recenty, they have quadrupled production, in part because of access to irrigation and government loans; they have also increased exploitation of the middle and poor peasants (a factor often discussed by the latter groups) by cornering the distribution of seeds to poorer groups and acting as conduits of capital to the rural areas. This process has been analyzed by Dow (1973), Franke (1974), and Roseberry (1976) for other parts of the world.

A family of four or five children is still thought to be desirable by most rich peasants, but the pattern of extremely large polygynous families among the kin group leaders is changing. One leader who has twenty-six children and three wives is often scorned and people now comment that they are making him poor. Another young leader, his brother, has deliberately settled on three children and one wife, stating that he wants his children to go to college. This reflects a radical change in family size and philosophy.

Some rich peasants have acquired windfall incomes by renting absentee landlords' properties and managing them on a two year contract. Most, however, cannot compete in a sustained manner. They use capital for local marriage alliances and thus do not have liquid cash necessary for a fluctuating market. Additionally, the large capitalist farmers have a cotton marketing cooperative that does not include the rich peasants. Thus these peasants must usually return to their patrilineal lands after a few years. The richest man in the village in 1965 was in debt when I returned five years later.

Although their strategies of corporate land ownership allow rich peasants to take risks, the increasing economic stratification in the plains area also threatens them. Numerous children are not as great an advantage as they once were, as cash begins to compete with social relations as a source of power, and there is no available land to pass on to heirs. Too many children become a liability. A more recent popular strategy is to educate the boys in town and get them out of the village, their education being considered their share of the inheritance. Many of the boys have become primary and secondary school teachers with the aid of a government sponsored program, or they have gone to technical schools. Their incomes do not add to their fathers' income, as they are not high and are needed to raise the son's own family in the cities. Nor are these positions politically advantageous. Nevertheless, the sons' jobs are viewed with some pride (although they are not viewed as upward mobility because of the low pay), as education has a high value among religious sheikhs who are literate in the Koran. Some boys are now marrying city girls, which results in their female cousins (the traditional marriage partner of choice) remaining unmarried for long periods. This had caused nervous conditions such as ulcers, tensions, and acts of violence among the girls. Since the lineage will not marry girls to lower-status peasants, it is likely that there will be a reduction in the birthrate among this generation of rich peasants.

Sharecroppers and Ex-Sharecroppers: The Sub-Proletarians

Sharecroppers are at the opposite end of the scale from rich peasants. Under semifeudal conditions sharecropping meant children were not beneficial, since the landlord controlled all forms of production and the sharecroppers controlled their own labor. Their share of the produce did not substantially increase with the input of more family labor. Sharecroppers had access to some subsistence, but the households had no access to wages, and thus the children could not add to family income. Thus sharecropper households had the smallest number of children (averaging 3.0 for household heads over thirty-two years). Capitalist penetration has resulted in increased family size in all categories: some were given land and became middle peasants of the second type; others rented land, taking on financial risk, which obliged them to supplement their income with seasonal wage labor; still others relied solely on low-paid wage labor picking cotton, which is viable only if it involves the labor of the entire household, including the children. In all categories, the marriage age seems to have dropped.

Households of the older generations, whose primary occupation had been sharecropping, averaged 3.1 children (in Village B) and 3.0 (in Village C). They had virtually no polygyny and married later in life, since it was difficult for them to accumulate cash. The usual age of marriage was eighteen to twenty years for women, and twenty-five or older for men. A man could leave his share to only one son; the others were forced to search for their shares elsewhere, most often on other estates. The estates were close together and I found much mobility, with an average of six years spent on any one estate. Landlords also preferred not to have large kin groups on their estates and thus acted against clustering to ensure better control. In most villages no more than three or four nuclear families would be related. The typical arrangement might be for one son to live near his father, father-in-law, or uncle. The majority of marriages are outside the kin group, and among those inside the group, there is only a slight preference for the father's side. Also, most children did not marry within their own village. The far-flung nature of kin and nonkin networks were useful, however, in finding jobs on other estates.

It is important to distinguish these sharecroppers from those peasant sharecroppers in Egypt and Java who work on estates but also have their own small plots. White (1973) and Hussein (1973) found that such peasants were obliged to have numerous children in order to farm their own plots for subsistence and simultaneously work on plantations, because of the small return on the plots. As a result, children became important for cheap labor for rice and cotton production. Peasants in both areas were also involved in production for export and had intensive irrigation cultivation, thus being less dependent on weather conditions than peasants on the Amouk Plain, whose access to irrigation is not year-round. Wheat production was primary in this area and cotton, secondary until the expansion of cotton production, irrigation, and mechanization of cultivation in the 1950s.

The second generation of sharecroppers that remain in the area are obliged to have many children. From Table 1 we see that the sons of laborers and small renters average 3.8 and 3.6 children respectively, that is, more than their older sharecropping fathers. Those who are forced to rely on wage labor alone are subject to periods of unemployment because of fluctuations in the market and the weather; their income depends on what they can earn during the busy season and the number of pickers in their family. They state bluntly, "If you have four children, and you and your wife pick cotton, you each earn $50, or a total of $300 a year, and you can get by. Otherwise you can't." They also cite changing conditions wrought by external aid; "You Americans have slit our throats. Many have died. . . . So and so landlord was bad, but it is worse now. We have no sure credit, no security at all."

In the case of renters, they must pay out cash ahead of time and assume the risk of the market price. They claim they cannot rely on the changes in the weather and the market, and often must pay 100 percent interest or more to get cash for planting. It is a highly speculative business, and they feel that they need to have children to pick cotton for security. Children are a cheap investment, since they can pick cotton at a young age. This is true for both boys and girls, and as Mamdani found in India (1973:94) girls are now appreciated almost as much at birth as boys.[3]

In sum, the landless are forced to rely on short-run strategies in unstable market conditions over which they have no power. Children are a source of additional cash. Marriages are earlier and brideprice figures have become related to the market. Economic and health conditions are little better, and women must now work harder as laborers in addition to their previous jobs as food processors and mothers, adversely affecting maternal health, and giving them less time for child care.

New Middle Peasants

Initially, those peasants in Village C who received the ten acres of land did well. These families (age category 1) were able to rent additional lands with their capital, and incomes varied greatly, ranging from $900 to $2500 yearly, with most closer to the first figure. Some of the wealthier also lend out money in bad seasons, and a few have bought tractors, renting their tractors out to other farmers.

In terms of family size, the contrast with previous generations of sharecroppers is startling. The families have doubled the number of children to 6.4. Apparently the new lands encouraged them and they felt they could use family labor on the new areas. In part they may also have been imitating rich peasant family life. They have little polygyny however—10 percent compared to 42 percent for the rich peasants—and thus the number of children per wife is higher than it is for rich peasants.

Both new landowners and poorer workers spend about 10 percent of their annual income on medicine, compared to about 5 percent spent by rich peasants, medium peasants, and share-croppers who live on higher ground. Yet health conditions in Village C are quite bad, despite this expenditure, worse than in those villages on higher ground.

Unfortunately for the children of these new middle peasants, there have been no additional land grants, and some have had to resort to renting land or working as seasonal laborers when they get married. The birthrate of the second generation is similar to that of the second-generation sharecroppers. In fact, among all the peasant and worker categories, in the second generation we find they have more children at the age of twenty-seven than their sharecropping fathers had at the age of forty-eight.

Middle Peasants

This category consists of peasants who own land and occasionally work it as a family, hiring people for seasonal labor. The amount of land they own is usually less than the rich peasants, but the main distinction is who works the land. In the surrounding mountain villages there are numerous examples of a stable class of middle peasants. But in the plains villages (Village D), these peasants were often forced off their land by rich peasants and landlords, either migrating to other areas or becoming share-croppers (Aswad 1971). This middle-income category earns an average of $1000 yearly compared to $1700 for the rich peasants. They try to imitate the rich peasants, although they have less polygyny and thus an average of smaller families. They align themselves politically with rich lineages trying to marry their daughters into these more powerful families. If forced off the land and into the category of sharecroppers, they have small families. From Table 1 we see that these middle-income peasants average 4.6 children for eighteen families in the older age group and 3.4 children for nine families in the younger group. This group is pessimistic about the future. Their lands are being increasingly threatened by agrocapitalists and the rich peasants who dominate the local avenues to the market. Their children are not in urban schools,[4] and they do not want to be laborers, even on their own lands. The somewhat lower birthrate may reflect this view.

Poor Peasants

There are, in fact, few poor peasants on the Amouk Plain, because of the extensive use of sharecroppers in the area. The few that exist live in the villages alongside rich and middle peasants (Village D), where they own small amounts of land and work for the rich and middle peasants. Some had been middle peasants who lost their lands to those with more capital or through inheritance divisions. They resemble Egyptian and Javanese peasants in that they need children to work their own small plot and simultaneously work others' lands. The children often stay in the village after marriage, forming extended families, and thus are not as mobile as sharecroppers' children are. Most recently they are filling some of the odd jobs left vacant by expelled sharecroppers in these villages. For them, children have always been valued as workers, and the number of children they desire is high.

Conclusion

The results of this investigation have helped to demonstrate the important relationship between changing economic conditions, household strategies, and family size. Increased use of money and credit, access to small landholdings for previously landless sharecroppers without further economic assistance, and increased dependence on unstable markets have all brought an increase in the number of children desired for most categories of peasants and workers, and a reduced number desired for only a few—primarily some members of the rich peasant class. These findings add to an understanding of the reasons behind the current world increase in population in areas of peripheral capitalism.

Notes

1. It should be mentioned that this data was not collected with the intention of analyzing population variables, and thus important data such as mortality, birth, and abortion rates were not collected. It may be stated, however, that the availability of medical services is virtually nonexistant locally, although much effort is spent riding buses to obtain services in distant towns. The effects of government policies on birth control, child labor, and other areas is negligible. Only rich and middle-income peasant children go to village schools, although this does not preclude their participation in picking cotton if necessary, since the harvest season is in the summer.
2. In these villages, land is not part of a daughter's inheritance, unless there are no sons. In that case, the daughters get half and the other half goes to their male cousins on their father's side, whom they usually marry, thus keeping the land within the closed patrilineal unit.
3. The desire for children is contrasted to the Gross and Underwood (1971) study of peasant families in northeast Brazil who switched to sisal production for the export market. There the strength requirements of sisal harvesting meant that children were not beneficial until they were teenagers or adults. In that case, the investment period was long, and during periods of food shortage children were not fed well.
4. There were no members of the families in this study who had worked as laborers in foreign countries. That pattern seems more typical of middle peasants of the mountain or persons who have migrated to the cities and have obtained some capital. A new steel mill was constructed on the coast, and it is partially staffed by the Russians near Iskerderun on the coast. But so far only one person, a son of a rich peasant, was working there. Most laborers who work at the steel mill come from villages closer to the mill.

Population Policy, Family Size, and the Reproduction of the Labor Force in India: The Case of Bombay

Karen L. Michaelson

Any mention of India evokes discussion of "the problem of over-population," and, indeed, India has become synonymous with the dismal picture of the teeming, starving masses of Asia. The interest in the problem of population is not just the concern of outsiders who wish to guide India's development: population planning has long been a significant part of India's development planning. The Indian government was one of the first to adopt a family planning program at a national level, and the campaign to slow population growth continues to be a key feature of long-term development planning. My visit to India in 1969–1970[1] revealed a constant media barrage extolling the virtues of the small family and advertising the availability of family planning services. No film was shown that did not have the familiar red triangle symbol of the family planning program flashed on the screen at least once. No newspaper or magazine lacked advertisements for the two-child family. Posters with the smiling faces of two parents and two children (one boy, one girl) met the eye at every juncture. It is estimated that by 1970 about 80 percent of urban people and 60–70 percent of rural people were aware of population planning and the means to achieve the small family norm (Mandelbaum 1974:6).

Despite these massive efforts, India's population increase of 24.7 percent for the 1961–1971 census period was the highest ever. Obviously there has been a gap between public interest in population planning and private self-interest in family size—between the availability of family planning services and actual use of these services.

An earlier version of this essay was presented in the symposium on population anthropology at the Seventy-fourth Annual Meetings of the American Anthropological Association in San Francisco, December 1975.

In April of 1976, under the Emergency Rule of Indira Gandhi, a new national population policy was adopted with the goal of reducing the annual birthrate from 35 to 25 per 1,000 by 1984. Under the direction of Prime Minister Gandhi's controversial son Sanjay, the new policy included legislation to raise the minimum age of marriage, deny subsidized housing and medical care to government employees who did not voluntarily undergo sterilization after the third child, and increase incentives to men voluntarily undergoing sterilization (Frankel 1978:565). Between April and September of 1976, 3.7 million people were reported sterilized.

But the abuses and charges of coercion associated with this new population policy led not only to disillusionment with the massive national sterilization effort, they also contributed substantially to the downfall of the Gandhi government. After the Emergency, birthrates crept from 33 to 34 per 1,000, and by 1979 there were 630 million Indians, with a daily net increase of 35,000. More than 40 percent of these Indians are under fifteen years old, with the reproductive years still ahead of them.

This study analyzes that population growth, as exemplified in Bombay, and puts it into the context of the historical and social features of the reproduction of the labor force in a capitalist economy. The focus is on the microprocesses of family-size decisions, which produce the high birthrate characteristics of India's population growth. It avoids a discussion either of the aggregate data of such population growth, available extensively elsewhere, or of the awesome projections of that data. Such aggregate data, while informative in terms of the description of population dynamics at a macrolevel, do not reveal the underlying processes that stimulate rapid population growth, or the variety of factors that appear to make large families desirable at a microlevel. After all, demographic events do not take place in the aggregate: child-bearing decisions are made at the individual, or at most, the familial level. Additionally, when population becomes "overpopulation" in concept, it does so in terms of a set of resources—pressure on subsistence in Malthusian terms, or more precisely in a capitalist system, pressure on employment.

The focus on Bombay, one of India's major—and most modern—

cities, points up the way in which the process of capitalist development affects urban population growth just as it does fertility in the rural areas. Population theorists, citing Europe's "demographic transition," expected birthrates to fall once the nations of the Third World "modernized." One index of that modernization was thought to be the level of urbanization, the city being the site of industrialization and the major point of contact with the ideas and technology of the West. Yet birthrates have not dropped rapidly in India, in rural or in urban areas. In this study, the factors that structure urban birthrates, especially among the poor, are revealed to be similar to the contexts in which rural fertility decisions are made. When the rural family moves to Bombay, or when generation after generation of "hutment colony" dwellers reproduce their labor power under near-starvation conditions, their structural position in the capitalist economy and the choices that they face remain very much the same as for those who remain in the countryside.

The other focus of this study is an analysis of the processes within the capitalist system of production that stimulate the rapid growth of population in the absence of a concommitant expansion of the economy to absorb it. According to Marx, surplus population—the so-called reserve army of the unemployed—is both a product of capitalism (through such factors as mechanization, boom-bust cycles, urban migration), and at the same time essential to its system of exploiting workers. Thus family-size decisions are analyzed as part of the larger process of capitalist development in India.

The final section of the study examines the assumptions underlying India's population planning policies in the context of the features of capitalist development.

Population Growth and the Dynamics of Colonialism

It is an error, historically, to presume that current high birthrates in countries such as India are a function of irrational behavior in the face of scarcity, or "native inability to control their basic urges." Rather, they are a result of the historical processes of colonialism—the external factors that made high natality a rational solution to labor needs (Polgar 1972:207). In India, as in much of the rest of the colonized world, the colonial administrators needed a large supply of productive labor to produce raw materials for the mills and factories of the West. Additionally, they needed a market for their manufactured goods. Thus population growth in the colonized areas was encouraged. It was only when the need for a cheap labor pool became less pressing, and the poverty of the colonized masses rendered them unsuitable as market consumers, that population control became an issue. But by then the stage was set for high natality and the means of lowering mortality, resulting in continued rapid population growth.

The actual transformation of the Indian economy, a long, drawn-out process, was a direct result of the political and economic policies adopted by the British government and the economic penetration of India by British capitalism (Desai 1959:28). This historical development is well documented by Bettelheim (1968) and others. Of particular concern here are those national and international policies that lead to local decisions to have large families, and consequent perception of overpopulation.

The establishment of industry and commerce opened vast numbers of jobs to the Indian labor force. These jobs, however, were located mostly in urban centers, such as Bombay. Thus job opportunities, plus deteriorating conditions in the rural areas (including commoditization of land, transition to a cash economy, and so forth), caused a rapid population influx to the towns, giving rise to enormous shortages in housing, employment, and a variety of social amenities.

Recruitment of the labor force to these new opportunities was largely on a preexisting caste basis: "the caste groups who had access to better jobs used ties of caste and kinship to fill future job openings and solidify their group's positions" (Michaelson 1976:290).

In the post-Independence period, the legacy of British rule resulted in a highly stratified society, beset by a variety of shortages—in education, housing, and employment opportunities. Migration to towns and cities has continued, while industrialization has not developed rapidly enough to provide adequate employment. Elsewhere (Michaelson 1976) I have documented the ways in which the scarcity of resources encouraged continued reliance on caste and family ties to achieve individual and household economic stability. The continued impoverishment of the countryside, together with pressing shortages in the urban areas, set the stage for present population growth and now provides the context in which individual family-size decisions are made in India.

Rationale for Family Size: Household Economics

The decision to have a large family emanates from social and economic conditions that make it advantageous to have such a family at the level of the individual household.[2] At the most basic level, people are not poor because they have large families; "quite the contrary, they have large families because they are poor" (Mamdani 1972:14). It is necessary to realize, in this context, that the family remains the basic unit of work and economic security in India. No account can be made of individual income or well-being without taking into account the family as the wider budgeting unit. This holds true whether the family lives in a nuclear household or a joint one, for where economic (and thus family-size) decisions are concerned, most families may be considered as joint entities. Those who earn a little more contribute to the support of less fortunate kin, whether they reside within the household or not. Owens (1974:25) points out that in his sample of those with below-subsistence incomes, over 60 percent lived with families in which other incomes raised theirs to a more or less viable level. Thus it is necessary to look at the totality of a family's strategies for making a living in examining family-size decisions.

The labor of children (from an early age) plays a significant role in the economic strategies of poor families in India, in urban as well as rural areas. In an underdeveloped economy, small children perform productive tasks that are of great service to the family. "Often these services are of little importance in themselves except that somebody has to do them and if they can become the responsibility of the younger children, then the parents and the older children are freed for more productive pursuits" (Clinton 1973:53-54). In rural India children at a tender age tend livestock and do household chores. In the city they gather dung, small bits of coal along the railroad tracks, bottles, and other saleable debris; they can also beg, and to a degree, run errands. In both cases, female children can be expected to care for still younger children (or cousins) and free their mothers for either domestic labor or an outside menial job.[3]

As children get older the opportunity for outside employment increases. In rural households older children engage in seasonal agricultural labor alongside their parents. For those families, the cost of maintaining many children is usually less than the benefit of their work contribution during the seasonal peak of high labor demand (Polgar 1972:208). Mamdani estimates that a child between the ages of five and sixteen can earn Rs 150–200 per year ($18–$25), plus food and clothing. Parents thus have little economic burden from a child, whose income goes to swell the family coffers. It is important to note in this light that while I was in India the poverty line was considered to be Rs 1200 ($145) a year for a family of four, so that a young child might be expected to earn a fair amount of the total family income, while at the same time not costing the parents a great deal. Farm families must also consider the possibility that several children will take employment elsewhere, such as in a nearby town, and contribute their wages to the family's well-being.

Much the same may be expected for urban children. In 1969–1970 opportunities for youthful employment in Bombay were extensive. Their jobs ranged from vendoring of a variety of goods (small-scale vendors and shopkeepers find it advantageous to have a number of sons to tend the store), through household service, to more formal employment. A common strategy is to place a child as a servant in a well-to-do household where he or she will earn real income and be reasonably well provided for.

One household in my research population employed a fourteen-year-old boy servant at Rs 50 a month, Rs 45 of which was sent directly to his parents. He was provided with more nutritious meals than he could expect at home and several changes of clothing. He lived in the household and was provided with his personal effects. Children as young as eight years old were employed as household help. Several such children, or perhaps a few who attached themselves to a factory or office as junior peons or messengers, can increase a family's income substantially. Laborers are not unaware that even a youngster may bring home wages that can make a difference of considerable import in the house (Mandelbaum 1974:19). Thus at the household level a large family seems the best way to meet present financial exigencies. Marx aptly notes that the premium set on the exploitation of children leads to their production (see Meek 1971:108). In a society where the economic system does not necessarily reward increased education with greater financial remuneration, it is rational to have many children, at a low cost per child, and put them to work early for maximum benefit.[4]

Contrary to the beliefs of many population planners, the poor have many children not because they are uninformed or irresponsible, but because they *want* them. Children are perceived by the poor as a means of "getting ahead." Through their labor they provide capital with which to invest in expansion of various types. For those who wish it, older children can be expected to contribute their wages to the education of younger children. Or all family members may pool their income to educate one child, who will then use his or her (hopefully increased) income to help the others: the latter strategy was common in Bombay among the poor. The more productive workers in the family, the greater their ability to support one child through the unproductive educational years.

Because the labor market is fragmented by differential recruitment by caste into coveted jobs, the educationally equipped son of a poor family may need to buy his way into the "modern sector," using family resources for "donations" to get a foot in the door. Once in a better job, the young man creates an outpost through which he hopes he can bring other relatives in—and keep unrelated poorer castes out (Breman 1976: 1906). Thus, where a rich man invests in machines, a poor man invests in children (Mamdani 1972:113).

Additionally, even with the limited expansion of opportunities in industry, many laborers feel that the more children they have, the more chance there will be that at least one of them will make good. The as-yet-unborn child might be the one to "make it." Everyone seems to have examples of two-child families where both children had turned out badly (Poffenberger 1975). And there are always counterexamples of large families who, despite lack of education, had one lucky scion whose success lifted the whole group out of poverty.[5] The hope of such success, although almost never achieved, spurs the desire for many children. For most, the strategy does not work out as planned, for unemployment and obligations of dowry and debt prevent substantial savings.

Children are wanted, additionally, for security: in old age, in sickness, or in case of some unnamed disaster. Women, in particular, are anxious for sons to care for them in old age and give them status as mothers-in-law and grandmothers. But even a daughter can be expected to contribute to her parents' maintenance. The more children born, the more chance that at least one will survive and be able to support aged parents. This phenomenon is common not only to India:

> Economic investigation shows clearly that once people are compelled to undertake wage-earning activities in order to pay taxes and to gain some cash, if the capitalist system does not provide adequately for old-age pensions, sick-leaves and unemployment compensation, they have to rely on another comprehensive socio-economic organization to fulfill these vital needs. . . . In this light, it is clear that demographic expansion, which is the logical means to face the social security requirement, comes as a response to colonial pressure. (Meillassoux 1972:102-03)

The lack of social services in urban areas accentuates the feeling of needing security. A common belief is that in rural areas, many social overhead needs were "taken care of by the village" while in the city, a family had to muster all its strength simply to survive in the competitive, and sometimes hostile, environment. Many Bombayites feel that an elderly or disabled person has a place in village life, and would not be allowed to starve no matter how many of their family survived. But in the city, a family can rely only on itself.

The familial base of social and political power as well as economic strength provides a further justification for the larger family. Having a large number of children is a valuable asset to poor Indian families, not only as a wage-earning strategy but as a means of gaining power and prestige. Many sons give power in a dispute; the marriage of daughters also increases the network of relatives who may be relied on in times of need. Because kinship brings power, prestige, and economic gain, a large family network is advantageous to those at the lower end of the socio-economic distribution system (Benedict 1972; Marshall 1972). Mandelbaum neatly sums up the factors which make large family size a rational choice for the masses of Indian poor:

> Many in India share these values about having children, believing that the more sons they have, the greater the family's chances for economic gains. Those who are concerned about their childrens' education commonly reckon . . . that if they have many sons, some of them will help pay for the education of others. Those who find that they have more sons than their land or trade can support hopefully expect that some will find jobs elsewhere and return part of their wages to the family purse. All know that a flourishing set of sons provides insurance in case of sickness, credit against debt, and the best kind of strength to meet social obligations. (1974:21)

Class Differences in Family-Size Decisions

The economic pressures that weigh upon the poor and create conditions favoring large families do not affect the more educated, wealthier Indians in the same way; their access to more varied resources and opportunities does not require reliance on a large number of children. In a recent national survey, urban couples with the highest income averaged 2.84 children per woman on completion of the reproductive cycle, while poor families averaged 4.53 children (Mandelbaum 1974:43). In both cases women tended to bunch births in the first ten-to-fourteen years of marriage, but wealthier women tended to stop having children sooner and to space their children more. Given massive media campaigns, this difference cannot be explained by differential access to family planning information alone, although it is true that such information reaches the somewhat wealthier segment of the population more effectively. (For example, information on tubal ligation, IUD, or other contraceptive devices is frequently provided in maternity homes—immediately after delivery of a child—when a woman is liable to be most susceptible to the advantages of postponing future pregnancies. The poorest women tend not to deliver their children in these maternity homes.) Rather, differential fertility can best be explained by differential access to resources.

The security factor is a case in point. Data from my research among Bombay's middle class[6] indicates that provision for later life income—and even the need or desire for the income from child labor—drops off as a justification for childbearing. For example, the elderly parents of one woman (whose husband held a low-level managerial job) had ceased having children after only two daughters had been born. This had been considered a daring move, when even now most middle-class couples will try for a male heir in the third child. The old man's justification was that in his line of work he was eligible for a pension and hence had less need of sons. Yet he also carefully married his two daughters, at a very high dowry cost, to families with many sons, so that one son-in-law at least is now available to them in their old age.

Most couples in the research population expressed an ideal family size of two sons and one daughter. Couples under thirty appeared to space children at four- to five-year intervals and postpone the birth of the first child until at least a year and a half after marriage.[7] Of households with two children, most used some form of contraception, and several women with three children had had tubal ligations after the delivery of the last child. While women forty and over in the research population had an average of four living children, most younger women and their husbands desired small families and were taking action toward that end. Because middle-class families are reasonably assured of infant survival, they need not have six or seven births to ensure desired family size. In fact, overly large families or too close spacing of children were roundly criticized by middle-class informants, both in terms of national needs and the ability to provide adequately for children.

To middle-class families children are not income earners, they are costs. Educating a child through college requires extensive expenditure, making more than three children a financial hazard. These households, however, already possess sufficient resources to keep their (fewer) children in school; they need not count on the labor of additional children, as is the case in lower-income households. Even desire for sons is outweighed by cost considerations. After three daughters, one could still have more daughters, and dowry would lead the family into financial ruin.

Family planning has become a part of urban middle-class ideology: urbanites characterize themselves as "people who plan" and castigate the poor for their prolific reproduction. Yet decisions to limit family size work only in the context of the resources open to those who are already middle class: for those who hope to rise, more children mean more potential.

Interestingly, even the poor couples I interviewed or observed differed in their contraceptive behavior according to the relative security of their occupation. Blue-collar workers in factories and other "formal" work contexts tended to try to limit births in their families, although these were larger than those of the middle class. Men and women with more casual employment (hawkers, servants) tended to have large families with little or no attempt to space their children. The difference can be attributed in part to the incentives many workplaces provide for males willing to undergo vasectomies, which include cash payments and paid leave time. But the government also provides incentives for vasectomy candidates, employed or not. The difference in fertility behavior certainly is not due to a differential in knowledge of contraception, since female household servants, in particular, are quite aware of the intimate details of their middle class employers' lives. One twenty-three-year-old servant, pregnant with her sixth child, told me that she knew about "the planning" and thought it was a good idea to space children, since her own children were "weak" (one died shortly after birth; another was crippled). But she felt she could not use any contraceptive method, because her husband's family wanted more children.

Reproduction of the Labor Force

The concept of the reproduction of the labor force used here moves from the historical conditions of scarcity, which motivate family-size decisions in a particular historical form of capitalism, to an analysis of the underlying dynamics of capitalism as a structural system. Using this analysis we can see that individual choices are not made by chance but result from the structural properties of the system in which the individuals live. This approach draws heavily on the work of Godelier, Althusser, and Balibar, and combines both structuralist and materialist perspectives. "For Marx as for Lévi-Strauss a structure is *not* a reality that is directly visible, and so directly observable, but a *level of reality* that exists *beyond* the visible relations between men, and the functioning of which constitutes the underlying logic of the system, the subjacent order by which the apparent order is to be explained" (Godelier 1972:xix). Understanding the economic context of family-size decisions explains the surface phenomena better than the assumptions of population planners who see lack of technology or motivation as causing population increase. But that analysis does not explain the workings of the system in which those family-size decisions are made. The notion of reproduction destroys the appearance of individual or even groups of individual acts as isolated phenomena and places them within the continuity of the productive process.

The phrase "reproduction of the labor force" means that every society must reproduce the conditions that enable production to go on at the same time that it is producing its material needs

(Althusser 1972:242). The conditions of production mean not only the material factors of production (such as raw materials and machinery), but also the reproduction of the productive forces, that is, labor power. Reproduction is thus the continuity of the elements of the productive process: with no pun intended, the "pregnancy of the structure" (Balibar 1970:258). One may thus speak of social reproduction—the reproduction of the human component, the actual bodies that provide the labor for the system, in every system of production including capitalism.

But at the same time that the actual bodies are being reproduced (or replaced) the social relations of production, which allow it to function as such, are also reproduced (Balibar 1970: 270). Reproduction thus means the continual reproduction of the relations between the classes, both in number and in their relationship to one another. In this light, biological reproduction—and particularly differential fertility—can be understood as not only peopling the Indian subcontinent, but continuing the system of social class as it presently exists there.

Reproduction and Surplus Labor

In the analysis of family-size decisions I noted that the poor have more children than the middle class or the wealthy because the poor lack other resources with which to raise their status, or even to survive. How do these relatively larger numbers at the lower socioeconomic levels of society serve to reproduce the capitalist system? It appears at first glance that the system is "over-reproducing"—creating more workers than it can possibly absorb and thus creating the concern with overpopulation.But just as in other modes of production appropriate labor is reproduced as required, so in the capitalist mode of production this redundant population of workers—what is called the reserve army of the unemployed—is required by the system to meet the labor requirements of its cyclical fluctuations and to maintain a labor force willing to work for low wages. Marx stated in *Capital*: "The overwork of the employed part of the working class swells the ranks of the reserve, while conversely the greater pressure that the latter by its competition exerts on the former, forces them to submit to overwork and subjugation under the dictates of capital" (cited in Meek 1971:100).

That this phenomena operates in India, and in particular in Bombay, is obvious both to the casual visitor and through the analysis of economic data. Joshi and Joshi (1976:30) note that the openly unemployed in Bombay number about 5.9 percent of the labor force potential. This figure, however, does not include the underemployed, those who work in low-productivity tasks, disguised through too many workers per job, mismatches of education and occupation, and abbreviated work hours (Owens 1974).

Overall in India, the total of jobs generated within the so-called "organized sector", characterized by steady employment and in legally constituted enterprises, had stagnated to about 500,000 per year by the mid-1970s. This lack of expansion in both the public and private sectors faces a projected 65 million entrants into the labor force by 1986, building on an existing backlog of 18 million unemployed (Frankel 1978:495). While most of these organized sector jobs are in urban areas, access to them, as noted before, is highly structured by caste and kin ties, and the majority of the poor are excluded from them.

Joshi and Joshi note that over half the workforce is "employed" in this unorganized sector, and that number is increasing rapidly. Personal services occupy much of the surplus army of the unemployed and underemployed in the unorganized sector. There are more than 13,000 *dhobis* (washermen) and 11,000 barbers (Joshi and Joshi 1976:52), most of whom work on a casual basis without formal business premises. Even cursory observation reveals itinerant priests and astrologers, self-appointed car watchers, grindstone sharpeners, private tutors, street dancers, and animal trainers, whose numbers swell the ranks of the surplus army. In commerce, hawkers, dealers in scrap, old bottles, and newspapers, and an assortment of beggars ply their trade on Bombay's streets. Hawkers may have small stands, or simply spread their handful of goods on the ground before them. These enterprises vary in prosperity, frequency and scale of operation, and degree of legality. In manufacturing, casual employment is found as daily labor, as messengers, or in small firms. Transport and commerce absorb numbers of part-time drivers, rickshaw wallahs, and coolies. The tiffin carriers, who transport lunch for middle-class workers from home to office, form a small army of informally employed men.

The large families of the poor take advantage of this unorganized sector to find casual employment for family members. But the high fertility of lower income groups, while seeming to provide upward social mobility for individual families, creates a reserve army of the unemployed and underemployed in India, which depresses wages and working conditions for workers. The middle class, which has accepted family planning in line with the smaller need for their numbers in the present Indian economy, faces somewhat different employment pressures. Much of the surplus of that class is absorbed by prolonging education where there are no jobs (Owens 1974:8). Even with that means of diverting a portion of the labor supply, the economy's inability to absorb the educated provides a surplus population, thus keeping wages depressed for white-collar workers as well as for laborers. Those who have invested in education for their children often find that these children have to take jobs much beneath their skills. In addition to depressing wages the pressure of this surplus army also serves to stabilize the labor force, as the fear of job loss is great.

Reproduction and Class Ideology

It is not only through acceptance or nonacceptance of family planning that the labor force is reproduced in numbers appropriate to the needs of the capitalist system in India. The ideology of elite population planners also separates middle- and lower-class workers. The middle class accepts the ideology of the elite planners—that the poor are unmotivated to control their numbers—and uses this as a continued reason to deny further programs of social welfare to the poor. The supernumerary presence of the poor is ascribed to their irresponsibility, and their poverty-stricken state to excess fertility rather than to the inability of the system to absorb this surplus population. Both Mamdani (1972) and Mencher (1970) note the negative light in which middle-class family planning workers and researchers view the intelligence and rationality of the poor. The author's research among the middle class in Bombay (Michaelson 1972) indicates a similar attitude: the poor are incapable of maintaining a standard, and programs for their betterment are well-nigh useless until they are motivated in middle-class terms. Because the educated middle class of Bombay is active in promoting family planning, this bias tends to make effective appeals to the poor difficult—and the failure of such programs reinforces middle-class conceptions of the irresponsible behavior of the poor.

Thus not only the numbers of the classes, but also their social relations, are reproduced. At the same time, the concept of lower-class irresponsibility causes the middle class to see their interests as separate from the working class, with whom they might otherwise ally themselves.

Family Planning Efforts in India

In the context of this discussion of the dynamics of capitalism and the motivations for family-size decisions we can now examine the successes and failures of India's family planning programs. By and large, excessive population in India has been seen as a malady, and family planning has been viewed as the cure. Family planning programs in India have emphasized the medical aspects of population control: the diversity of contraceptive methods, contraceptive information and appliance delivery systems, and the numbers of acceptors of family planning services. Family planning has been perceived as an educational effort, with medical research to "build a better contraceptive" taking up a great deal of the research funding. This situation is not exclusive to India, but has held throughout most of the Third World:

A look at the budget of USAID, the largest funder of population related research, yields some interesting findings. Of the $10,701,000 spent on research in 1971, 59% went toward the development of improved technological devices for contraception, abortion and sterilization; 24% was spent on the development of systems to deliver these devices, while only 17% was allocated to the study of population dynamics and descriptive demography. . . . Less than 4% of AID's budget in 1971 (and this is true of the entire 1966-71 period) was spent trying to determine the socio-economic conditions which influence fertility behavior. (Godwin 1973:135)

There are two fundamental reasons for this medical approach to population planning in India. The first has to do with the kinds of research that have been used to support public policy, for the choice of research methodology largely determines what types of policy recommendations will be made. The second factor has to do with which groups have been in control of population policy and planning.

The idea that people generally desire small families and need only to be provided with appropriate contraceptive techniques comes largely from the widespread use of Knowledge, Attitude, Practice (KAP) surveys of individuals in target populations on matters of family-size planning and contraceptive techniques. If the KAP survey's findings reveal that most women want fewer children than they have (and this is frequently the result), then it is assumed that the problem is a failure of education and availability, rather than a lack of motivation to reduce family size.

Such studies, however, have built-in problems as a methodology for approaching population and family-size decisions. In the first place, KAP surveys, which indicate a desire for a smaller family, do not account for the meaning of the question to the respondee. Most poor women in India never really give thought to how many children would be ideally desirable, and the notion of limiting family size absolutely (for spacing of children is frequently desired) is a non-issue. The desire for a large family, after all, has a rational economic source. Additionally, a poor woman faced with a well-dressed family planning worker may well give the answer she knows is desirable, rather than the one she really feels. Thus the "expressed" desire for a smaller family (even though the smaller family may still be above what is desirable on a national scale) is misleading.

Given the earlier analysis of the socioeconomic circumstances motivating large-family-size decisions, it is obvious that KAP surveys do not provide the basis for understanding family-size decisions in a social context. They lead to solutions which are essentially "to disseminate contraceptive devices and to 'educate' individuals about the importance of using them, rather than to seek to alter the social circumstances and thus to change the social base of the individual act" (Mamdani 1972:20). KAP surveys and the assumptions which underlie these studies almost invariably lead to findings supportive of existing policies and socioeconomic relationships.

That this should be so is not surprising, for the persons who have devoted the largest amounts of time, energy, and money to the population issue have been the economic elites, which have been able to "mobilize bias in favor of those policies which do not threaten the existing power structure." "By implying that the only need is the invention and distribution of new technological devices, family planning programs do not disturb the elites" (Godwin 1973:136). It is interesting that the enlarged population, which originally provided abundant labor and local markets for the capitalist, became "overpopulation" when the mechanization of industry made such labor unnecessary, and the impoverishment of the masses made them a poor market for producers' goods. It is at that point that population policy became an elite concern and family planning became an integral part of India's development policies.

The elite concern with population control is not unique to India. From the time of Malthus, population control has been concerned not merely with the regulation of population, but with the regulation of *the population of the poor*, lest they become an unruly, and potentially revolutionary, mass. If poverty is "caused" by fertility, then regulation of fertility is the solution. Such a solution is considerably cheaper than economic aid or measures to redistribute income (Segal 1973:175). And under the Emergency, with its emphasis on control of "undesirable elements," family planning efforts focused even more on the poor:

> Inevitably, as the pressure on state officials to set higher targets for sterilization increased, and as district officials and government employees . . . were assigned quotas of numbers of persons they were to pursuade to undergo sterilization—or risk their own jobs, salary increases and promotions—the family planning programs degenerated in many areas into a terrifying campaign of forced sterilization. As always, those who were most powerless were the most vulnerable to arbitrary power. . . The tribals, the Harijans, the minorities and other members of the Backward Castes and classes were the first victims of forced sterilization. (Frankel 1978:565)

In recent years there have been a number of criticisms of the overmedicalization of India's family planning program. Liberal theorists have attacked family planning efforts in India and elsewhere by explaining that the problem is not technological but one of lack of motivation to reduce family size (Polgar 1973:21). These criticisms, however, do not escape the class bias which underlies the whole issue of family planning. They shift attention from "what programs and policies will be effective in reducing population" (for no one denies that population is *a* problem, if not *the* major problem in development), to "what type of *family planning* program will be most effective." The assumption here is that the poor are not acting rationally in having large families and need to be educated so that they will understand the value of the small-family norm. Rather than focusing on programs and policies of socioeconomic change that would motivate small-family-size decisions, this new emphasis continues to focus on family planning programs, now seen as a form of education rather than simply technology.

Yet it is difficult to expect the disadvantaged masses of India to be motivated to reduce family size by appeals to the national good or world betterment. Many of the alleged advantages to individual families are "probably more apparent in theory than in practice; unless other conditions are changed, and at any rate the masses in the high fertility areas will have to be shown, not told, that such advantages exist—they have been exploited too long and too consistently by those in more privileged positions to take on faith any advice from these sectors" (Clinton 1973:6). Not only do the poor have more immediate problems to deal with, they have the least to gain from promoting the so-called collective good and preserving the present inequitable distribution of social advantage. The fact that family planning programs are at present advocated by those who most benefit from that inequality does nothing to inspire their confidence.

Reproduction, Choice, and Population Policy

Family planning theorists, like most liberal theorists, have stressed consumption and distribution in their analysis of population, rather than the role of particular segments of the population in the production process. Thus family planning programs have stressed the consumption of contraceptive services and have looked at the choice of a child versus other wanted items as a consumer issue. Such a view does not place these choices within the wider socioeconomic system, nor does it explain the role that so-called overpopulation plays in the capitalist system. Choice, to liberal economists, is based on maximizing return, and its exercise presumes that such choices are possible and free.

The assumptions of the Indian family planning program that result in an emphasis on technology or motivational increase are thus drastically misplaced. Past declines and increases in fertility have had little if any relationship to advances in contraceptive technology. To the extent that fertility relationships are understood, they seem bound up with personal and economic interests at an individual or familial level (Godwin 1973:136). Individual families, after all, are not trying to solve *population* problems. They are trying to solve *poverty* problems, even if the solution to those problems is to have a large family, and even if individual decisions to reproduce appear to run counter to class interests limiting numbers to reduce surplus labor. Since such behavior is a rational byproduct of the socioeconomic conditions in which these individuals live, motivation to reduce family size comes not from attitudinal change through propaganda but from changes in the socioeconomic circumstances of family life.

This analysis in no way implies that birth control information and assistance should be denied to those who desire them. But family planning programs must be combined in India and elsewhere in the Third World with profound changes in the social and economic structure, changes that will then alter the way in which the labor force is reproduced. Only such changes will provide the conditions under which poor families, in urban as well as rural areas, will have fewer children.

Notes

1. Field research for this essay was supported by a Fulbright Fellowship and conducted over a year's time in a suburb of Bombay. The data upon which the empirical portions of the study are based were gathered from some 300 households, about 25 of which were visited on a regular basis (once a week), and 7 or 8 of which were visited daily.

2. This seems to presume that a real "decision"—to have or not to have a child—is made. In many cases, little thought is given to whether or not to have a particular child, especially among the poor. When the desire for a small family is expressed by poorer families, it is often after the fact, when opportunities have already been closed off.

3. The contemporary norm is still for women to remain in the home as much as possible. Typically, only the poorest women, whose income-producing capacity cannot be spared, work outside the home. The slight increase in women workers among the middle class is probably as much economic pressure as any real notion of "women's liberation." An economy that can hardly absorb male workers tends to reinforce conservative attitudes toward women's outside employment.

4. Issues of relative costs and values of children—the high quality child versus quantity—presume a largely Western model of what a "quality" child is. The Western emphasis on a carefree childhood, and its attendant high costs, should not obscure the fact that in many other countries children take on responsibility at a much earlier age than is common in the United States, and thus begin showing "benefit" or value much earlier in life.

5. I never met one of these proverbial families, despite the fact that my

work was among the middle class, where such success stories should have surfaced. A few families in my sample had increased their means over time, but none—for several generations back—had been really poor. If a single member of a very poor family is successful, that member typically becomes so enmeshed in increasing family responsibilities, for a widening circle of kin, that his increased income makes little real difference because it is so spread out.

6. The term "middle class" must be used cautiously in the Indian context. For my purposes, I used the research population's definition: incomes between Rs 200-1000/month (depending on family size), nonmanual occupations, and a life-style characterized by the maintenance of a perceived "standard" of consumption and propriety. In real terms, this population consisted of wage earners, not owners of the means of production or even high-level managers. Despite their real status as workers, however, members of the research population defined their interests as different from those of manual laborers. The issue of the reality or place of the middle class in Indian society is too complex to deal with in the context of this paper.

7. Age at marriage has also risen for middle-class Indians. The average age at marriage in the research population was males, twenty-eight to thirty, females, nineteen to twenty-three. The parental generation was characterized by brides of about sixteen to eighteen years. This increase of age at marriage, particularly of females, has also lowered the number of births per couple.

Part II

Labor Migration and Population Growth

Cross-National Labor Migrants:
Actors in the International Division of Labor

Elizabeth McLean Petras

> A surplus labouring population is . . . the lever
> of a capitalistic accumulation . . . a condition
> of the existence of the capitalistic mode of
> production.
>
> —Karl Marx, *Capital*

During periods of rapid capital accumulation, when the demand for labor power is great, "capitalistic production can by no means content itself with the quantity of disposable labor power which the natural increase of population yields. It requires for its free play an industrial reserve army independent of these natural limits" (Marx 1967:635). Without the availability of surplus labor, the process of accumulation that presupposes the expansion of production cannot proceed. In the context of this argument, three sources of labor reserves are traditionally considered: (1) the floating reserve, which is repelled and attracted through cyclical and technological unemployment and employment patterns; (2) the latent reserve, generated by the release of agricultural workers who are displaced by the introduction of large-scale machinery into commercial production and thereby reduced to wages that are inadequate for household survival; and (3) the latent reserve composed of the ever-present irregularly employed working poor.

This surplus is structurally necessary for the expansion of capital, just as it is structurally produced by the contraction of the same accumulation process (Sweezy 1968:83-94). At times, in certain geographic areas, these traditional sources of labor *appear* to exist no longer, but the successful accumulation of capital ultimately must overcome spatial barriers. Therefore when local developments, such as the temporary depletion of an adequate labor source within geographic and national bounda-

131

ries, seem to have halted its growth, capital finds other means of satisfying its labor needs. The process of accumulation thus continues by turning to an exogeneous source of labor, outside the local surplus population.

International migration is thus stimulated by much the same group of conditions that set internal migration, especially the rural-to-urban movements, in motion. Within the framework of a modern world capitalist system, the driving tendency toward capital accumulation is realized internationally as a single division of labor existing within a multiplicity of policies and cultures (Wallerstein 1974). In the process of global capitalist development, surplus or reserve labor is drawn across national barriers toward the most flourishing, healthy centers of accumulation. Generally, free labor moves from those nations located in the peripheral areas of production to the core or metropolitan centers.

Structurally, the relationship between the core and peripheral countries is defined by uneven development. Uneven development is born of the natural drive of capital toward concentration and centralization and is nurtured by intercapitalist competition and political relationships between advanced capitalist countries of the core, the dependent capitalist countries of the periphery, and the less advanced, although not necessarily dependent, capitalist countries of the semi-periphery. Viewing the separate nations as regional aggregates, some regions are major importers of labor while others are major labor exporters. Through the exchange of population (as well as in a variety of other relations) the periphery, the semi-periphery, and the core regions are locked together in much the same manner as are labor and capital.[1] Although they are at opposite poles, the status of each is determined by the status of the other: they are linked through the bond of combined and uneven development. Thus linked, the expansion of the whole proceeds on the basis of disharmonious rates of growth among (and within) the regional aggregates. Major migration patterns tend to correspond to the global relations among regional aggregates, while more subtle shifts in population occur in response to cyclical economic rhythms within individual countries.

Classical and neoclassical theories of migration also state that labor will move from regions with surplus labor and low wages to regions with high wages and excess demand for labor. Orthodox theory may take into account only private free market forces (for example, wage rates and per capita income) or it may be expanded to include public variables (social services, welfare payments, and so forth). The assumption is that as the unemployment pressures are reduced within the labor-export region, the wage rate will rise and, conversely, with the reduction of labor demand in the importing region, wages will fall, until the per capita income differentials between the two diminish or are eliminated. The same equilibrating forces will reduce the differences between welfare payments, social services, and other public expenditures. Thus orthodox economists and demographers focus on the homogenizing effects of immigration but do not test their theories against the larger historical and international trend toward the concentration and centralization of capital.

Orthodox economic studies are typically limited to an examination of fluctuating population flows from one country to another, sometimes measured against the rise and fall of capitalist business cycles within specific dispatching and receiving countries. However, neither supply-and-demand interpretations nor cyclical analyses locate international migration within the more complex network of capital flows within a world economy. Consequently, they commonly fail to account for the social and economic disadvantages incurred by the labor-dispatching countries, which often deepen the already unequal relations between the poles.

Historically, the internationalization of production took the form of moving capital out of the advanced capitalist countries into the labor-rich colonies or dependencies, where it was invested in raw-materials extraction or cheap production of goods. The transport costs of moving raw materials or durables to market locations generally were offset by the utilization of inexpensive, unorganized labor. This arrangement involves relocating only the small number of managers, technicians, supervisors, and bureaucrats who accompany capital and technology to the "poor country" in order to supervise production there. In some cases, however, the transport costs of moving the product to the market location can be prohibitive (Harvey 1975). Additionally, political struggles inevitably emerge as populations begin to resist the exploitation of their labor and their raw materials. Thus by *importing labor* to the location of capital and the capital plant, capitalists in the core not only cut circulation costs but reduce the political and social costs of production as well.

The Role of Foreign Labor
in the Capital Accumulation Process

In the large-scale shift of labor toward capital-growth poles, those who move, the workers, quite naturally anticipate gains from the move. Given higher wage and living standards in the regions to which they move, some relative betterment may in fact be realized. To concentrate on potential relative advantages to the immigrant or their countries of origin, however, is usually to ignore the disadvantages incurred by both. In addition, such a focus glosses over the special advantages to capital in the receiving countries that are realized from the employment of foreign workers. It binds our understanding to a classical theory of economic evolution involving gradual and relative changes in wages, working conditions, and economic development, rather than illuminating the underlying economic laws that govern and maintain the social organization and relations of production and the structural relations between the core and the periphery— all of which lead to the process of immigration (Sweezy 1968). Thus, this analysis focuses on the impact on the political, economic, and class structure in both labor-receiving and labor-dispatching countries and on the specific influences on capital accumulation in the core.

Within the core states, the use of an imported labor force offers many advantages, which can be identified in several aspects of the accumulation process. Three of these areas will be considered here: the rate of exploitation of labor; the social costs of production; and the ongoing political struggles between capital and labor.

Rate of Exploitation

The rate of exploitation or, alternatively, the rate of surplus value refers to the amount of profit received by an employer from the products of a worker's labor, over and above the actual wages and benefits that the employer must pay that worker. It is determined by three factors: the length of the working day; the real wages paid for the performance of a specific task; and the productiveness of the worker. The amount of profits an employer derives from the labor of an individual worker can be increased if the rate of exploitation can be intensified. In simple terms, this may involve the extension of the working day, a lowering of the real wage, the increase of labor productivity through speedups or the introduction of technology and automation, or some combination of these three factors. Additional profits may be generated by lowering the amount of constant capital invested in the methods and machinery of production, as in the case of labor-intensive rather than capital-intensive production. Intensification of exploitation is particularly critical in three areas of production: the less efficient, less productive competitive sector; sectors in the process of moving *toward* economies of scale and dominance in the monopoly sector; and some locations at the bottom of the job hierarchy within the monopoly sector during periods of especially rapid expansion.

To the extent that cross-national reserves of labor have been concentrated in those sectors of production that offer the lowest paying, least skilled, most irregular, and most undesirable jobs, which are nevertheless *essential* to the ongoing functioning of the economic system, capital has been able to extract a higher rate of surplus value from these workers. Newly arrived waves of immigrants and migrant workers, either temporary or permanent, clandestine or legal, often form the most exploited, least privileged stratum of the working class. Construction, public works and services, hotel and restaurant industries, agriculture, and industries in the least rationalized or competitive sector of production have traditionally been open to immigrants. The low-paid service sector in Western European countries such as France, Britain, and Switzerland, for example, have relied heavily on foreign labor. Construction, an area of seasonal work particularly sensitive to fluctuations in business cycles, also depends on imported labor in Europe. During the 1960s, the British construction industry employed large numbers of Irish workers; West Germany's building trades were dependent on Yugoslav workers; Switzerland employed many Italians, while France employed workers from Spain, Portugal, and Northern Africa in building occupations. Historically, foreign workers are employed seasonally during agricultural harvests, and they return home once labor demands recede. California agriculture, for example, has employed Chinese, Hindu, Japanese, Filipino, and most recently Mexican workers to supplement the indigenous labor force, which draws heavily on rural southern whites, blacks, and youth.[2] Similarly, on the East coast of the United States, the agricultural migratory streams are fed by labor reserves recruited from the Caribbean islands. Manufacture of textiles and clothing, known for its low pay and poor working conditions, has depended on foreign labor in a number of instances. The most well-known case is the employment of poor European immigrants in the U.S. textile mills and garment industry at the turn of the century. Today, the profit margin of the North American garment industry leans heavily on the cheap labor and piecework performed by Chinese, Puerto Ricans, and West Indians. Where labor costs and demands for better working conditions have threatened profits in this industry, it has traditionally reverted to the use of foreign labor—shipping production directly to labor-rich periphery states such as South Korea, southern Italy, or Taiwan. The rate of exploitation can be intensified through the use of foreign labor by combining low wages with extended hours in the use of capital plant and equipment. In the British woolen industry, the employment of male Pakistani workers in the night shift which British women, who predominate in this industry, refused to work has permitted almost constant production (Castles and Kosack 1973:38). Availability of this foreign labor reserve, needy enough to work under conditions rejected by domestic workers, means that valuable time or equipment is not lost to capital.

Immigrant workers in labor-intensive and inefficient sectors of production permit production to expand without investment of profits in mechanization and automation of the capital plant. This is critical in production areas not easily rationalized or where the costs of better organized, technical methods are prohibitive, such as the construction, hotel, and restaurant industries or services, where economies of scale are difficult to organize because of the necessarily small units of production.

Second, foreign workers have frequently been important in the early stages of the capital accumulation process or in individual areas of production, which are dominated by small and therefore less efficient firms, but which are in the process of rationalizing. Lacking political rights and fleeing from poverty and unemployment, the workers' vulnerability renders them more docile and therefore dependable at a time when capital is attempting to increase control over all aspects of production and marketing. The large-scale dependence of U.S. capital on immigrant workers from the mid-nineteenth to the mid-twentieth centuries marked a period when production moved from the sphere of individual enterprises to one controlled by a large-scale corporate sector. In the fifty years following the Civil War, the United States came to dominate over one-third of the world manufacturing capacity, with a corresponding concentration and centralization of financial and industrial capital. Since rapid capital accumulation is always accompanied by an increased demand for available workers, the shortages among those recruited from the native working class had to be filled from other sources. Without the mass of low-paid foreign workers recruited from the surplus populations of Europe, where they had been displaced or unabsorbed as productive labor, the emergence of monopoly capitalism in America could not have proceeded at the rate it did. Indeed, it is quite likely that this stage would never have been completed at all.[3]

The period of rapid capital accumulation following World

War II in Western Europe shows striking similarities with that in the United States: the European case involves an advanced stage of capitalist development, while the U.S. case represents the period of monopoly emergence. While large intra-European migrations are not new to that continent, they take on special dimensions during the postwar period, in part because of their massiveness, but more importantly because of the particular role they play in facilitating the rapid growth of Western European capital during this period, and because of the core-periphery relations within which this labor flow occurs.

Today, it is estimated that one out of every six workers in Western Europe is an immigrant. In some extremes, such as that of the small Swiss nation, nearly one-third of the labor force are immigrants and one-sixth of the entire population are now foreigners (Berger 1975). The structure of the European labor market represents one of the most advanced cases of an international division of labor, in which exogenous labor reserves are attached to an indigenous working class (Castells 1975; Castles and Kosack 1973; Nikolinakos 1975). Workers from the less-developed capitalist countries of southern Europe, North Africa and, to a lesser extent, the Middle East, Southeast Asia, Asia Minor, and the Caribbean have taken up jobs in Western Europe. The major exporters of labor are the poorer Mediterranean countries—Greece, Turkey, southern Italy, Spain, Yugoslavia, and Algeria—plus Ireland, Trinidad, Jamaica, India, Pakistan, and Ceylon, which have heavy immigration flows to Great Britain, and Tunisia and Morocco whose workers move to France. Importing the bulk of this labor are France, West Germany, England, and Switzerland, which together absorb over 75 percent, and Sweden, Luxembourg, and Belgium, which employ most of the remainder.[4]

Stimulated by large amounts of international public capital, plus substantial investment of private capital, both primarily from the United States, the Western European region underwent a remarkable development surge between 1945 and 1952.[5] At the same time, the decimation of the labor force because of the war was exacerbated by continuing low birthrates. By the 1960s, the capital accumulation process was so rapid that an expanded labor force was needed to maintain its pace. In West Germany, the volume of industrial production rose by one-third between 1953 and 1961, almost entirely as a result of immigration. By 1972 an intricate recruitment system in the Mediterranean area provided about two-fifths of Germany's annual inflow of foreigners, and among all those emigrating from the Mediterranean region, Germany absorbed between 50 percent and 90 percent.[6]

The majority of these foreign workers absorbed the slack at the bottom ranks of the labor market. At the same time, production was undergoing rapid technological changes. These same immigrant workers in the less efficient competitive sector of industry contributed directly to the increasing rationalization and domination of the monopoly sector. First, the high rate of surplus value extracted from foreign workers provided capital necessary for the scientific and technological reorganization toward which many industries were moving. Ironically, the same automation and technology that permits a rise in productivity also decreases the demand for active labor. Thus the capital produced by labor which permitted increasing rationalization of production at the same time tended to create unemployment and redundancy among the very labor that produced it. Second, the influx of a cross-national reserve army of unemployed during a period of rapid economic growth helped prevent the uncontrolled rise of domestic workers' wages. Because they are willing to work for lower pay at longer hours and under worse conditions, immigrants provide a competitive element in the labor market, which prevents indigenous workers from continuing to accelerate their pay and benefit demands. At the same time as they perform jobs that free domestic workers for some degree of mobility, the presence of foreign workers also serves as a check on the wages and working conditions of that mobility.

The Social Costs of Production

Labor Force Reproduction

Social costs of production refer to those individual and collective expenditures and investments in the education, health, housing, and general welfare necessary for the production, maintenance, and reproduction of a workforce. Social costs can be greatly reduced through the use of immigrant labor. To begin with, since foreign workers are predominantly young males (frequently single) that have recently reached the age of labor market entry, the costs of rearing and educating these workers, however minimally, have already been absorbed by their country of origin. So in addition to providing the receiving countries with the potential source of surplus value, to be realized from the labor of an immigrant worker, the peripheral countries also provide social capital stored up in the form of each person who leaves. In a 1979 study, the U.S. Department of Agriculture estimated the cost of raising a child born in 1960 to the age of eighteen at $34,300. The cost of raising the same child born in 1979 was calculated at $165,300 (including both public and private capital) (Moore 1981). For the individual arriving in a U.S. city as a young adult from Latin America, say, to take a job in the restaurant or garment industry, those social costs will have already been borne by his or her country of origin, albeit at a lower rate. More striking is the case of a young professional or technician from Latin America arriving to establish eligibility for licensing, education and professional training already in hand. If the immigrant possesses some special skills or training, even greater benefits accrue to the core country at the expense of a periphery nation.

Literature on immigration in Western Europe is sprinkled with estimates of the actual social investment embodied in the form of each worker. Suzanne Paine's carefully documented study (1974) on the migration of Turkish workers to West Germany estimates that each immigrant represents about $2000 of congealed social capital at the time he reaches the labor market in the metropolitan country. A recent study by the Organization for Economic Cooperation and Development places the human capital embodied in a single foreign worker at $10,000 and the total yearly capital represented by immigrants in Europe at $50 million (Castells 1975:47).

Magnifying the social costs borne by the labor-exporting regions is the selective nature of migration, which constitutes a skill drain as well as a capital drain. Those who leave are typically among the more vigorous and ambitious young workers. Referring again to the Turkish case, it is those with the greatest technical training and literacy levels who have moved to West Germany. One Turkish survey Paine reports found that, contrary to the popular image, 74 percent of the emigrants had backgrounds in industry, while only 11 percent came directly from agricultural production (Paine 1974:47).[7]

General good health among those who emigrate adds to further selectivity. Careful medical screening required by the core nations ensures that those who enter legally will not have serious health problems, and in some locations they are probably more healthy as a group than comparable national workers. Turkish workers going to West Germany must undergo a medical examination before leaving Turkey. Switzerland and Sweden both require migrants to take medical examinations on arrival, before work permits are granted. If workers are in poor health, or if they fall ill while abroad, they may either be denied entry or returned to their home countries. In either case, their ill health and its costs are exported back to the periphery.

Ironically, however, precisely because they are forced into jobs in which the health and safety conditions are the most treacherous, immigrant workers suffer a disproportionate rate of occupation-related mental and physical ailments. Industrial accidents are excessively high for a variety of reasons, ranging from the language disorientations suffered in a strange setting to the long work hours, often compounded by intensive physical strain. In France, for example, the accident rate is eight times higher among foreign workers than among indigenous workers (Berger and Mohr 1975:126). Studies in Western Europe report that, in addition to those deported for bad health and accidents, among those who otherwise return home, the unskilled form a disproportionately large group.

Activity Rates and Dependency Ratios

In addition to the savings in the social costs of producing an immigrant worker, the labor-importing country also benefits from savings in the social maintenance of a foreign workforce.

Among the unmarried males of prime work age who predominate among immigrant groups, somewhere between two-thirds
and three-fourths fall in the age group of fifteen to forty years,
with propensity to migrate being highest among the group aged
twenty to twenty-five. The result is a high rate of economic
activity and a low rate of dependence among migrants in the
receiving country (Thomas 1959:524). Personal or legal restrictions on family immigration produce a high rate of involuntary
bachelorhood among many immigrants. The result is often a
disruption of sex ratios and marriage rates. For example, prior to
World War I, there were upwards of 10,000 Hindu workers in
California (McWilliams 1971:19). With the Immigration Act of
1917, which barred entrance from certain zones, further Hindu
immigration ceased, and since most of the original workers were
men, they were forced to return to India if they wished to marry.
In the case of Filipino farm workers, most elected to remain in
California rather than return home. Today, the high concentration of aged Filipino bachelors has become a major concern of
the United Farmworkers Union, since these men are now beyond
working age and have no families for social or economic support.

Although the employment rate is high among foreigners
during their tenure in the metropolitan countries, they are
not unaffected by unemployment. Indeed, recent recessionary
unemployment figures among immigrant workers in Western
Europe indicate that they are apt to be hit as a group even harder
than domestic workers. Upon being unemployed any length of
time, most return to their country of origin, either voluntarily or
because they no longer possess work permits. Likewise, during
the successive economic recessions in the United States at the
turn of the century—1884, 1893, 1907, and 1914—immigration
statistics indicate substantial waves of return migration as the
depression-related unemployment was deported back to the
countries of origin (Rosenblum 1973; U.S. Immigration Commission 1911).

The counterpart of this high activity rate is to be found among
the labor-exporting countries, where the elderly, the (future)
wives and children of migrants, and the unemployable who
remain behind all add to the social costs of maintaining depen-

dents. Even without attempting any calculations of the human capital contributions of the periphery to the core nations, the low-dependency, high-activity rates alone confirm the fact that the social costs of production are lowered for the recipient nation. These costs are borne by the dispatching states or incorporated into the general level of poverty and misery reproduced among those who remain in the periphery.

Health, Education, and Welfare

The shameful standards of health, education, and welfare to which foreign workers are often subjected has been the topic of many compassionate accounts (Berger and Mohr 1975). That immigrant workers tend to live in poorer housing, experience worse health care, and receive inferior education for their children when they are accompanied by their families arises from a complexity of political, economic, and cultural causes. The relative rise in the standard of living experienced through the act of migration may offset the poor living standards, however inferior they may be to those of native workers.[8] Since so many foreign workers expect their foreign work tenure to be only temporary until they accumulate savings for the return home, perhaps their lives in bare rented rooms and bunkhouses may seem more tolerable. On the other hand, even when these conditions are rejected as unacceptable, the absence of political rights and representation prevents migrants from availing themselves of organized political pressure for protection. In Argentina, for example, large numbers of Bolivian and Paraguayan workers live in the crowded villas de miseria. Most males are unskilled and general laborers, often working in construction or irregular employment in stagnant industries (Marshall 1979; Kritz and Gorak 1979). To further complicate their precarious status, many are working and residing in the country illegally or on provisional visas. Despite their poverty, they are relatively acquiescent politically. They had no active or organized voice in the Peronist unions and, of course, could not vote in state elections (in those instances when elections have been permitted during recent years). Such acquiescence is often mistaken for satisfaction with conditions as they are.

When disenfranchised immigrants organize over living conditions, action by the state is often swift and irrevocable. In France, for example, approximately 2.5 million foreign workers, mostly from Africa or Portugal, were in residence in the early 1970s. If they were not living in *bidonvilles*, the urban slum settlements, they tended to occupy state-operated housing units, six-by-ten foot rooms for which the state demanded $60 rent per month. The workers, rejecting these rates for such inadequate conditions, declared they would pay no more than $40 per month. They were neither organized nor defended by the trade unions, despite the left-wing politics of these unions. Thus, when over 12,000 recently united behind their own immigrant workers' leaders on this issue, after nearly twenty years of relative passivity, the response of the state was repressive. Police were sent into the industrial suburbs and sixteen of the leaders of the fourteen-month strike were rounded up and deported. While pledging support to the strike, the unions did not use the leverage of political sympathy strikes. Hence, the foreign workers were left with the only political weapon usually available to the disenfranchised: confrontation and disruption.[9]

Direct and indirect benefits to capital of low social costs have two aspects. First, the low investment in schooling, the cheap and inadequate housing, and the paucity of demands from the workers for a higher standard of living all combine to permit a lowering of labor force maintenance. Second, the low living standards, combined with the low level of consumption resulting from self-enforced savings, means that productive foreign workers do not add much to the inflationary trend of capital expansion periods (Castells 1975:56).[10]

Finally, the reduced social welfare benefits which foreign workers receive is an additionl source of social cost-cutting. Many foreign laborers and their families do not qualify, or are not aware that they qualify, for the social welfare coverage commonly available to the domestic workers of most industrialized nations. Add to this the number who are ineligible because of their illegal status within the country, the number who return precisely at such time as they might receive coverage such as unemployment or disability insurance, and the large numbers of dependents who have not accompanied workers during their employment abroad and are therefore not covered by social welfare legislation: the savings to the core nation, both relative and absolute, become substantial.

Unemployment Costs

While capital draws in foreign labor reserves to fill the gaps in production during periods of expansion, it is equally eager to have them disappear during periods of contraction: such reserves play a unique role in helping maintain an equilibrium for capital during periods of economic fluctuation. Persistent attempts to locate and deport aliens working without legal status in New York State suggests the manner in which an excess workforce is "gotten rid of" legally at a time when the economic pressures of recession stimulate potential social and political pressures as well. From the immigrants' perspective, the essential elements of the story involve a long-hoped-for move to the United States, a period of irregular work at low pay and long hours, a final loss of job combined with the realization that no fortune was being accumulated, and a disillusioned return home.

In Western Europe today, most countries have provisions that restrict the length of stay for a foreign worker to such time as he or she maintains legitimate employment, often with a specific employer. The worker pays unemployment and social security contributions; only a few ever draw their benefits, for these contributions are lost if a worker loses his or her job and therefore must leave the country. Retention of the legal right to deport any worker who is unemployed permits the importing state to maintain a flexible labor force, which can be recruited and expelled according to the demands of the accumulation momentum. This is particularly useful in seasonal production, such as agriculture or construction, where capital can slough off the cost of unemployment and readmit workers when production resumes.

Subtle advantages to capital accrue from the fact that immigrants, concentrated in unskilled jobs that are more heavily hit by unemployment, suffer disproportionately from cyclical unemployment. A proportionately greater part of the cost of supporting unemployment is transferred to the periphery, where such costs are magnified, given the already high unemployment and welfare programs. What emerges is a contradiction between the drive for maximizing private profit in one instance, and the adequate provision for social security and welfare protection for labor, specifically immigrant labor, in another. When recession, industrial accidents, or bad health hit, the migrant often discovers he or she has all of the disadvantages of working in the metropolitan country and none of the advantages.

Jerome (1926) has demonstrated that migratory movements correspond to fluctuations in available employment stemming from contraction and expansion of the internal business cycle.[11] A slight lag of anywhere from a few months to a full year will occur in both the accelerating and decelerating process. Specific conditions such as agricultural failure or industrial depression within the labor-dispatching country do influence the lag, but conditions in the receiving country essentially dominate the rhythm and location of the migratory flow. This is because of the ability of the receiving state to formally regulate the movement of workers into its labor market. As a supplement to labor contracting and recruiting stations abroad, a variety of incentives to immigrate are offered during high-demand periods. During low-demand periods, the state ceases replenishment of the foreign workforce by denying new admittances or reentry of workers among those who are constantly returning to their home countries, or by placing formal restrictions on specific immigration. The most outstanding example of the latter was the gradual closing of the gates to foreign immigration to the United States culminating in the final establishment of quotas in the 1922 immigration act. Today in Western Europe, West Germany was the first to take formal measures to discontinue labor importation by imposing the *Gastarbeiter-Stop*, whereby labor recruiting offices were closed first in Portugal and Spain and later in Yugoslavia, Turkey, and Greece, and by decreasing the issuance of work permits requisite for entry. Additionally, in order to rid itself more rapidly of a potential source of political opposition as a result of rising unemployment, the German state has provided payments to thousands of workers to facilitate a return home and has refused residence permits in areas designated as already overcrowded with foreigners.[12] One after another, the European labor-importing states have followed this example.

It is frequently observed that in order to see the slums of Berlin or Paris one must travel to the outskirts of Athens or the impoverished villages of Andalusia. By the same token, in order to fully comprehend the magnitude of the current economic crisis of monopoly capitalism, and therefore the levels of unemployment suffered by its working classes, one must look beyond the official unemployment statistics of the core nations and turn also to the agricultural villages and urban slums of the periphery and semi-periphery. One might go so far as to argue that the great international movements of labor constitute something akin to a form of development aid given by the poor countries to the rich (Castles and Kosack 1973).

The Politics of Class Struggle: A Metropolitan Working Class and Its Reserve Army from the Periphery

The advantages in the use of foreign labor may vary for different sectors of capital. For small capital, or the competitive sector, the need for ready, cheap labor is satisfied. For big capital, or the monopoly sector, the need for a degree of planning and regulation of production may force the regularization of immigration through some minor economic and social security measures. Both sectors, however, have common political needs, which grow out of the contradictions between labor and capital: the withholding of political and trade union rights for immigrants, in order to thwart their capacity to participate in class struggles. A cleavage is thereby created between immigrant workers and the political organizations of domestic workers, and the historic role traditionally played in democratic politics by the working class is effectively denied. Just as employers' governments deport industrial accidents or unemployment, they also retain the power to deport political dissidence. Any protest or overt political activity can potentially result in the loss of jobs and subsequent deportation. The absence of active political support from the trade unions leaves few alternatives between acquiescence and passivity and semispontaneous actions aimed at securing concrete political rights. The situation was summed up succinctly by a foreign worker in a French Citroën plant: "If we open our mouths to protest (about anything), we are threatened with being fired and thrown out of the country" (Coryell 1974:17).

Unions, Parties, and Foreign Workers

It seems that no phrase ever written by Marx has been so trivialized and abused as his call for international workers of the world to unite. But it is difficult to imagine a situation in which it would be more appropriate than in the case of the metropolitan working classes and their reserve labor armies from the periphery and semi-periphery. Nonetheless, a schism remains, maintained by economic self-interest combined with racist and national chauvinist ignorance, and aggravated by the fear that the foreigners might take their jobs and eat their bread.

Union policies toward immigrant workers thus reflect a series of contradictions. Many explanations have been offered for their ineffectuality: xenophobia and racist attitudes among indigenous workers and their leaders, hostility toward the competitive role of foreign workers in the labor market, as well as in their potential for strikebreaking. Divisions and lack of contact are also encouraged, because foreign workers are isolated in certain categories of the occupational structure (often occupations which have not been traditionally represented by strong unions), because of the transitory, seasonal work patterns many immigrants are bound to, and because of cultural and language differences. Furthermore, the work experience of immigrants in their home countries has not typically involved contact or commitment to workers' unions and organizations. The immigrants themselves often feel that union policies and struggles do not usually focus on the immediate difficulties they face as a semimarginal work-force or sub-proletariat; hence there is low motivation for them to subject themselves to the regulations and dues of the unions.

Of equal importance is the strategic interest of trade union bureaucrats in maintaining their relationship with capital as labor elites, which causes them to sacrifice one sector of the working class (foreign workers) in order not to disrupt that arrangement. The International Ladies Garment Workers' Union has a close working relationship with employers in the industry, for example, but at the same time does not put up any real fight over the conditions and wages under which Puerto Rican and Caribbean workers are laboring, since the organizational inter-ests of the bureaucracy frequently take precedence over the real needs of the workers.

Performance of low-paying jobs by foreigners contributes not only directly to capital's accumulation but indirectly to the mobility within the occupational hierarchy that is thus made available to domestic workers. Just as labor in a sense "belongs" to capital, so do its reserve armies "belong" to an employed working class. However, the exploitative relationship of the first to the second is qualitatively different from the relation-ship of the working class to its reserve armies. In fact, by serving as a wage check, a foreign reserve periodically and ultimately becomes a disadvantage to that working class within the labor market.

A further factor in the lack of active union organizing among foreign workers involves the politics of pro-labor and left politi-cal parties where they exist. Tactically, both unions and the parties that represent them concentrate their energies on certain crucial points of production. Since the revolutionary program of the left relies on a large, organized, urban proletariat, their unity in militant strike actions is a vital source of power for both unions and political parties, especially those of the left, to have access to and influence over. When machines halt in major industries, the accumulation process is impeded not only in that industry but also in other productive facilities and areas of the economy. In contrast, the combined power at the point of pro-duction of those at the bottom ranks of labor—the service workers, the small groups of workers employed in backward, nonunionized shops, the irregularly and seasonally employed— is greatly diminished in comparison to that of the organized industrial worker, since they control no stable and vital means of production. Politically their potential is weak in matters relating to struggles over control of the means of production, and thus they are less likely to be courted by labor unions and labor parties. While the voting allegiance of these marginal workers could be extremely significant to labor and left parties, especially when this sector is numerically large, foreigners carry no weight in parliamentary or electoral challenges because they have no voting rights. Thus the degree to which left and labor parties have failed to use their base within the trade unions to develop policies aimed at the specific problems of immigrant workers may be a function of the fact that they are not viewed as "important," either for their strength over production-related struggles or for the electoral support they embody.

A seemingly logical reaction from the trade unions and the parties oriented toward the working class would be an immediate demand for the full political rights of all workers, foreign and domestic. The relative absence of such demands seems to return us to the question of whether the unions are operating essen- tially to protect a section of the working class that represents a privileged strata. So long as foreign workers can be deported or kept out during contractions of the business cycle, they are reduced as a potential threat not only to capital but also to the indigenous working class. The highly competitive character of a reserve army is always intensified during economic downswings. But this role diminishes when the reserve army contains large numbers of foreign workers who can simply be removed from the labor market. This diminishes the imperative for incorpor- ating reserve labor into workers' organizations, an imperative that logically heightens during economic crises.

In periphery nations, with high birth and unemployment rates, low standards of living, and sharp class divisions, migration may siphon off latent social disturbances and rebellion, which are always a potential under the oppressive conditions of under- development. A safety valve is opened by out-migration, which draws off precisely those active young males who are just at the point of seeing their life's aspirations blocked and who, as a result, could provide that energetic mass which has traditionally been in revolt against backward and repressive regimes. The draining off of this vital sector from the periphery, and the corresponding reduction in unemployment and frustration, may contribute to the control maintained by many reactionary, repressive, and often fascist governments. The existence of such regimes is in the interests of monopoly capital in the advanced capitalist states, since they help maintain that precarious fulcrum on which the world capitalist system balances.

Notes

1. International flows of labor power tend to move among five groups of countries: advanced or core countries with large net inflows (e.g., the U.S. and Western European countries); advanced countries of the core with large net outflows (mainly European countries such as Norway); core countries with large two-way movements (e.g., Canada, U.K., or Switzerland); intermediate or semi-peripheral with large net outflow (e.g., Turkey, Greece, Iran, Spain, or Portugal); and peripheral or underdeveloped countries with large net outflows (e.g., Colombia, Mexico, the Caribbean states). Because of the complexity of these movements, especially involving the dominance of intermediate countries as exporters of labor power to Western Europe, and the patterns of two-way or fill-in migration among many intermediate states, it seems important to identify this group as a distinct category. I have borrowed the terms employed by Wallerstein (1974) which designate this group of states as semi-peripheral.
2. This pattern appears to be altering as more winter crops are being grown by U.S. companies across the border in Mexico, where labor is not only cheap but unorganized (see Baird and McCaughan 1976).
3. Between 1800 and 1930, over 40 million Europeans emigrated permanently overseas, mainly to North America. At the height of this population shift—between 1880 and 1914—the number was approximately 22 million (Baird and McCaughan 1976:16).
4. A small percentage are employed in the Netherlands, Austria, Norway, and Denmark, and lately northern Italy, where the process

of uneven development has produced both an expulsion of emigrants and an attraction of immigrants within a single nation.

5. The net flow of some $22.8 billion in public capital from the United States alone to Western Europe during the ten years following the war created a tremendous expansion in productive capacity (Thomas 1961:35-38).

6. In 1961 Italians alone comprised over 40 percent of the foreign workforce; by 1972 both Yugoslavs and Turks outnumbered Italians (Böhning 1972:33).

7. Undoubtedly, this statistic masks the initial move of many migrants from the country to the city within their home states and their work experience in industry as a benefit of an earlier geographical and occupational move. The step migration patterns become even more pronounced when the portion of migratory moves which are intergenerational in nature are also included.

8. The initial willingness of most immigrants to work for less than the importing country's "average wage" and accept a standard of living which is below the prevailing threshold of standards which indigenous workers can be forced to accept, reflects the fact that for many workers migrating from peripheral zones, the conditions and wages which they can expect within the labor market of destination still represents a relative improvement over those to which they are bound "at home." The deprivation and exploitation which they experience at the point of destination is less relative to the prevailing conditions within the labor market of origin, than when measured against the prevailing conditions of the labor market of destination as a point of destination.

9. Residence permits and work permits are issued simultaneously upon arrival in France, making the right to residence dependent on possession of a one-year contract with a specific employer. But the fact that any protest can result in the loss of jobs and subsequent deportation, combined with the failure of the unions to actively support the workers, probably contributed to the inability of these semispontaneous actions to secure any concrete political rights.

10. There is by no means uniform agreement on the contribution of immigration to deflationary trends, however. See, for example, the arguments with regard to contemporary Europe between Böhning (summarized in Paine 1974), C. P. Kindleberger (1967), and Castles and Kosack (1973) versus the opposing views that immigration does not tend to have a deflationary impact, proposed by E. J. Mishan and L. Needleman (1966) writing on Britain.

11. This relation seems to hold true not only for the economic short cycles, which Jerome analyzed, but for the long cycles as well (see Thomas 1972).

12. Quoted in the *New York Times*, October 25, 1975, p. 2. One German official, the head of Nuremberg's federal labor office, explained, "We're quite aware now that 2.6 million foreign workers was too many, and 2 million is probably the most our economy can handle. . . . We could have acted like the Austrians, who threw out 100,000 of their 280,000 foreign workers in a year. That would be the equivalent of us throwing out a million. It might have kept down unemployment, but it wouldn't have been good for peace in the streets." Speaking in the same code, a Bavarian government official, referring to the hundreds of thousands of foreign workers in his state, declared, "We have nothing against some of these people deciding to go home. The rule is that German workers have preference for the jobs that are available."

Population Dynamics and Migrant Labor in South Africa

Marianna Edmunds

Introduction

The African population of South Africa has one of the highest growth rates on the entire continent; at 3 percent a year (van Rensberg 1972:6) it is well above the world population growth rate of 2 percent and above that of Africa as a whole, which is 2.8 percent (Environmental Fund 1979). If the present trend continues, South Africa could have the highest population growth rate in the world by the year 2000. Population dynamics, however, are more than growth rates, and in South Africa the political economy of migrant labor and apartheid have established a set of demographic patterns that not only pose contradictions for the maintenance of the regime, but have had long-term and serious effects on the reproductive structures of the African population.

Population dynamics in South Africa cannot be explained outside of the context of global economic processes. Specifically, an understanding of birth and mortality rates, fertility, and migration patterns demands an examination of the penetration and development of capital in South Africa. Rapid population growth and chaotic population movements are specific responses to a socioeconomic system in which the producers have lost control of decisions affecting their production and reproduction. In South Africa the official policy of population control takes on genocidal implications.

This essay was originally written for a population symposium at the Seventy-fourth Annual Meetings of the American Anthropological Association in San Francisco, December 1975. It was considerably revised, updated, and rewritten in September 1979 for publication. I am especially grateful to Professor Jim Faris for his editorial advice and overall support.

Social Production and Population

"In order to live, people obtain food, build dwellings, and adopt various means of livelihood. In doing so, they act cooperatively, joining together for combined activity, which lends production a social character and leads to the establishment of definite relations among people" (Guzevaty 1974:77). The fundamental characteristic that differentiates all human societies from other animal populations is the process of social production, the ability to transform nature through production. For this reason, unlike other animal societies, human societies do not need to use population control as their primary response to nature. The process of production in turn enables human groups to regulate and plan labor activity and thereby the reproduction of producers (Faris 1975:249). Thus it is the process of social production that determines the reproductive structure of the population.

Throughout history, human societies in general have tended to higher birthrates in times of productive stress than in times of relative security. When the means of subsistence is threatened by drought, flooding, war, conquest, or impoverishment victims commonly respond by increasing their numbers to ensure survival and continuation. And social production, with its constant innovation and planning, has historically enabled societies to accommodate the resulting population pressure.

Ester Boserup (1965) discusses the ways in which different societies have handled population increase. Countering the popular Malthusian concept that population growth diminishes a finite supply of resources and leads to impoverishment and starvation, Boserup argues that agrarian societies accommodated growth by developing new technology and intensifying the level of agricultural productivity for the increased numbers. Despite Boserup's refreshing anti-Malthusian thesis, however, her contribution still fails to explain the source of population increase, positing population growth outside the system of production as an independent factor to be dealt with by upgrading technology or productivity. For Boserup, structural social change in the forces and relations of production appears to be an effect rather than a cause of population change. In this essay, I suggest that we must examine the concept of the social relations of production to explain population dynamics.

Within the context of social production, human demographic patterns are seen as socially rather than biologically determined. As such, there exist no universal laws of population. Instead, population dynamics are a response to the system of production that generates them and are relative to their historical time. According to Marx, "Every special historic mode of production has its own special laws of population, historically valid within its limits alone" (1967:632). Thus population dynamics must be understood as an expression of a particular set of social relations of production and productive forces in a specific era.

Under capitalist social relations, population dynamics take on certain identifiable forms. To receive a sufficient rate of return for the reproduction of labor power, human beings must sell their labor, thus losing control over the means of production and the product. They also effectively surrender control of their reproductive patterns, except for the effort to survive. As Faris puts this: "Producers no longer control decisions about their labor potential . . . and become subject to new and different population requirements over which they have no effective control" (1975:254).

Demographically, capitalist production generates two forces: the demand for producers to reproduce labor power as cheaply as possible, and an additional demand for labor power to expand and increase productivity. In the early stages of capitalism, this means an increase in the labor force itself, hence in the numbers of workers. On the other hand, the ratio between variable capital (wages) and fixed capital (machines, plant) must favor increased mechanization for profits to continue to rise.[1] The increase in capital as a whole, or rise in productivity, has the appearance of increasing the population of laborers, as it is a process that ejects workers from production, creating what seems to be a redundant, or surplus population. "The labor population produces along with the accumulation of capital produced by it, the means by which itself is made relatively superfluous, is turned into a relative surplus population; and it does this to an increasing extent. This is a law of population peculiar to the capitalist mode of production" (Marx 1967:631-32).

Thus capitalist production creates its own surplus population by the very nature of its development. Marx's explanation for the overall importance of this redundant population is relevant for South African population dynamics:

> But if a surplus laboring population is a necessary product of accumulation or of the development of wealth on a capitalist basis, this surplus population becomes conversely the lever of capitalist accumulation—a condition of the existence of the capitalist mode of production. It forms a disposable industrial army that belongs to capital quite as absolutely as if the latter had bred it at its own cost. Independently of the limits of the actual increase of population, it creates, for the changing needs of self-expansion of capital, a mass of human material always ready for exploitation. (1967:632)

Capitalist Development in South Africa

The economic development of South Africa in the twentieth century has been based fundamentally on the exploitation of African labor for a mining economy. This has been accomplished through a system built on migratory forced labor and wage slavery. Migrant labor supplies at least 70 percent of the entire labor force of South Africa (Transkei Study Project 1976:7); it is also used to bolster apartheid, South Africa's sociopolitical and legal system of racial segregation. Through apartheid an immigrant white minority is able to dominate and oppress an indigenous black majority. This system legalizes the underpayment of African labor and the prohibition of permanent residence by the majority of Africans.

Through the legal mechanisms of apartheid and the importation of cheaper migrant labor from neighboring countries, South Africa has kept labor's return to capital at an artificially low rate, thus ensuring the increase in profit rates for capitalist investment. Because of its highly labor-intensive economy, South

Africa has experienced an extraordinarily high rate of return on capital for over half a century. At the same time, in accordance with the classical dynamic of redundant wage labor noted above, the South African economy has been ejecting laborers from production, thus creating a high level of unemployment (Simkins and Clarke 1978:41, 67, 70), albeit at a slower rate than in other maturing capitalist systems.

This continual pressure on subsistence and the reproduction of labor power has engendered an increase in numbers to ensure survival. In South Africa, the African population has shown a growth rate of 2 to 3 percent since 1904 (Lorimer 1961:89), a rate that would have been considerably higher had it not been offset by high death rates as well. Population dynamics in South Africa are a direct response to capitalist development, manifested in the demographics of the most exploited sector and the principal producers—the African population. High growth rates, high mortality (especially infant and child), high natality, low life expectance (because of dangerous work conditions and impoverished living conditions on the reserves), compromised fertility (high incidence of stillbirths and veneral disease), and unregulated birth spacing because of migrant male workers all testify to a chaotic reproduction system generated by capitalist social relations of production.

My interest thus is to analyze the migrant labor system's influence on the population dynamics of the African community and the concomitant manifestations of impoverishment and underdevelopment in the context of capitalist development in South Africa.

Early Capitalist Penetration

African social formations were integrated into the emerging capitalist system as early as the seventeenth century (Amin 1974), but full-scale European capitalist penetration in South Africa did not occur until the end of the nineteenth century. In the process, developing political formations were crushed or stunted.[2]

Dutch immigrants settled the Cape Colony as a refreshment

station for the Dutch East India Company in the mid-seventeenth century. Their immigration itself may have been in part a response to population pressure in northern Europe caused by the growth of mercantile capitalism. The Dutch immigration interrupted the development of existing African societies by pushing their populations north and appropriating their labor for the establishment of small states based on petty commodity production.

> In the Cape colony and the Boer republics, pure peasant economy prevailed until the 1860's. For a long time the Boers had led the life of animal tending nomads; they had killed off or driven out the Hottentots and Kaffirs with a will in order to deprive them of their most valuable pastures. . . . When the Boers spread further east they came in conflict with Bantu tribes and initiated the long period of the terrible Kaffir wars. These god-fearing Dutchmen regarded themselves as the Chosen people and took no small pride in their old-fashioned Puritan morals and their intimate knowledge of the Old Testament; yet not content with robbing the natives of their land, they built their present economy like parasites on the backs of the Negroes, compelling them to do slave labour for them and corrupting and enervating them deliberately and systematically. (Luxemburg 1951:411)

The British arrived in the nineteenth century in the course of national capitalist expansion and the search for primary accumulation. This time, however, capitalist expansion was assisted by state power: African states were conquered and their lands annexed outright. In Africa, the difference between the small Dutch republics and the British colony was that between a patriarchal peasant economy based on outdated small-scale slavery and large-scale industrial capitalism (Luxemburg 1951).

Two events significantly determined the capitalist transformation of South Africa: the discovery of the Kimberley diamond fields in 1869 and the discovery of gold in the Transvaal between 1882 and 1885. Under Cecil Rhodes, the British South Africa Company accelerated the transformation of South Africa so much that within ten years, by 1895, over 100,000 British citizens had emigrated to Witwatersrand alone. The company further annexed African land and appropriated African labor in major proportions, building railways through rebellious districts.

By the last quarter of the nineteenth century the British had completely subjugated both the earlier Dutch states and the African societies yet unconquered. Ultimately, the dominant capitalist interests—British industrial expansion—forced the bankruptcy and collapse of the Dutch states. However, the conflict between the British and the Dutch was surpassed in 1910 by that between capital and labor, as the two colonial powers entered into an alliance against the African population, which has lasted up to the present. The Dutch bourgeoisie was allowed to dominate the agricultural sector, while the British controlled the mining, finance, trade, and other major industrial interests. Because of the extraordinarily low productivity of South African agriculture under the Dutch, however, the British virtually controlled the interests of capital in all sectors.

By the early twentieth century capitalist penetration was almost complete (Mafeje 1973), which Amin (1974:559) claims was only possible because of the "potential periphery ready at hand" when South Africa reached its industrial stage.

The Development of Migrant Labor and the Bantustans

> We are trying to introduce migratory labor as far as possble in every sphere. That is in fact the entire basis of our policy as far as the white economy is concerned.
>
> —House of Assembly, 1968

As this quote from Rogers (1972:7) demonstrates, the key to the South African system has been the control of labor; the mechanism for controlling labor has been control of land. Following conquest and colonization, Africans were forced from their traditional lands onto reserves through a system of taxation and land legislation or forced to migrate to the white cities for employment. The Land Act of 1913 allocated about 8 percent of the total land surface to the African population, calling these areas native reserves. In the 1920s, with the establishment of presidential power over the reserves and the reversion to migrant labor the structure of the present bantustans was laid down

(Rogers 1972:11). By the 1930s the self-sufficiency and social fabric of the African societies had been all but destroyed through impoverishment, and the regime had succeeded in establishing a pool of ready labor for the mines, farms, and developing manufacturing industries. Anderson (1962:98) has pointed out that "the South African gold industry could not manage without the resources and African labor power maintained through the reserves at the level of pre-capitalist existence. Rand ores are of a very low grade and lie so deep that under normal conditions their extraction could not even approach economic viability . . . but the presence of Africans in the native reserves ensured a subsistence work force." The other side of this policy was the permanent devastation of the population made to live on the reserves: "Brought in from the reserves in their youth and shipped back in their old age, the migrant laborers spare the mining industry a whole range of social costs, the burden of which is shifted to the poverty-stricken reserves" (Magubane 1979:95-96).

Critical to understanding migrant labor in South Africa is the fact that the migrants are paid less than subsistence wages on the grounds that their income is supplemental to their subsistence efforts. At the same time the recruitment of labor in neighboring countries increased at various periods, not only to supplement the labor force but more importantly to keep wages down by creating a perfectly elastic labor-supply curve for the mines.

Although migrant labor existed in South Africa on a small scale prior to the discovery of gold and diamonds, the gold industry dramatically changed the area and transformed the population into one of migrant labor pools. The Bantu Authorities Act of 1951 established the reserves—bantustans—as formalized units of apartheid, with 12.9 percent of the country's total land allotted to 77 percent of the country's population. The remaining 87.1 percent of land was allotted to the minority white population.

This act institutionalized a scheme whereby every African will eventually belong to a homeland, stripped of his or her South African citizenship. The stated aim—"to eliminate all residential rights and transform all African labor in industry, commerce, agriculture . . . into migrant labor" (International

Defence and Aid Fund 1969:5)—has two objectives: to establish a permanent supply of cheap labor for the mines, farms, and factories, and to maintain apartheid through the creation of "new nations"—the African Homelands program—the residents of which will be migrant workers and their families. Resettlement in the 1960s included the aged, women with dependent children, the unfit for work, and all those who did not qualify as useful or necessary for residence in the white areas. As of 1981, three bantustans have been declared "independent" by the South African government—Transkei, Bophuthatswana, and Venda—and six more are planned.

Constituting approximately 13 percent of the total land of South Africa, for close to 80 percent of the population, these areas are small, strategically scattered outside the major production centers, and incapable of offering adequate employment or subsistence. They have the poorest and most unproductive land, with no mineral reserves and a scarcity of water resources. Migratory labor in the mines, factories, and farms provides the primary means of subsistence. By 1971, nearly 3 million people had been forcibly moved to the bantustans and by 1977 nearly half of the African population, over 9 million people, were defined as residents of the homelands. The remainder were settled on farms, in the towns, or for a major portion of the year, in the white areas as migrant laborers. A recent study of the Transkei (TSP 1976:3-4) showed, however, that only 57 percent of the homeland population actually lived permanently there, while 32 percent lived permanently in the white areas and 11 percent were temporarily absent migrant workers.

By all accounts, the population living in the homelands is insufficiently supported by the land and resources available. Hance (1970:413-16) summarized the situation on the reserves in 1970:

> Overworked, overgrazed, and ... damaged by erosion. Almost none are self-sufficient in food production, several of the larger ones being dependent on white farms for at least 25-40% of their supply. ... The government has found it impossible to remove all the surplus families from the land, which has led to the splitting of units and the perpetuation of uneconomic holdings. In 1966, only

33,007 Africans were in paid employment in the Transkei (out of a projected population of over 3 million) . . . compared with an estimated 258,000 employed outside the bantustan, including 118,000 migrant laborers.

By the end of the 1960s these former reserves had deteriorated into rural slums, suffering the pressure of overpopulation of up to 66 percent and landlessness of up to 25-44 percent (Mafeje 1973:19), with an industrial proletariat domiciled in the country-side. By 1975 Hance claimed that at least one-half of the population in the homelands was unsupported (1975:520). Moreover, because of the agricultural resources, which are entirely inadequate to sustain the population even under the most scientifically rational land methods, and because of the poor opportunity for employment, the reserves will continue to experience excessive demographic pressure (Hance 1970:413-16).

The Effects of Migrant Labor

To appreciate how population dynamics reflect these conditions, let us look at some of the social and economic effects of migrant labor after seventy-five years.

Social Effects

The impact of migrant labor on the African population's dynamics has been pervasive, threatening the viable reproduction of labor power in the societies involved. The dilatory effects have long been documented. Schapera's 1943 study, "Migrant Labour and Tribal Life in Bechuanaland," describes the unfavorable effects of migration on the peasant economy of the reserves, with 40 percent of the African male population away so much of the time: "A few men who have learnt skills abroad are able to practice them at home, but most of the occupations learned abroad are irrelevant in the home environment. . . . Because of migration, many people are no longer available to attend to the routine tasks of tribal life, and as a result both animal husbandry and agriculture have suffered. . . . Men from every tribe are now living abroad" (UNESCO 1956:207).

Hance (1970:193) claims that the loss of the working male population caused agriculture to deteriorate owing to the reduced number of plots farmed, a more simplified crop complex, and consequently a reduced amount and variety of food produced. Further, he argues that when the ratio of females to males exceeds two to one, serious disruption of economic and social life begins. In 1976, the ratio of females to males in the Transkei was 3:2 (TSP 1976:68).

Structural changes have also occurred because of the migrant labor system. Monica Wilson attributed the shift among the Xhosa from a strongly patrilineal system to a matrilineal system to "the disruption caused by migrant labour" (in Thompson 1960:71-86). The disruption of family life also led to broken homes, desertion of wives by husbands and parents by sons, a loss of respect for the elder system, and a distorted birthrate (Schapera, in UNESCO 1956:208).

Social effects of the migratory labor system have even been documented by the regime itself. In the 1965 Cape Synod Report of the Dutch Reformed Church, patterns of neglect and moral disintegration of the workers' families, attacks on women, and increased poverty in the reserves were attributed to the social disintegration caused by migrant labor (Hance 1970). Lack of health and medical services have added to the impoverishment of the population. In particular this has allowed for an extraordinarily high infant mortality rate in the homelands, reportedly between 250 and 400 per 1,000 live births (Friedman 1977:12). Additionally, the introduction of venereal disease and the spread of tuberculosis are cited as direct effects of the migrant labor system.

Economic Effects

The economic strain and impoverished living conditions create the context for an increased birthrate, despite the high infant mortality rate and the compromised fertility rates. These strains are reflected in the economic realities of the African population's living standards.

The typical migrant in 1960, as drawn from 193 employment histories, is a man who has spent two-thirds of his working life, from age sixteen to forty-seven, in employment away from home. In those thirty-one years, he has had thirty-four different jobs, remaining an average of forty-seven weeks on each job (Houghton 1960:180-81). No official figures are available on the number of migrant workers, but the Transkei Study Project (1976:68) estimates that nearly half of all economically active black males in South Africa are migrants. The majority work in the mines or on the farms. Mining labor, which employs 11-15 percent of the African labor force in South Africa (FAO 1978:9), is almost totally migrant, and half of it is drawn from South Africa alone. Agriculture employs 40 percent of South African workers, the majority migrant.

Overall, migrant wages are the lowest in the economy and account for 70 percent of the gross national income in the Transkei alone (TSP 1976:66). The lowest per capita income derives from farming, which is reportedly lower than it was sixty years ago (UN 1977:22), while mining wages did not rise from 1911 to 1970 and possibly fell (Hance 1970:22; SACTU 1970). In 1966 Africans received 18.8 percent of the national income and at that time mining wages were the lowest (Langschmidt 1968/69:2). However, miners' struggles in the early 1970s did force wages to rise in 1975-1976.

In 1972 the average wage for African miners was $343, while for the white miner it was $6,250 (Hance 1975:525). African earnings in 1977 constituted 14.3 percent of white earnings in mining of all kinds and 13.1 percent of white earnings in gold mining (ILO 1979:14-15). In sum, two-thirds of the African workforce earn less than one-seventh of the wages of their European counterparts (ILO 1979:12) and in some cases this ratio is more than doubled. In 1975 the per capita income for Africans was approximately $245 per annum compared to $4,200 for whites, a ratio of 18:1, white to black (Friedman 1977:19-20). With the cost of inflation African earnings and standard of living actually decreased in the 1970s, while the income growth rate for whites exceeded 110 percent between 1966 and 1975 (Friedman 1977:19-20). Africans' share of the national income amounted to 10 percent in 1970 in current income, while the white population grossed 85 percent. Since 1970, many observers claim that this difference has widened. By all accounts, the average wage paid to Africans is less than the Minimum Living Level determined by both black and white councils in South Africa.[3]

But it is the reserves that uphold and support the development of South Africa's white cities. According to Mafeje (1973:19), the urban areas actually hold the rural areas to ransom. Magubane underscores this point: "What would it mean to the mining and agricultural industries to be without labor from the reserves? Black African labor means a difference of profitability and bankruptcy. Out of exploitation of reserve labor comes the surplus value that is invested in urban-based industries" (1979:87).

In the bantustans the standard of living is even worse than in the urban areas. Migrant labor, depleted land, and grossly inadequate health services have led to an impoverished population under great pressure to reproduce and continue as its only means to survive. Thus survival has meant an increased birthrate to offset the high death rate, producing a net population growth rate of 3-4 percent.

Another factor affecting the population dynamics of South Africa is unemployment and underemployment, both of which are characteristically high for the African population.[4] South Africa provides no regular official statistics on the total level of unemployment for the population as a whole. Figures for non-Africans are published regularly, but these are only an index for the state of the business cycle, not for overall unemployment, which is disproportionately concentrated among the African population (Simkins and Clarke 1978:1). Figures are calculated for the white urban areas and farms, but no records are published for unemployment or underemployment in the bantustans, where it is reportedly the highest and from where the bulk of migrant labor is drawn. For example, one Institute of Race Relations report estimated that in the latter half of 1968 unemployment in Transkei was 22.5 percent (Simkins and Clarke 1978:70) and migrant labor amounted to 11 percent.

Although unemployment dropped in the urban areas in 1970-1976, it rose on the white farms because of falling employment levels and mechanization (Simkins and Clarke 1978:70), making the total unemployment rise from 6.1 percent to 10.9 percent during this period. This figure is estimated to be an absolute minimum. Another statistic for the increase of unemployment and cumulative increase in underemployment in the bantustans during this period was from 32,000 to 396,000 (van der Merwe 1976:54). Of the more than 1 million new workers that entered the labor force between 1970 and 1976, at least 57 percent faced unemployment (Simkins and Clarke 1978:5).

It is interesting to note that during this period (1969-1976) mean annual growth in output, total employment, and labor productivity dropped in South Africa, while labor supply rose (Simkins and Clarke 1978:36). With the reserves and migrant labor, agricultural underemployment rose from 24 percent to 38 percent while nonagricultural unemployment declined very slightly from 15 percent to 14.2 percent. The resulting picture is one of increasing agricultural underemployment.

Overall unemployment between 1960 and 1977 increased from 1.2 million to 2.3 million or from 19 percent in 1968 to over 22 percent by 1977. This is attributed in part to the increase in labor supply and falling employment growth rate from 33.7 percent to 23.7 percent during the same period (Simkins and Clarke 1978: 32, 41) and to shorter periods of productive activity among migrants in recent years.

The strain on the African population is felt even more by the shift in the racial composition of the workforce in the past two decades. Coloured, Asian, and white workers increased from 26.9 percent to almost 29 percent between 1960 and 1976. To date, the regime has ensured almost full employment for whites while the level of unemployment and underemployment for the African population continues to rise.

The social implications of a high rate of rising unemployment is one reason the South African government is so eager to stem population growth on the reserves. With a current annual increase of 128,000 African males (60,000 from the homelands and 68,000 from the white areas), combined with the 3 percent population growth rate, the government still only provided jobs for some 8,300 African males by 1975 (TSP 1976:5). Even for a regime based on an unending supply of cheap labor, this has raised serious questions.

Changing labor needs accentuate the conflict between South Africa's development as a capitalist power and its policy of apartheid. By 1980 the demand for unskilled labor is projected to be up from 1.37 million in 1970 to over 2 million (*Financial Mail*, July 4, 1967). At the same time, the view that more and more Africans were occupying skilled technical and managerial positions was proved false. According to the Department of Labor's Manpower Survey of February 1978, between 1975 and April 1977 the proportion of Africans in almost every class of skilled positions dropped from 2.9 percent to 0.4 percent. Simultaneously, the proportion of whites in these positions rose from 94 percent to 97 percent and the share of Coloureds and Asians dropped marginally (*Financial Mail*, February 24, 1978).

Among professional, semiprofessional, and technical staff the percentage of Africans also dropped, while that of whites rose. Even in the bantustans, the percentage of black artisans and apprentices dropped from 2.5 percent to 2.1 percent and clerical workers dropped from 13.4 percent to 13.2 percent. The total amount in just these two years was a fivefold decrease. Thus Africans were not only *not* being advanced into higher level positions, but the higher the position, the less chance there is for mobility at all. Two reasons often cited for this downward trend were the economic recession of 1977 and the South African government's master plan to whiten its urban areas (see, for example, Simkins and Clarke 1978).

On the other hand, the false labor shortage created by prohibiting Africans from holding skilled positions has made industry desperate for skilled labor, essential for an expanding industrial economy. Even South African economists recognize that there is no real shortage, but rather a wastage and misuse of labor power which has actually inhibited the South African economy from realizing its potential. A key structural trend and an explicit policy of the South African mining industry has been the generalized displacement of labor in production. This process has been manifested in two forms: the substitution of local for foreign labor (a Chamber of Mines objective since 1975) and the substitution of capital for labor. From 1973 to 1976 South African miners increased from 82,000 to 193,000, replacing foreign laborers (Simkins and Clarke 1978:67-68). Total displacement is not desirable, however, according to Clarke, if only for wage savings. Despite a 30 percent increase in permanent jobs, increasing unemployment in the bantustans far outweighs this addition to the labor force.

Despite differing statistics and percentages of growth and decline, it is generally agreed that unemployment and underemployment is high and rising for the African population. The high population growth rate in the 1960s and 1970s is a direct response to this employment structure and promises to continue as the crisis of unemployment and underemployment intensifies under the dynamics of capitalist development.

Population Dynamics and Labor

Population growth figures for the African population are uncertain and vary because of nonexistent or poorly kept records. Although registration of births and deaths was made compulsory in 1952, two-thirds were registered between 1952 and 1961, and from 1961 to 1975 most went completely unrecorded. However, a more than 2 percent growth rate since 1904 (Lorimer 1961:89) is probably a good estimate, given the rapid rate of capitalist development. Africans outnumber whites by a ratio of 4:1, and the major concern of the apartheid regime is that this ratio will continue to widen under present economic conditions.

In the first decade of this century, as South Africa was on the verge of industrialization geared to development based on mining profits, the African population increased by 640,000 from 1904 to 1911 (Setai 1975:144), despite the frequent and erratic absences of men from the rural areas as well as the return of diseased or injured migrant workers. High fertility rates were also a response to the employment structure and accelerated urbanization rate. Between 1960 and 1967 fertility declined from a much higher rate in the 1950s to a low of 40 per 1,000 women, in part because of the disruptive effects of the large-scale removal of nearly 1 million people to the bantustans between 1959 and 1969 (Rogers 1972:39). However, high fertility in the 1950s may also have been a response to offset high infant mortality, as Unterhaler points out: "In a society where there is a large number of infant deaths, the conscious or unconscious desire to compensate for this loss may be a factor in the high fertility rate" (Unterhaler 1955:7).

It has also been suggested that fertility declined among African women in the rural areas because of the long absences of the men, often up to two or three years. Again, a contributing factor may have been delayed marriages owing to the difficulty of paying the *lobola* (or brideprice), stemming from the general economic deterioration and overcrowding on the reserves. Even more significant for inhibited fertility has been the lack of basic and adequate medical services on the reserves.

Overall, however, fertility rates of the African population of South Africa have been high, particularly in the rural areas. Unterhaler (1955:95) conducted his research when the rural population was three times that of the urban, revealing an overall birthrate of 44.39 per 1,000 women and general fertility rate of 186.4 per 1,000. In one township, Alexandra, high death rates offset the gross reproduction rate of 2.8 percent, producing a net growth rate of only 1.8 percent.

Infant mortality and death rates are good indicators of the well-being and general living conditions of a population. In South Africa, the high infant mortality rate reflects subhuman living conditions, impoverishment, and poor health services. "It is the operation of socioeconomic factors . . . which vitally affects infant deaths" (Unterhaler 1955:8). No formal or official data have been kept on African infant mortality since the mid-1950s, and what was kept has been fragmentary and incomplete. But infant mortality has been high throughout the century—both in urban and rural areas. One survey in 1966 reported that *half* the children born in a typical African reserve died before the age of five (quoted in Friedman 1977:12).

Overall infant mortality estimates range from 200 to 450 per 1,000 live births. In a 1949 Public Health Department report, the rate from 1942 to 1946 averaged 216 per 1,000 with the highest being 275 in 1942 (Hamer 1962:20). In another report, infant mortality in Ciskei was registered at 164 per 1,000, while in the Transkei it was 280 per 1,000 (Fox 1937). Unterhaler's 1955 study showed the Pretoria Public Health Department reporting a rate of 282 per 1,000 African children up to three years old, compared to 30 per 1,000 for white children. In areas where there were clinics, the rate for Africans was lower, but still high, such as in Johannesburg where it was 141 per 1,000. In the Alexandra township, the rate of 131 in 1953-1954 was attributed to "lack of medical services, overcrowded and unsanitary living conditions, and low wages coupled with illiteracy," and at a health center in Natal, Unterhaler claimed that the rate of 113 would have been 244 per 1,000 had there been no clinic (1955:85). By 1970 the rate ranged from 110 to 140 per 1,000 in urban areas—at least five times that for whites. The latter figures are generally considered underestimates, since they are based on statistics for the Coloured population who fare slightly better in living conditions in South Africa.

Death rates for the African population in South Africa stand as some of the highest in the world, despite varying figures and degrees of validation. A 1968 estimate is from 27 to 32 per 1,000, with 49.6 years of life expectancy for men and 54.2 years for women (UN 1975). High death rates are a result not only of poor living conditions but of dangerous and debilitating work situations. In 1978 at least 737 miners died on the job and 29,000 out of 226,000 workers were injured. In the last five years, the death rate has been affected by the police attacks and violence bred by escalating tensions in South Africa.

Another population dynamic generated by capitalist development has been the rapid and massive urbanization rate; at 5.1 percent it is estimated as one of the highest in the world (Africa Guide 1978). The rural population declined accordingly: from

82.5 percent in 1970 to 80.5 percent in 1977. From 1936 to 1968 the urban population almost tripled, 1.2 million to 4.3 million, with the highest rate of increase—126 percent—between 1946 and 1960. Despite restrictions on African urbanization, and even after thirty years of apartheid, the majority (53.5 percent) of Africans live and work *outside* the bantustans rather than in them. Most reside in the rural areas, but Africans still outnumber all others, including whites, 80 percent of whom live in cities (Friedman 1977:6). N. J. van Rensburg (1972:3), a South African advocate of strict population control, argued that 75 percent of the African population will be urban by the year 2000, based on his figure for African urbanization from 1951 to 1970: an increase of 15 percent (from 24 to 29 percent) in less than twenty years!

Apartheid notwithstanding, Africans in the urban sector have been crucial for South Africa's development. Former Prime Minister Vorster recognized the economy's need for blacks in the cities when he spoke to the House of Assembly as early as 1963: "Despite the ideal of separation, the fact of the matter is this: we need them because they work for us" (in Rogers 1972). And again in 1972 he expressed South Africa's priority concern: "We would like to reduce them . . . and we are doing our best to do so, but at all times we would not disrupt the South African economy" (1972:7).

The South African government regards the ability to control the black population as a major political goal. African labor power is needed in the cities and on the farms, and migrant labor from the bantustans is favored since it is cheap and unlimited. The bantustans, which help to reproduce such labor, thus represent a direct and indirect form of population manipulation and control. According to Magubane, they are "deliberately designed so that the people who reside in them have no choice but to seek employment in the capitalist sector," and are thus a means of providing the necessary supply of cheap labor and also a "dumping ground for the human waste discarded by the urban and mining industries" (Magubane 1979:87). Moreover, as capital replaces labor in mining and other industries (such as manufacturing) and masses of unemployed Africans begin to threaten political stability, the bantustan policy also serves to curb the

African population growth rate (Sadie 1972:37). Not only is mortality greater in the homelands, but these areas set up fixed geographic enclosures where subsistence production is impossible, and at the same time offer little opportunity for local industry and labor-intensive employment, increasing the pressure of population against subsistence. In sum, a cheap labor supply, a dumping ground for redundant population, and population control are important by-products of South Africa's bantustan policy.

Reproducing a healthy labor force is essential for capitalist expansion, particulatly in a labor-intensive economy. Disease, high mortality, and widespread malnutrition do not contribute to this end. At what point do the diminishing returns of such a policy no longer make it profitable in reproductive terms for continued capitalist development? Magubane's description of the bantustans raises serious questions about the viable reproduction of labor power on these reserves, which are "concentrated areas of poverty, disease, and ignorance, where all activities or thoughts that the white rulers fear or dislike are repressed and extra-economic coercions and controls can be swiftly applied. The reserve system represents the ultimate in deliberately conceived human retardation" (1979:87).

Because of the strain on the reserves to support an increasing population, and the instability of the family units caused by migrant labor and apartheid, the dynamics of the African population express the growth rates of a particularly distorted form of capitalist penetration.

South African Population Policy

According to van Rensburg (1972:7) for every white born in South Africa between 1960 and 1970, there was a corresponding increase of 7.2 nonwhites. The expressed government concern is that: whites are a dwindling minority; a population explosion of an unsurpassed rate is presently taking place in southern Africa, and South Africa's population is increasing at the highest rate in the world; the present population is going to accelerate appreciably in the near future; and this has very serious disadvantages for all humans in this part of the world.

By mid-1978 the South African population numbered 26.9 million, with an annual birthrate of 46.6 per 1,000, which promises to double by the year 2000. The average number of children per family between 1975 and 1980 was 5.6, which the South African government regards as unacceptably high. It intends to reduce this figure by actively supporting population control (IPPFF 1979). Van Rensburg (1972) and Sadie (1972), two South African proponents of this policy, set out its goals and implementation.

The major reason for the concern over the "dwindling white minority" is the fear of loss of political power. This is clearly expressed in van Rensburg's *Population Explosion in South Africa:* "The proportion of whites in the population could drop to about 10% in the year 2000 and to about 1.3% by 2070. A similar reduction of white political authority in the country must therefore also be considered a distinct possibility" (1972: 10-11). But in the same book, van Rensburg claims that this could never happen because certain events would make it impossible, such as mass starvation, political chaos, or population planning. Professor Sadie, from the University of Stellenbach, underscores this plan with the following:

Bantu are due to increase their majority from 70 to 74% in 2000 and to 77% by 2020. If the white population is not going to be strengthened by immigration it will be exceeded in size by the Coloured population by the year 2010 . . . from the point of view of economic development, the relative size of the white population, which provides the major proportion of the entrepreneurial initiative—and the Asian population, which is assuming an increasing role in this regard—is very important. These two groups constitute 20% of the aggregate population in 1970. If demographic tendencies continue on their course, these two will have 16% share in 2000 and only 13% in 2020. *This way lies the relative impoverishment of the Bantu and Coloureds even while their per capita income could rise. They have, for practical purposes, only their labor to offer whose employment is dependent on the enterprise and capital supplied by the other two groups. The need for a substantial and vigorous family planning program which will reduce fertility more rapidly than is implied in our projections is obvious.* (1972:37, emphasis added)

The official position attributes all social ills and health inadequacies to overpopulation, using studies in the United States as a model for explaining the direct correlation between a high birthrate and a low income level.

Overpopulation leads to malnutrition, undernourishment, and famine. This leads to poverty, lack of educational facilities and concomitant ignorance and inability of greater achievement or of a greater contribution to economic growth and development. This in turn leads to diminishing opportunities for employment, unplanned urbanization, uncontrolled pollution of air and water, further deterioration and degeneration into slums, which again leads to greater social decay, extra-marital births, uncontrolled population growth and even greater poverty. (van Rensburg, 1972:xvi)

The overriding question for the regime, according to these population-control proponents, is whether South Africa can support a population of over 700 million in less than a century. (This dubious figure was projected from the 3.4 percent growth rate between 1960-1970 by van Rensburg.) Van Rensburg's concern is obvious from the following statement: "As of 1960, whites were the single largest group . . . by 1970 [they] had dropped to third behind the Zulu and Xhosa. This will lead to a ratio of 5-6 Africans to 1 white by 2000 and this would be disastrous" (1972:9). But the reality behind this concern with numbers is the implication that the social structure will change with black population growth, in a way that would alter the precarious dominance that whites now exercise. To counter this trend, van Rensburg used the classical Malthusian argument that the doubling of resources in 20 years—necessary for the redoubled population—will be impossible, leading to a rapid decline in the standard of living, which will have "very serious political, social, and economic implications as well as adverse effects on human relationships" (van Rensburg 1972:11). He then links the policy of the homelands to the need for population control, saying "the more successful the policy of separate development is (with the concomitant increase in the percentage of whites in the white areas), the more successful the policy of development of the homelands will have to be (with the concomitant increase of blacks there)" (1972:13).

Van Rensburg warns that unless the population growth rate is reduced, Africans' need for land could well lead to armed conflict: "Now it is a fact that the African farmer achieves a very much lower level of producivity than does the white farmer. Such an abandonment of white agricultural areas would therefore ultimately be detrimental to the food production for all South Africans. A situation could very well arise where the whites would have to safeguard their land by force of arms" (1972:14). The obvious answer for all this, he argues, is immediate family planning for the African population, combined with positive action by the whites. "Are we," he asks, "through our passivity, our indecision, and lack of purposeful action going to allow such an unrealistic growth . . . a growth which must inevitably lead to poverty, undernourishment, bankruptcy and ruin in South Africa?" (1972:viii).

One relatively unsuccessful government effort to counter the demographic effects of capitalist development on the African population has been the attempt to increase the white community by immigration. A goal of 33,000 annually between 1960 and 1970 failed; net immigration between 1948 and 1973 amounted to 25,000 to 30,000 (Friedman 1977:11; Sadie 1972:10). And since 1973 white immigration has dropped to its lowest level ever. The purpose of creating "independent" entities out of the bantustans is more evident in this light: this population would no longer be considered officially part of South Africa, removing the responsibility for reproducing it from South African jurisdiction.

The policy of bantustan "independence" simply shifts the burden of reproduction of labor power totally to the African population, who will still need to migrate to work for white enterprises, while maintaining a veneer of separate development to the world. Additional attempts to satisfy international and domestic pressure to reduce or eliminate apartheid have yielded numerous reports on improving the face of South Africa but the social and economic relations remain substantively unaltered.[5]

Conclusions

Continued capitalist development in South Africa faces increasing tension and confrontation with the political system of apartheid. It is evident from population projections that bantustans as part of a larger apartheid plan "fly in the face of powerful economic and demographic forces and are not at all likely to achieve their stated goals" (Hance 1970:121). They cannot succeed in the overall objective of engineering the population, restraining urbanization, enclosing the majority population, and reducing the black-white ratio, since "even if separate development is implemented with unimaginable success, 'White' South Africa will still be more than ¾ non-white. Nothing will have been solved" (Rand *Daily Mail*, April 18, 1970).

Some of the strains are already apparent: the need for more skilled workers than are available in the white population; inhibited productivity because the migratory labor system requires the continual training of new workers, since migrants cannot stay long enough on any one job to develop skill or expertise; and little or no buying power because of exceptionally low wages in an increasingly overproductive society. South African businesses today have more products to sell than an affluent white population needs or demands.

Thus the bantustans, so necessary for South Africa to maintain its level of economic growth based on exploitation of cheap, mainly unskilled labor for low-grade ore mining and agriculture, are at the same time a serious inhibition to growth, especially in the expanding industrial sector. While the bantustans must support the urban industrial centers and respond to employment pressures by high fertility, the conditions for subsistence are practically nonexistent. In fact, conditions are so poor that they provide a good argument that population management and reduction in South Africa is by starvation.

Migrant labor, institutionalized by the homelands policy, is the very backbone of capitalist accumulation in South Africa. It is also the source of impoverishment, underdevelopment, substandard living conditions, and population pressure. The 53 percent of the African population which is rural is forced to depend on the migrants' income and at the same time bear the costs of the maintenance and reproduction of labor power for the cities. The demographic profile of the African population reflects this exploitation. Indeed, population dynamics serve to elucidate the fact that the very reason South Africa was able to develop into an industrial power—the value of its labor power— is the very source of the conflict that threatens its further growth as a capitalist society today.

The present crisis in South Africa reflects some of the contradictions generated by capitalist development. In South Africa, as in the rest of the world, overpopulation is not the *cause* of underdevelopment, but is itself a consequence of expanding capitalist development, which leaves in its wake poverty, underdevelopment, and chaotic population growth. Control over reproduction is but one aspect of peoples' control over their lives and their productive activity. Therefore, sound family planning and reduction of uncontrolled population growth can only be established when producers regain control of their production and product.

Notes

1. The demand for labor is determined not by the amount of capital as a whole but by its variable constituent alone. That demand falls progressively with the increase in total capital, instead of in proportion to it, as previously assumed (Marx 1967:629).

2. Stevenson (1968) pointed out in his study of state societies and the onset of colonialism that population dynamics reflect social and economic processes in nineteenth-century southern Africa. At that time, greater population densities existed in state or incipient state societies of the Zulu, Ngwato, Tswana, and Bemba than in nonstates because of the three-way nexus between trade, trade routes, and developing political and social organizations. In all these societies, population density was dramatically reduced with the destruction of state formations brought on by the intervention of colonial rule. Another argument that supports the thesis that colonialism inter-

rupted existing population dynamics is made by Faris (1975:257-58), who claims that prior to colonialism African state forms may have been viable and continued for a good many years without evolving to other modes of production because they contained the mechanisms to resolve their contradictions—accumulation of surplus and increasing population—through military expansion and technological innovations such as crop diversification.

3. For a family of five in Soweto, the Johannesburg Chamber of Commerce calculated R87.22 as the Minimum Living Level, while the Urban Bantu Council calculated it to be R117.82 (1 Rand = $1.35). The Bureau of Market Research at the University of South Africa and the Institute of Race Relations conducted studies on median urban household incomes and concluded similar results—that the average urban income for Africans was significantly below the official Poverty Datum Line (Friedman 1977:19-20).

4. Underemployment includes those who are able but do not work full time; whose wages are abnormally low; whose income could be raised if they worked under approved conditions, or were transferred; whose jobs do not permit full use of their capacities or skills; or who are employed in establishments whose productivity is abnormally low (van der Merwe 1976:50).

5. Cf. the Weihahn Commission Report of May 1979 and subsequent pronouncements by South African Prime Minister Botha on relaxation of apartheid restrictions.

The Effects of Plantation Economy
on a Polynesian Population

Eric H. Larson

The Pacific Islands have served as a kind of controlled laboratory in which analysts could impose limits on the number of variables affecting human population size and distribution (Vayda and Rappaport 1970:5-8). Owing to an island's physical isolation and dimunitive size, the interrelationships between such variables as population and distribution, resources of the local environment, and the level of productivity have been assumed to function within the confines of an island itself, free of intrusions from beyond the immediate shores. This assumption permitted the conclusion that people, nature, and human technology existed in a state of internal equilibrium.

While such a perspective lends itself to elegant statements on population dynamics, it fails to acknowledge the fact that the Pacific Islands participate in the modern world economy and that such participation has an impact on these population dynamics. Successive visits and settlement by explorers, whalers, missionaries, traders, planters, migrant laborers, exiles, the military, and most recently, tourists have changed the face of Oceania, and it is difficult today to rediscover the innocent paradise described in earlier times (Oliver 1961). This study looks at a Polynesian people, the Tikopia, as they have been influenced by their post-contact development as a plantation economy. Specifically, it will examine the ways a plantation sets up conditions under which the Tikopia population is encouraged both to grow and to disperse, and how population, rather than being an independent variable, responds to even moderate changes in other variables. Plantation capitalist enterprise is defined here as the employment of a wage-labor force whose

This essay is based on fieldwork carried out in the Solomon Islands between June 1964 and July 1965.

Movement from Tikopia to Russell Islands (since 1949)

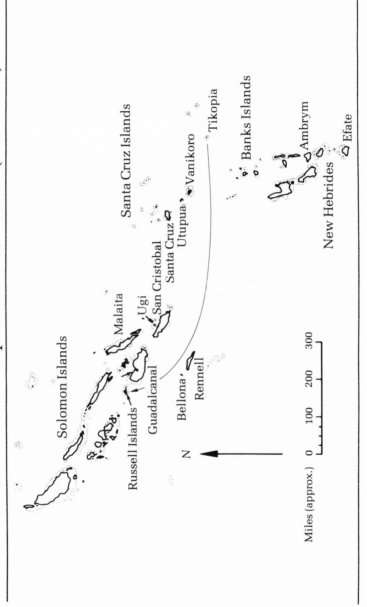

Solomon Islands

Malaita

Ugi
San Cristobal

Russell Islands

Guadalcanal

Bellona
Rennell

Santa Cruz Islands

Santa Cruz
Utupua
Vanikoro

Tikopia

Banks Islands

Ambrym

New Hebrides

Efate

N

Miles (approx.)   0   100   200   300

function is to produce tropical crops on company-owned estates, usually in developing countries, for ultimate consumption in industrialized nations of the temperate zones. It will be assumed that in this case population growth can be stimulated or impeded by instituting a plantation, as well as by technology and environment, factors traditionally considered important in demographic studies (Cowgill 1975:505-25).

Background and History

The Tikopia live on a tiny Polynesian outlier, itself called Tikopia, on the remote southeastern tip of the Solomon Islands archipelago (see map). Much of the Polynesian culture has been maintained on Tipokia. The people divide themselves into four clans, each of which is headed by a hereditary chief. Membership in these units is determined by the recognition of blood relationships through the male line. Within the clans, extended families constitute the groupings actually responsible for holding and maintaining property, raising children, and exploiting the land and sea for survival. Subsistence is almost totally dependent on resources obtained from the local environment, where the islanders cultivate vegetables in the gardens, collect wild fruits and nuts, fish in an inland pond, the reef, and the sea, utilize local timber and vegetation for house construction, canoe-building, and mat weaving, and—with the exception of steel tools obtained from the outside world—live by their own skills and devices. Since 1949, however, the Tikopia have been migrating in significant numbers to the Russell Islands,[1] located in the central Solomon Islands, to work on Lever's Pacific Plantations, a subsidiary of Unilever Corporation.[2]

In 1965 Lever's maintained 15,000 acres of coconut estates, located mainly on the islands of Pavuvu and Banika. Twelve European managers supervised a labor force of 1,100 men in planting new estates, cultivating older ones, and performing all tasks necessary for the production of copra, a raw material used to produce such items as soap, margarine, and other edible fats. Plantation workers were recruited from throughout the Solomons, although a majority came from the relatively heavily populated island of Malaita, and a few specialists were enlisted from Fiji and the Gilbert islands. Tikopia laborers constitute 13 percent of the workforce and reside separately from non-Tikopia in two labor compounds, Samata and Pepesala, and the Tikopia village of Nukufero on Pavuvu Island.

Between 1955 and 1965, during which time the migration to coconut plantations had shifted into full swing, the Tikopia population grew substantially. A 1952 census of Tikopia situated throughout the Solomons recorded a population of 1,750 (Firth 1959:53); by 1955, after a devastating epidemic of malaria and influenza struck the home island itself, the overall number dropped to around 1,350 (Larson 1966:3). In 1965, however, the figure rose again to 1,611, a 19 percent increase within a decade. Most significantly, the age group 0-10 years amounted to 450, constituting 25 percent of the total population. Even a casual observer could not fail to see that Tikopia children were prominent in social life, and Tikopia of all ages not only expressed fondness for young people, but stated a desire to raise large families. Yet before labor migration to the Lever's plantations began, when people were largely confined to the tiny home island, a scarcity of land and resources prompted elderly males, fearful of overpopulation, to ask younger ones to postpone marriage and remain celibate. Those needing to gratify sexual desires were encouraged to practice *coitus interruptus*. Abortion, infanticide (burying an infant's face in the sand), the loss of people who ventured out to sea, and intraisland warfare were other checks on population growth (Firth 1936:373-74).

At present, with a substantial number of Tikopia residing in the Russells, the islanders no longer view population growth as a crisis. Indeed, they express the desire to expand in numbers and disperse in space, a change which can be interpreted as stemming from the labor demands of Lever's coconut plantations, and the policies undertaken to secure a Tikopia workforce. The difficulty of enticing large numbers of Solomon

Islanders to work on a regular basis on the plantations led the company in the early 1950s to encourage a steady flow of Tikopia labor to the estates. At first they were unsuccessful.

James Spillius, an anthropologist doing fieldwork on Tikopia in 1952, reported that few of the people signed up when European recruiters called on the island. Returning workers discouraged would-be recruits by expressing a dislike of work routines and quotas set by management, and of the inadequacies and over-crowded living conditions in a single large building situated in a labor compound that accommodated workers from throughout the Solomons. They spoke with resentment of the scorn heaped upon them by Melanesian co-workers, a people of different race and culture, who saw them as primitive and naive about modern ways. Moreover, they alleged that the Melanesians had practiced witchcraft on them. They also resented the cold, impersonal treatment by the company, a coldness compounded by the suf-fering from diseases, boredom, and homesickness on the planta-tions (Spillius 1957:92).

Migration and Labor Policy of Lever's Plantations

In fear of losing a potentially rich labor source, Lever's sought advice from Spillius on methods of accommodating and increas-ing the flow of personnel to the plantations. Spillius suggested first that Tikopia, and not European recruiters, be made respon-sible for selection; he argued for the inclusion of traditional leadership in any decision to sign on people from the island. He advised the company to play upon ethnic identity by having Tikopia and Melanesians reside in separate labor compounds. He suggested also that the workers be housed in smaller indi-vidual quarters, with living arrangements set up among them-selves. Finally, he called for greater flexibility in job assign-ments, so that Tikopia might organize into small groups and cooperate in work tasks as they do on the home island.

Lever's accepted these suggestions and began making changes to ease the workers' transition to wage laborers. First, Tikopia were included with Europeans as part of the recruiting team. Initially they simply assisted, but later they were given full responsibility. By this time they were competent in explaining conditions on the plantations, having worked there, and were able to predict with accuracy the relative chances of adjustment of prospective workers. On an island where every person knows everyone else (no one lives further than one mile from his or her most distant neighbor), recruiters knew whom and whom not to approach. They knew, for example, of those wanting to earn a target sum of money with which to buy certain amenities not available at home,[3] or of people who wanted to send children to a school located close to the plantations, or of others who needed better medical care available in the central Solomons. Since Tikopia lacks docking facilities and a ship in anchorage risks the danger of being damaged on the fringing reef, labor recruiters were required to sign on workers within a short time. A recruiter who knew the likely candidates was more efficient and yielded a relatively larger number in the time allotted. Moreover, a would-be recruit who independently decided to sign on felt more trustful of someone known than of a strange European who could not speak the native language and who might be intimidating.

Lever's agreed further to recruit labor under the constraints imposed by Tikopia leadership. The highest level leadership is conferred upon four chiefs, each of whom heads one of the four clans, and who together hold the loyalty of all the people. Before Anglican missionaries converted the island's people to Christianity, each chief officiated at rituals in which the respective clan deities were worshipped and vegetable totems made sacred and set aside as tabooed objects for a specified time in the year (Firth 1940). Chiefs were also said to have had the power to condemn incorrigible offenders of the social order to almost certain death by banishment to sea. Today, such condemnation is deemed incompatible with a Christian ethic and against codified Solomon Islands law. Still, the chiefs do hold titular ownership of the entire island and can render final decisions over production, distribution, and consumption of local resources. Chieftainship as an institution also represents the apex of an islandwide kinship structure, in which the complex of normative behavior guides practically the entire range of social life. Given this tradition, and current respect for the chiefs, a prospective migrant was expected to ask his clan leader for permission to leave the homeland. A chief, however, granted leave only reluctantly, since, as indicated, his function is to hold the society together, and it was expected that the chief would make at least a token argument against leaving. A chief would take real action opposing the departure if the person seeking to leave had no willing kinsman remaining to care for his house and gardens. Or a chief might regulate the number and kinds of people departing, as they did in 1964, when they decided that no more than forty men with their immediate families could migrate. Within any quota, high-ranking men may also be restricted, since by custom they help their respective clan chief in governing the community. These men are related by close family ties and, especially at community meetings that draw large gatherings, advise a chief and articulate rulings of islandwide importance. A chief is thus able to determine who genuinely needs to go to the plantations and who should remain to tend to business at home. Hence, migration was a rational act based on the needs of Tikopia, not the plantation, and departure was seen as a legitimate alternative within the range of appropriate social behavior. Such legitimacy yielded a fairly predictable number of recruits each year, and Lever's itself gained by submitting to the chiefs' final approval of migration to the plantations.

In another measure to stimulate migration, Lever's decided to separate the Tikopia from Melanesians on a single plantation and to modify time schedules and inflexible work quotas set for the Tikopia during the early days of discontent on the estates. This separation heightened morale insofar as feelings of oneness coincided with a strong sense of ethnic pride and loyalty to one another as a people. Raymond Firth, the well-known anthropologist who has written extensively about the Tikopia, entitled his classic ethnography, We, the Tikopia, having heard these three words of the book title uttered by natives repeatedly in all kinds of situations. As he notes, "[the expression] is constantly on the lips of the people themselves, representing that community of interests, that self-consciousness, that strongly marked individuality in physical appearance, dress, language, and custom which they prize so highly" (1936:xv). Firth wrote of this pride as he observed it in the late 1920s; at the time of my own investigation, it persisted with the same vigor on the plantations, and the possibility of building a new, exclusively Tikopia community in the Russells has stimulated a new sense of frontier in which to expand in both numbers and tradition.

An example of expanded tradition was seen when Lever's modified labor procedures for the previously disgruntled Polynesians on the estates. As indicated, the Tikopia initially perceived plantation labor as being boring and rigid. On Tikopia itself, work groups are organized to achieve given ends in a relatively spontaneous and informal way. People come and go, whether the task is completed or not, and someone is likely to replace one of the original participants. A job may be completed at some indefinite time in the future. Work groups tend to be small in number and comprise both men and women. The division of labor within these groups is apportioned equally between the sexes, so that both cultivate gardens, fish in the reef, prepare meals and care for children, build houses, and work together in the other activities essential for maintaining the society. Lever's shrewdly employed this model: both males and females are now permitted to work together in small groups and set up their own schedules.

Work on the coconut plantations involves weeding beneath the evenly planted rows of palm trees, collecting the ripened and fallen nuts, splitting open the husks and shell and extracting the coconut from the shell, putting the coconut into sacks, and transporting them to a drying mill. There the coconut is dried into copra and then picked up by cargo vessels headed for processing plants in Australia and Japan. These tasks conform to those on other modern plantation enterprises in which most production has been mechanized, yet Lever's allots up to 60 percent of operating expenses to wages (Courtenay 1964:53). Production on Lever's plantations is labor-intensive and the jobs require little skill. Lack of skill specialization in turn allows the Tikopia routinely to assist one another. Examples of such assistance can be seen when children spend up to half a day collecting dispersed coconuts on the ground, or when a wife joins her husband wielding a machete to cut down the tall grass surrounding the palms. Workers who tire of a job, say, in the drying mill, may switch to collecting sackfuls of coconut in a truck or sit beneath a tree gouging out the coconut from shells someone else has previously split open. Such assistance and job exchanges go on frequently and with a moment's notice; the European manager may or may not know of the proceedings, but in any case the responsibility of maintaining job discipline rests with the Tikopia overseer. These overseers are selected by the company mainly because they represent authority in the Tikopia social order. If, on occasion, work drops off, a word from one of them is usually enough to set matters straight. Also, extracting the coconut and weeding constitute over 90 percent of the work, and these tasks are paid by the amount of work done, not by the hour. So from the company's standpoint, the chores will eventually be completed and the Tikopia are seen to be relatively happy. The Tikopia see their own burden mitigated by following a work procedure familiar to them since childhood on the home island.

The modification of labor recruitment on Tikopia and relaxation of rules on the plantations improved the Tikopia attitudes toward wage employment and helped to increase the number of migrants. However, most migrants still spent no more than from one to four years on the plantations, living there in the labor compounds, before returning home for an indefinite period. The company, on the other hand, wanted a permanent workforce, available at all seasons. In order to facilitate this, it decided to give the Tikopia outright 200 acres of land on which to build a community and plant subsistence gardens. The Tikopia accepted the land grant and in 1965 began staking out the village of Nukufero. Nukufero gradually developed, as Tikopia came in ever-increasing numbers from the home island, the plantation labor compounds nearby, or elsewhere in the Solomons to clear the area of tall trees and jungle brush, construct leaf houses, a school, and a church, lay extensive pipes to bring water from its source in the bush, and plant and cultivate gardens that would serve the basic subsistence needs of the workers or those simply settling in the community.

At present, the village is seen as an attractive place to live, a home away from home where traditions can be carried on. The Nukufero headman, for example, represents the authority vested in the four chiefs and can serve only by receiving their prior approval and continued support. One of the headman's main functions is to allocate land to new arrivals, and land itself constitutes a basis for maintaining tradition. In effect, the land tenure system on Tikopia has been extended to Nukufero. On Tikopia, extended families several generations in depth and related through the male blood line jointly own land that is dispersed throughout the island. For example, a father and three sons, each with a wife and children, may own a grove of coconut trees near the shore, a plot or two of swamp taro, and stretches of upland gardens planted with sweet potatoes, yams, and bananas. These areas are owned collectively by the father and sons, and each with his nuclear family is free to cultivate and take food from any one of them. Thus a nuclear family does not own a single plot outright but lays claim to discrete parcels located in different areas. Such a land tenure system promotes extended kinship ties, since the various nuclear families that constitute larger corporate family structures cooperate in maintaining the holdings and reciprocate in giving and sharing in the fruits of the land. The system expands and contracts, depending on the number of nuclear families and landholdings plugging into it. On special occasions, such as a large feast honoring the four chiefs, the whole island may be viewed as a single extended family, with everyone contributing food from all the gardens.

The basis of kinship, then, is the joint ownership of land, and land in Nukufero, as on Tikopia, is said to bind people together. Land owned in Nukufero is owned also by those on the home island. Any single Tikopia is said to have land in both locations. Gardens and house sites are dispersed over the face of the home island and across an expanse of 500 miles of sea to Nukufero. Thus in contrast to moves to plantations in other parts of the world, in which migrants are forced to break away from their traditional social order (Mintz 1957; Norbeck 1959), the Tikopia are able to maintain the vitality of kinship by reconstituting a community in the new location. Lever's, it may be noted, benefits from this same system. The company has limited the land to be turned over to the migrants to 200 acres, since with additional land the Tikopia could grow their own coconuts for commercial copra production. They could earn, at least potentially, significantly more than they do now and still grow subsistence crops, thereby not only reducing Lever's workforce but constituting potential competitors. As it is, the land available for food production suffices only to meet the subsistence needs, yet frees the workers from dependency on a monetary wage for survival. As a result the company is faced with little pressure in labor demands for better wages.[4]

Tikopia Perceptions of Labor Migration

The movement of the Tikopia to the Russell Islands serves the interests of both laborers and management. The Tikopia view migration pragmatically as an opportunity to earn a target sum of money on the plantations while maintaining cultural traditions, obtaining additional lands, and raising large families. They are not blind, however, to the inequities of the plantation system. Since piece-rate pay predominates, in 1965 Tikopia workers earned around $.18 an hour, computed on the actual time put in, or approximately $6.25 a week. By comparison, European managers received from $125 to $200 a week. In addition, the managers, unlike the workers, qualified for such liberal fringe benefits as paid travel fares and four-month vacations every two years to the country from which they were hired, retirement benefits after twenty years with the company, and access to cheap domestic help, which only they could afford. Added to the difference in wage and fringe benefits were inequities resulting from racism. Except on those exceptional occasions when Tikopia workers and European managers competed in soccer matches, or when a European passed briefly for a "walkabout" among the Tikopia community, the two groups had little personal contact. Europeans belonged to Club Banika, a facility reserved almost exclusively for Caucasians, with a swimming pool, tennis court, bar, and billiard tables. Housing was also segregated, with management living in cheerfully furnished six-room dwellings situated on grounds carefully maintained by "garden boys" (adult Solomon Islanders), while workers lived either in thatch huts in Nukufero or in labor compounds on the plantations. These compounds consisted of one-room dwellings built of corrugated iron (which retained the tropical heat), of about 350 to 500 square feet. They were laid with concrete floors and lacked plumbing and electricity.

Yet Tikopia were unable to effectively articulate misgivings about the system. In discussing the economics of plantation labor, workers expressed mistrust over management's intended actions, as, for example, when they said they believed that management could dismiss and repatriate them to their home island without notice. Despite legal ownership of Nukufero, the Tikopia believed the power of the company was strong enough to break any agreement set by law. The plantation was seen as a white man's enterprise, a somewhat complicated aspect of an already complex culture which Tikopia could not wholly comprehend and had to accept on management's terms. Given the limited alternatives available for earning money in the Solomon Islands, the Tikopia accepted migration as an alternatve to simply spending their lives confined to a single and remote home island.

Lever's plantations in turn saw the Tikopia workforce as one element of the total production process. The enlightened labor policy extended to the Tikopia was rationalized according to a European bias about democratic ideas, moral probity, and bourgeois standards of stability. At the same time, the company feared a possible threat emerging out of growing nationalism and socialist aspirations in the Solomon Islands (Davenport and Coker 1967:123-275). The contradictions of the plantation system, expressed in foreign ownership of local property, minimal capital formation within the region, diminished purchasing power of the people resulting from increasing inflation, lowered export of raw materials caused by the world recession, and balance of trade deficits is not likely to disappear by virtue of an image of liberal, progressive, and beneficent enterprise.

Conclusion

To conclude, the ethnographic data in this chapter lend support to a theoretical perspective that posits specifically social and economic explanations for population increase or decrease. They support Marx's notion that every historical mode of production has its own special laws of population, historically valid within its limits alone (Coontz 1967:178). They do not tend to support the idea that population numbers, per se, are the independent variable or prime mover of social change, nor do they support a view of population growth rates as relatively inelastic, that is, relatively unresponsive to moderate changes in other variables.

In the specific case of the plantation as a socioeconomic institution, the data speak to the importance the plantation places upon nonmarket mechanisms for mobilizing and controlling the labor force, and ultimately for creating conditions under which population growth is stimulated. Plantations have mobilized labor in various forms of economic organization—slavery, indentured labor, sharecropping, and wage labor—and the case of Lever's discussed in this chapter points to the adaptability of a system that can sustain the characteristic monocrop production through granting perquisites to workers. More generally the company helps reproduce the existing organization of production by establishing abundantly cheap and unskilled sources of labor, thereby continuing to maximize profits while failing to develop a fully sophisticated technology or raising productivity per individual worker.

Notes

1. Tikopia folklore cites prehistoric voyages to different Pacific islands and as early as 1904, government documents report Tikopia leaving home for a change of scene and wage employment in the central Solomons (Firth 1931; 1936:43; 1954). Emigration in those early days, however, was not undertaken on any mass scale.
2. The scope of Unilever's post-World War II holdings and activities is reported by Charles Wilson: "Unilever owned and directed more than 500 companies spread all over the world. It held a majority of shares in another 55 companies, and a minority of shares in several more. The value of the manufacturing and trade of these businesses was 603,633,000 pounds ... [companies] which traded in more places and in more products than any other concern in the world, which employed nearly a quarter of a million people, represented capital supplied by about 300,000 investors, and counted their customers not in the thousands but in the millions" (1954:xvii-xix).
3. By 1965, money was beginning to play a role in the Tikopia economy but was only of minor importance. It was used to buy such incidentals as tobacco, calico for colorful skirts, simple clothing that was worn on occasion such as men's shorts or a woman's blouse, steel hand tools, fish hooks, flashlight batteries, kerosene for lanterns, and a few other inexpensive items. Money was not circulated at all on the home island and was used only infrequently on the plantations.
4. The operations at Lever's Pacific Plantations have been unionized, but for reasons of inexperience and mistrust of union officials, who are Melanesian, most workers refuse to join. See Larson (1970:205) for a full discussion of Tikopia involvement in the union.

Neo-Malthusian Ideology and Colonial Capitalism: Population Dynamics in Southwestern Puerto Rico

James W. Wessman

> It is often said by those who are inclined to
> blame the Porto Ricans for being the main cause
> of their own misery that if they would retard the
> natural increase in population, the conditions
> of the masses would improve.
> —(Diffie and Diffie 1931:164)

The emotional pitch of the demographic arguments that occurred during the late 1960s and the early 1970s has abated, enabling us to evaluate more dispassionately both the social circumstances and the arguments of this period. If neo-Malthusian arguments were both socially and logically inadequate, radical responses to these arguments were not well formulated. Radicals tended either to deny that a population growth problem existed or, if admitting that there was such a problem, to assert that the demographic conditions would change immediately upon the imminent demise of capitalism. They failed to emphasize the contradictory nature of population growth, which may endanger anticapitalist movements as much as it threatens the continued expansion of the capitalist world economy.

What radicals failed to realize is that neo-Malthusianism is a social dogma that often cannot be disproved on the basis of publicly available information or historical analysis. Rather, it is an integral part of Western technocratic ideology, a mystification of demographic processes in a world system dominated by monopoly capital. Therefore, scholars who object to the social basis of the neo-Malthusian argument and who are made uneasy by its

An earlier version of this essay was presented as "Marxism, Malthusianism and Population Growth in Puerto Rico," in the symposium titled "Demographic Variables in Cultural Evolution" at the Seventy-fourth Annual Meetings of the American Anthropological Association in San Francisco, December 1975.[1]

facile logic must be satisfied with proposing equally plausible, testable, alternative explanations of population growth.

Neo-Malthusianism is based on the notion that because of the finite nature of economic resources (especially land), the economic well-being of a nation or population cannot be improved if there are too many people competing for those resources. It is based on the assumption that population will automatically increase unless measures are taken to limit it (especially among groups where "cultural factors" retard the acceptance of economic growth). Because this notion is ahistorical, it cannot be disproved; thus it may appear that the easing of demographic conditions in many areas has been a result of the implementation of population planning policies. This appearance is false, and it is incumbent upon radical scholars to make this point. This essay, which analyzes demographic processes in southwestern Puerto Rico, is one step in that direction.

The Puerto Rican Population in Political-Economic Perspective

Puerto Rico has seen more than its share of visiting "experts." A number of the best-known demographers in the United States have done research on Puerto Rico and Puerto Ricans. They have written about the island's population density (now over 1,000 persons per square mile), its migrant communities on the U.S. mainland (comprising 40 percent of the total population of Puerto Ricans), and its numbers of sterilized women (a third of the women of childbearing age). What has been lacking is an attempt to link the abundant data on the Puerto Rican population (e.g., Vázquez Calzada 1964) with a political-economic interpretation. Maldonado Denis (1972, 1978) and more recently the History Task Force (1979; Wessman 1980c) have published analyses of migration, while Ramos and Henderson (1975) have written about the island's population control progams. I will focus on the demographic evolution of a region during the twentieth century.[2]

Population growth often has been cited during the twentieth

century as the key to Puerto Rico's economic problems, especially during three more or less well-defined periods, all of which were also times of social unrest: the depression years of the 1930s, the decade following World War II, and the early 1970s. Of course, the growth of the Puerto Rican population was noted much earlier, but at the turn of the century, the stress was placed on the market potential of a million Puerto Ricans as consumers of North American products. In the second decade of the century, Fred Fleagle, the dean of the University of Puerto Rico, considered the island overpopulated and proposed that agrarian reform would resolve the resulting tensions. His comments were profoundly prophetic: "There is no particular reason to fear that the population will increase to such an extent that we shall be unable to support ourselves on what the island may produce; but *with the increase of population under present conditions, trouble between capital and labor and between workmen and their employer cannot be avoided*" (1917:26; emphasis added).

During the 1930s, the demographic interpretation of the island's problems was applied in analysis and policy by persons of differing ideological stances—primarily outsiders—ranging from Clark's academic liberalism (1930:xxiv, 59-60, 515), to Governor Beverly's administrative liberalism (cited in Gayer et al. 1938:11), to Gayer, Homan, and James' defense of imperialism in Puerto Rico (1938:11-13). The contradiction between capital and labor, as foreseen by Fleagle, was in part diffused by the ascent to power in the 1940s of the Popular Democratic Party (the *populares*) on the promise of agrarian reform.[3] By reestablishing a class of smallholders, many of whom did not own the land they worked and were thus dependent on the state, the *populares* provided the basis for an all-powerful bureaucracy. As in other Latin American countries, such as Mexico, bureaucratic support made land and other reforms possible but also prevented the evolving rural proletariat from acting as a class in its own interest.

In the early 1950s a number of social science reports on the issue of the Puerto Rican population were published (Hansen 1952; R. C. Cook 1951; Koenig 1953; Perloff 1950; Davis 1953; Hatt 1952; Stycos 1955). In general, these reports represent the efforts of some of the leading scholars from the island and the continent to focus attention on the issues of overpopulation and poverty and their solutions through industrialization and birth control, as well as to divert attention from such troublesome themes as Puerto Rican social class relations and the island's ties with the United States. The new element in the 1950s, not so much in evidence in the 1930s, was the semi-official policy of birth control, indicating that the ruling class had internalized the ideology broadcast from outside during the Depression.[4]

In the early days of industrialization, the promises of full employment and the elimination of poverty convinced many Puerto Ricans that commonwealth status was the only way to resolve the island's problems, although subsequent evaluation of the island's industrialization program indicated the equivocal status of the progress achieved. The explanations offered to the Puerto Rican people by the architects of the industrialization program, the Popular Democratic Party, began to emphasize a neo-Malthusian interpretation of Puerto Rican history, in accordance with the views of scholars from the developed countries, especially the United States. Neo-Malthusianism became governmental doctrine and, in the first years of the Hernández-Colón administration (1973-1977), the ultimate policy referent.[5]

This explanation of Puerto Rico's difficulties received strong ideological support when Luis Muñoz Marín, founder of the PDP and former governor, labeled population growth as the major obstacle to solving the island's problems (*El Mundo*, December 3, 1973).[6] In a speech before the Puerto Rican Family Planning Association, Muñoz Marín said that none of the problems could be solved without curtailing population growth, which prevented a just distribution of wealth. In spite of forty years of progress, he claimed, the rate of unemployment had not been lowered, owing to the high rate of population growth. He announced his support for a family planning program, which, he assured, would be purely voluntary, even if it must be carried out with the "necessary muscle."

Governor Rafael Hernández-Colón affirmed this position when he spoke to an audience at Johns Hopkins University, where he received an honorary degree:

> Of all the challenges with which man is confronted in his future, one of the most serious is the runaway population boom, which impedes the major part of the countries of the world from reaching a just balance between an infinite industrialization and a stabilized population. The growth in numbers of inhabitants is the principal obstacle in our succeeding to conserve our civilization. (*El Mundo*, May 27, 1974)

He made it clear that he was acutely aware of the issue of power and control, noting that population growth in the developing countries means dedicating "more energy to the maintenance of order."

In addition, Fomento, Puerto Rico's public corporation for industrial promotion, adopted a neo-Malthusian stance in a memo redefining the problems facing industrialization. This memorandum was written in a style unique to Fomento, ending with a further justification of its own existence and priorities.

> Puerto Rico's fundamental problem is overpopulation. The most acute social manifestation of this problem is the high rate of unemployment. Overpopulation also contributes significantly to related social ills, such as low income and inadequate health services. Given Puerto Rico's situation, the major attack on these problems must be two-pronged: (a) a program to stabilize our population and, (b) an aggressive, imaginative and well-planned program of industrialization whose principal goal is to increase employment in manufacturing. (*San Juan Star*, November 28, 1973)

Teodoro Moscoso, head of Fomento under Governor Hernández-Colón, referred to population growth in a spirited defense of the tax exemption program for foreign industries establishing factories in Puerto Rico (*San Juan Star*, October 11, 1973). Calling tax exemption the "developmental bone which keeps the economic dog happy and wagging its tail," Moscoso defended the program in spite of its admitted failure to eliminate unemployment, which he attributed to population growth.[7]

Perhaps the most comprehensive and convincing statement of the neo-Malthusian orientation of the Puerto Rican government under Hernández-Colón during the period 1973 to 1977 was contained in a controversial 1973 report titled *Oportunidades de Empleo, Educación y Adiestramiento*, prepared by a workshop team consisting of Luis Silva Recio (Secretary of Labor), Teodoro Moscoso, Ramón Cruz (Secretary of Public Instruction), and Amador Cobas (president of the University of Puerto Rico). This limited-circulation report (which received better distribution in the radical press) avoided the rhetoric of the previously cited public announcements, but it presented a detailed political program based upon the same kind of reasoning. In it, for example, emigration is posed as an escape valve "for those who *voluntarily* have decided to leave" (1973:4; emphasis added), while the proletariat is referred to as those with "low income and less education" (1973:10).

Its policy recommendations indicate how the Hernández-Colón administration intended to maintain the class structure and ensure its political hegemony. To reach the goal of 5 percent unemployment in 1985, the government intended to pursue a migratory policy that regulated the influx of foreigners and stimulated the eflux of Puerto Ricans; and an educational policy that maintained a higher proportion of students in the insular schools for longer periods of time (1973:9). In addition, the plans included a family planning program, the creation of additional employment in essentially unskilled areas, the reorientation of the system of higher education, and other related proposals.

By 1985, if the policies described in this report had been executed successfully, the *populares* would have been perched irretrievably at the top of an oligarchical technocracy—a colonial capitalist state—in which the government controlled the means of transportation and communication (namely, merchant marine and telephone-telegraph service); unemployment would be somewhat reduced because of a low labor-force participation rate[8] and an employment structure dominated by the manufacturing and service sectors; the public school system would retain in higher proportions and for longer periods of time those for whom government-sponsored employment is the only practical alternative; the university would feed the technocratic structure as it has fed the bureaucratic structure of the past; and, of course, the goverment would seek further aid for its designs from the United States government, thus "culminating" its unique status within the American union.

Of course, the *popular* conception of Puerto Rico in 1985 did not bear fruit. In 1976, rumblings within Puerto Rico over disastrous unemployment levels and low wages, at the same time the government was paring public employment in order to avoid a New York City-type economic crisis, placed the political hegemony of the Popular Democratic Party in danger. Their loss in the 1976 elections was not so much an endorsement of the New Progressive Party as a rejection of the way in which former Governor Hernández-Colón had run the island for four years under the banner of the *populares*. Their subsequent loss in the 1980 elections, although by the slightest of margins, suggests that the PDP may never regain the power and momentum it held for so long.

The failures of the *populares* in 1976 and again in 1980 served to discredit the neo-Malthusian interpretation of the island's social history, making it unlikely that any group will be able to resurrect such an interpretation in Puerto Rico for some time to come. However, since it remains the ideology of "development planners" from the UN and Western aid agencies, it will not soon disappear. Thus in order to prepare for and defend against its resurgence, it is important to develop other interpretations, interrelating wealth, poverty, power, and population.

Such interpretations must include relations between Puerto Rico and the United States, social class relations on the island, and the successive periods of Puerto Rican history—especially the periods of slavery and the plantation—in which agricultural labor came to have ideological connotations that have not been surmounted as of this date. These elements serve to put in perspective the ecological factors usually proposed to explain Puerto Rican economic conditions.

It is often claimed that the population in Puerto Rico has exceeded the "carrying capacity" of its resources: that is, there are too many people for too little land. Emigration and social problems (notably alcoholism, drug addiction, crime, divorce) are the purported consequences. However, emigration is an "escape valve," which alleviates the pressure of population on land only in an indirect sense. In a more meaningful sense, emigration alleviates pressure on the means of employment (cf. Engels in

Meek 1971:85-87). Those who emphasize the population-land ratio transform the historically specific conditions of Puerto Rico's employment structure—its low labor participation rate, the plantation and slavery legacy, and so on—into "natural conditions," and in so doing disguise the nature of the class conflicts.

Concerning Puerto Rican emigration, then, land is not the crucial issue; employment is. Since Puerto Rico imports an estimated 80 percent of its food, the land that produces this food is in Minnesota (corn), Idaho (potatoes), Florida (citrus fruits), California (rice), and elsewhere. Consequently, carrying capacity is not a useful concept for analysis, although it may have some utility in planning. Migratory movements from Puerto Rico to the United States, and the return movement to Puerto Rico (Hernandez Alvarez 1964; History Task Force 1979) are in part economic, in part political, and in part social. The basis for Puerto Rican migration is economic, a result of the unresolved problem of unemployment; it is political, because of the government's advocacy of emigration for the most depressed segments of the population; and social, because of the aspirations of social momentum established by years of such movement (Maldonado Denis 1972:203-324).

Thus an important component of political-economic relations is the exploitation of Puerto Rican workers by mainland employers, with the cooperation of the Puerto Rican government, and the social phenomenon of "making it" in the United States through education and other means of social mobility before returning to the island.[9] "Escape-valve" employment has in the past circumvented successful proletarian movements in Puerto Rico by offering the most oppressed a slightly better alternative (Julio Sabater, personal communication), even though the current proletarian movement is based partially upon the experiences of Puerto Rican workers in the United States. "If we forced them to stay here," said an unnamed political leader, "we'd find revolt inevitable" (cited in Turner 1973:161). Migration as social mobility has produced a conservative, pro-American sector of professionals and others whose interest is the status quo (Maldonado Denis 1972:316-17).

I argue that the basis of social class relations in contemporary

Puerto Rico has been the cooptation of the proletariat by a supposedly liberal government. Liberal institutions, such as the agrarian reform, the industrial promotion program, and the supervision of migrant labor, and such ideological expressions of these institutions as "Bread, Land, and Liberty" operate to maintain an infrastructure that capitalizes on relative surplus population. Under conditions of a disguised colonial dependency *(Estado Libre Asociado de Puerto Rico)* and a disguised class struggle *(juntos progresamos)*, a self-deceiving ideology has evolved that poses the insular government as arbiter, responsible to the people for solving social problems but hampered by the usual lack of resources in a developing society. This ideology is propagated on local television and radio programs and in newspaper editorials, and it is understood in everyday conversation.

The key, then, to understanding social class relations is the way in which a liberal government, representing the class interests of the social and intellectual heirs of the nineteenth-century planter class (Quintero Rivera 1972), tries to balance the pressures of the metropolis for its expansion with the aspirations of the proletariat and middle classes for better living and working conditions. Seen in this way, it is clear that neo-Malthusian ideology was merely one, temporary, tool in the maintenance of political hegemony in Puerto Rico. The promotion of new industry is rationalized in terms of "progress" and the generation of new employment, thus keeping the proletariat off balance. The result is a status-oriented consumers' struggle, which no one can win but in which the elites are relatively less scathed than the working classes.

The key role of liberal ideology makes the neo-Malthusian interpretation of Puerto Rican social history understandable as a means to disguise the island's class conflicts and its relations with the United States. Furthermore, it is only by unmasking these relations that the neo-Malthusian interpretation can be demonstrated to be inadequate.

Under the circumstances, it is not surprising that to some the principal contradiction of contemporary Puerto Rican society is that between population and technology (or, alternatively, between population and environment), as suggested in the ideology of the former Hernández-Colón administration. This contradiction is a reflection of the fundamental contradiction between productive forces and relations of production, in that it results from the incompatibility of seemingly boundless technology and private appropriation and manifests itself in periodic crises. The fact that Puerto Rico's productive forces are controlled largely from the outside means that partial social reforms cannot restore the essential balance between these forces and population growth. The *justa distribución de la riqueza* (redistribution of wealth), which the *populares* fervently claim to promote, does not resolve the issue of *how* that wealth is produced. That this confusion exists only serves to accentuate the point made by such radical scholars as Gordon K. Lewis: "any constitutional mechanism short of complete separation simply will not work" (1974:48). As long as technology is controlled from the outside, without a resolution of the island's political status, the class struggle continues to boil, while the poor stave off their hunger with the help of the ubiquitous food stamps.[10]

Marxist Political Economy, Population, and Plantations

The perspective on population proposed here is just one aspect of the theory of social change and of the interclass relations that promote and retard these changes. As Marx said, there is no general law of population (1967:631-32). What we can do, I suggest, is construct what some anthropologists call a "multilinear" theory, one that stresses alternative evolutionary pathways from specific social and historical circumstances.

The key term of the Marxist perspective is "relative surplus population." Marx argued that relative surplus population is a manifestation of the contradictory nature of capital accumulation, although it appears as a contradiction in the adaptation of the proletariat. Just as this class is responsible for the accumulation of capital, through its alienated surplus value, it also produces its own superfluity, and it does so to an always increasing extent. Relative surplus population serves to hold down the aspirations of the working classes. To quote Marx: "Relative surplus population is therefore the pivot upon which the law of supply and demand of labor works. It confines the field of action of this law within the limits absolutely convenient to the activity of exploitation and to the domination of capital" (1967:639).

The three classes of relative surplus population Marx proposed are the *floating*, referring to the movement between active and inactive labor armies in the industrial centers; the *latent*, referring to the movement from agricultural to urban proletariat; and the *stagnant*, referring to the active labor army with irregular employment (1967:641-44). Since these forms of unemployment and underemployment were devised to describe the historical experience of the European capitalist core, it is legitimate to ask whether these same categories adequately account for the experience of the plantation periphery. For example, floating unemployment would have to be redefined if it is to describe the plantation, which "is often as much a factory as a farm, and the labor force is likely to be both agricultural and industrial" (Mintz 1974a:54). Furthermore, the floating and stagnant forms are difficult to separate, owing to the highly seasonal nature of the plantation's labor process and the consequent movement from place to place during the annual cycle. The latent form consists of those small landowners who become urban proletarians. The stagnant form includes some rural toilers who move back and forth between peasant and proletarian adaptations.

The categories of relative surplus population are historically and socially *relative*. Categories are needed that describe the movement of capital, technology, and people in peripheral formations that are structured largely by their orientations to the world market, in which they supply certain agricultural commodities. These categories must express the essential *qualitative* changes in long historical spans, not merely the more-and-less of birth and death rates. Likewise, the categories must suggest something about the *causes* of demographic changes, including some conception of the historical necessity of relative surplus population for the operation of capitalism as a social and economic formation and as a world system. In fact, the categories should demonstrate something of how surplus value is generated, because ultimately it is not the *existence* of free labor nor the *presence* of markets (both of which are relative character-istics) that defines capitalism, but the *process* whereby surplus value (and not just surplus labor) is extracted and multiplied.

Precisely what categories of relative surplus population exist in a social and economic formation in which the plantation is the most prominent agrarian institution? Five categories may be identified, as follows:

1. *Seasonal:* the difference in the annual cycle between peak employment during the periods of planting, harvesting, and processing, and peak unemployment during the dead season. This category combines aspects of Marx's categories of floating and stagnant relative surplus population, without implying the permanent marginality of the stagnant variety.

2. *Transient:* the essentially linear disaggregation of small land-owners (as implied in the concept of "depeasantization") into either wage-earners ("proletarianization") or, to a lesser extent, petit bourgeois farmers and labor merchants. This category is similar to Marx's category of latent relative surplus population.

3. *Concealed:* the dialectical movement of persons between peas-ant and proletarian adaptations during their life cycles. It implies a certain resiliency of the social structure, as peasant-proletarians resist the expansionary tendencies of the capitalist mode; it also implies a certain amount of geographical move-ment, such as from highlands to lowland plantations and back.

4. *Superannuated:* the group of spent and obsolete workers, the "supernumeraries," as Marx called them, whose labor power has been consumed, as well as the disqualified workers who are unable to adjust to the changing technical and organiza-tional conditions of the "factories in the fields."

5. *Recondite:* those who at least temporarily leave the plantation periphery, with the unspecified possibility of returning. Those in this category partially relieve the pressure on the means of employment in that formation and may lead to the establish-ment of a "national minority" in the metropolis.

These categories, while imperfect, express the essential quali-ties of plantation labor: *it varies through time, it is expansive, it is resisted, and it exhausts the workers.* In addition, the classifi-cation does say something about the causes of population growth

Southwest Coastal Region of Puerto Rico

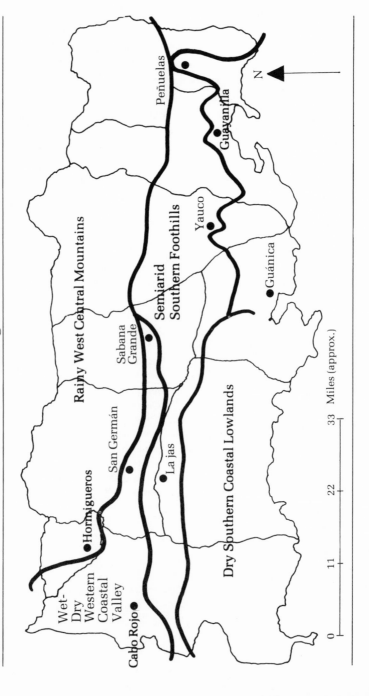

in such formations. Basically, the changes in demographic characteristics among plantation workers are most likely to occur in the categories labeled transient, superannuated, and recondite. The process of proletarianization is likely to be a more or less linear transformation that, once begun, is self-reinforcing, while the actual opportunities for employment in plantation agriculture are less dependable, since they depend on local environmental and climatic conditions and, more importantly, upon market prices in the capitalist world system. Stated differently, given the initiation of this process of proletarianization, the demographic growth of the dispossessed rural toilers is likely to occur largely independent of the demand for their labor (cf. Medick 1976). The question is, What happens to these people during the transition from smallholder to wage-earner and, later, from one category of wage-earner to another?

The Demographic Evolution of Southwestern Puerto Rico

The Southwest Coastal region of Puerto Rico consists of the nine municipalities between the crest of the Cordillera Central and the Caribbean Sea and between Mayagüez and Ponce, exclusive (see map).[11] The region encompasses 425 square miles and consists of four environmental zones (Picó 1974:357-84): the wet-dry western coastal valley, the dry southern coastal lowlands, the semiarid southern foothills, and the rainy west central mountains. The principal axis of environmental variation runs from northeast to southwest, following the distribution of precipitation which overlays the marked topographical features of the *altura* and *llanura* and the related geological soil series. The gradations of environmental variation, however, are accentuated by economic and social relations.

The relationship between environmental features, land use, and population distribution deserve a separate detailed analysis (Wessman 1976:151-205). For these purposes, it is sufficient to stipulate the following general relationships:

1. *Sugarcane subregion.* This area, comprising the municipalities of Cabo Rojo, Lajas, and Guánica, is and has been characterized by a high concentration of sugarcane, ranging from 85 to 97 percent of harvested farmland in 1969. In contrast, there has been little cultivation of coffee or grains, with only a small area dedicated to the cultivation of fruits. Land use has been fairly extensive, with a large proportion of land (usually 50 percent or more) in pasture. The farms are relatively large, ranging from an average of 80 *cuerdas* in Cabo Rojo to over 300 *cuerdas* in Guánica in 1969.[12] Historically, absentee ownership has been high, especially between the 1920s and the 1940s, when it accounted for between 40 and 80 percent of the farm area. Generally speaking, the municipalities of the sugarcane-producing coastal plains are the least densely settled of the region.

2. *Coffee and minor crops subregion.* This area includes the municipalities of Yauco, Guayanilla, and Penuelas and has been characterized by the reversal of the crop pattern in the sugarcane subregion. Here, a large proportion of the farmland—more than one-third since 1969—is dedicated to the cultivation of coffee. Sugarcane accounts for less than a third of harvested farmland. In addition, relatively high proportions of land have been used to cultivate fruits and grains. Land use has been more intensive, but with sizable areas of pasture. The farms have been intermediate in size, and absentee ownership of farmland has been approximately equal to that of the region as a whole. Population density is greater than in the sugarcane subregion, but it is quite a bit less than in the third subregion.

3. *Sugarcane and coffee subregion.* This area has been characterized principally by the cultivation of these two crops, as represented by the municipalities of San Germán, Sabana Grande, and Hormigueros. Land use has been much more intensive, with less than half the farmland in pasture, especially in recent years. Average farm size has been small, generally under 50 *cuerdas*, and absentee ownership has been relatively insignificant. These municipalities as a group have the highest population densities of the region, ranging from 442 persons per square mile in Sabana Grande to 984 persons per square mile in Hormigueros in 1970.[13]

Using census data and the system of vital statistics, it is possible to evaluate the assertion that the process of proletarianization and the emergence of relative surplus population provide

Table 1
Population Changes in Southwestern Puerto Rico, 1899–1970

Municipality	1899	1910	1920	1930	1935	1940	1950	1960	1970
Cabo Rojo	16,154	19,562	22,412	23,792	26,059	28,586	29,546	24,868	26,060
Guánica	3,511	7,773	9,948	10,238	11,606	12,685	15,630	13,767	14,889
Guayanilla	9,540	10,354	12,083	13,121	14,860	15,577	17,402	17,396	18,144
Hormigueros	3,215	3,887	4,584	4,872	5,700	6,098	6,916	7,153	10,827
La Jas	8,789	11,071	11,908	12,454	13,608	14,736	16,636	15,375	16,545
Peñuelas	12,129	11,991	13,598	13,278	14,539	14,789	14,931	14,887	15,973
Sabana Grande	10,560	11,523	12,305	11,881	12,592	14,146	16,097	15,910	16,343
San Germán	20,246	22,143	23,848	23,768	25,273	26,473	29,553	27,667	27,990
Yauco	27,119	31,504	25,848	27,787	30,115	30,533	33,708	34,780	35,103
Regional Totals	111,263	129,808	136,534	141,191	154,172	163,623	180,419	171,803	181,874

Sources: Censuses of Population and 1935 PRRA Census.
Note: Since several barrios have been reassigned to different municipalities during this century, the earlier census figures were adjusted to accord with the boundaries given in the 1970 census.

the appropriate context for understanding the evolution of the Puerto Rican population. Because these data are aggregative, a controlled comparison is needed to elicit the characteristics of the various social classes and other groups.

The Southwest Coastal Region currently numbers about 7 percent of the Puerto Rican population with 12 percent of its area.[14] The 181,784 inhabitants in 1970 were not evenly distributed throughout the region, as noted in the classification of subregions above. The relative sizes and densities of the municipalities have remained quite constant throughout this century, in spite of a 64 percent increase in population since 1899.

There is a marked correspondence between population size and density, on the one hand, and ratios of population composition on the other. These ratios describe the theoretically dependent population, according to age and rate of replacement.[15] Both where population density is low, along the coast, and where it is high, in the coastal valley (that is, the subregions where sugarcane production has been a dominant characteristic), the population is aging slowly. But in the coffee-producing municipalities of the higher mountains, where population density is intermediate, the aged population is being replaced rapidly and continuously by the younger population.

In 1965-1969, the Crude Fertility Rate (annual births per 1,000 population) was 25.3 in southwestern Puerto Rico, compared to 35.3 in 1888-1898, and 40.6 in 1930-1934. Fertility in recent years has been much lower in the coastal municipalities, but this situation has not held through time. In 1965-1969, the Crude Mortality Rate (annual deaths per 1,000 population) for the region was about 7, down from 32 in 1888-1898, and 10 in 1930-1934. However, mortality rates for the coastal municipalities were lower than those for the other municipalities for the entire period, except for the most recent years, in which mortality rates have become relatively uniform for the entire region. In general, the densely populated municipalities of the central coastal valley have had the highest rates of mortality.

Population growth in southwestern Puerto Rico can be approached from two perspectives: that of changes in population size and density, and that of changes in rates of growth. With regard to population size, the faster growing municipalities have been the coastal, sugar-producing municipalities, while the slower growing municipalities were in the interior, farthest from Mayagüez, the urban center on the west coast. The greatest increases in population density took place prior to 1935. There has been very little increase since 1950, because of the heavy out-migration of the 1950s and the slow recovery since then.

Estimates of population growth based upon fertility and mortality rates are more useful than the measures of size and density because the former estimates indicate the demographic components of the changes. For the region, the Rate of Natural Increase (crude fertility minus crude mortality rates) during the last decade of the nineteenth century was a mere 0.33 percent per year. However, this rate jumped to over 2 percent by 1911-1912 and with the exceptions of the period centering on 1924-1925 and the period immediately preceding the last census, the regional growth rate remained above 2 percent per year during the first seventy years of this century. The highest growth rates were experienced in the 1940s and 1950s.

According to notions of causality accepted by demographers, these rapid and prolonged population growth rates are explained by falling mortality, with sustained or only slightly decreasing fertility. Mortality declined by 78 percent during this seventy-year period, while fertility remained above 40 per 1,000 until the 1950s and had not fallen below 25 per 1,000 by the end of the period. However, demographic arguments regularly fail to account for the structural conditions that serve to maintain, decrease, or even increase a given level of fertility—specifically the logic of the reproduction of labor power. There are several reasons why these data should be analyzed within such a framework.

In the first place, according to the available data, an increase in both fertility and mortality occurred during the last decade of the nineteenth century. The increase in mortality was caused by a series of epidemics in the last years of the century. Although no information is available on the region's demographic rates before 1888, it appears that the subsequent decline in mortality and the eventual decline in fertility were not elements of the so-called demographic transition, as it is usually understood. It is more important to understand why fertility rose to over 40 per 1,000 in the early twentieth century and remained there for such a long time. That is, it is not a mystery why mortality rates fell during this century, but it is an open question why fertility reached such heights at the same time.

In posing these questions, I am keeping in mind Vázquez Calzada's comments (1968) about the inadequacy of the demographic estimates prior to the 1930s. Vázquez Calzada argues convincingly that the apparent rise in fertilty in midcentury actually was an artifact of an increasingly accurate demographic registry during a period of fertility decline. He claims that fertility has been declining since the turn of the century, and what seems to be a slight increase in fertility during the twenty years from 1930 to 1949 was in fact more complete coverage of births.

However, it is difficult to accept Vázquez Calzada's argument completely, in that *intraregional patterns* conform closely to what would be expected on the basis of the argument advanced here. I realize that the vital registration system increased along with literacy and other factors, but these are not the only changes that occurred during this century. In dealing with the island as a whole, the calculations made by Vázquez Calzada cancel out regional variations, which are the focus of this argument.

A second reason for looking at the structural conditions promoting population growth is that the patterns of contemporary intraregional variation are also found historically. While in the earliest part of this century these patterns were closely associated with disease cycles, aspects of which have persisted, more recently they have been tied to social and economic conditions.

At the turn of the century, anemia, tuberculosis, and tetanus were the major causes of death in the region, but a great deal of variation existed. Diptheria, yellow fever, and typhoid fever were secondary causes. Yellow fever was more common in the eastern, more mountainous municipalities, while dysentery was more significant to the west. A close relationship existed between the cultivation of coffee and mortality due to tuberculosis, and between the cultivation of sugarcane and mortality due to dysentery. Coffee cultivation involved respiratory problems characteristic of moist environments, while sugarcane production along the coast was characterized by diseases of the digestive system and by epidemics that flourish in crowded, unsanitary conditions. Certain epidemics spread from the coast to the mountains, probably because of intraregional migration typical of plantation systems.

During the first decade of the century, fertility rose while mortality fell, and the Rate of Natural Increase climbed to a rate of over 2 percent per year. The coffee-producing municipalities at this time increased most in fertility and decreased most in mortality, so that they were growing more rapidly than the other municipalities.

By 1924-1925 fertility and mortality had fallen, the former more than the latter, so that the rate of increase was lower. No discernible regional patterns emerged in this period of transition. The recent patterns did not emerge definitively until the 1950s.

Between 1930 and 1969 the regional fertility rate fell from over 41 to just over 25 births per 1,000 persons. Not much difference existed between the subregions in 1930-1934, after which time the populations of those areas followed more distinct trajectories. The sugarcane subregion remained relatively constant in demographic rates until 1945-1949, after which fertility fell to a low level, which has persisted until the present. The fertility rate of the coffee subregion increased until 1949, and the subsequent decline has been very irregular. In 1965-1969, the fertility rate of this area stood at almost 30 per 1,000 persons. The intermediate sugarcane and coffee subregion had the highest fertility rate until 1944, but after 1949 its rates fell sharply, and since 1954 little change has occurred.

Of course, general mortality decreased dramatically in the forty years between 1930 and 1969, but the specific causes of mortality underwent different trajectories of change, some increasing, others decreasing. Puerto Rico's mortality pattern was transformed from one characterized by deaths from infectious diseases (tuberculosis, dysentery, pneumonia) to one characterized by deaths from degenerative diseases (cancer, heart disease, and other diseases of a faster paced, industrial society). The same generalization is true of southwestern Puerto Rico, with allowances for intraregional variation.

In other words, specific causes of mortality followed complementary diachronic and synchronic patterns. The basic diachronic pattern consisted of a general reduction in mortality, accompanied by the replacement of deaths from infectious diseases with deaths from degenerative diseases, among others. At each point in time, a regional pattern has also existed. In the early period of the century, mortality from infectious respiratory and digestive diseases was higher in the interior municipalities. During the Depression, deaths from gastroenteritis and pneumonia increased. Even with the general decline in mortality from these diseases, the interior and sugar-producing areas suffered consistently higher rates from these causes.

In spite of the growth of the regional population during the forty-year period from 1930 to 1969, the Southwest Coastal region lost many of those born there to other areas. In addition to its own growth, the region contributed to the growth of other regions, the Puerto Rican urban centers, and the United States. This source of demographic renewal must be considered in the wide context of political-economic analysis.

Migration within the region between 1935 and 1940 was to a certain extent a sequential process, involving movement within the region toward the urban centers of Mayagüez, Ponce, and San Juan, and a further movement from Mayagüez and Ponce to San Juan. For example, the municipalities of Cabo Rojo, Lajas, and San Germán lost more out-migrants to Mayagüez than to Ponce, while the opposite was true of Guayanilla, Peñuelas, and Yauco. Guánica and Sabana Grande lost approximately equal numbers to both urban centers and Hormigueros actually gained in-migrants from Mayagüez and Ponce. The pattern for the period from 1940 to 1950 was quite similar.

The most significant migratory pattern involved the replacement by the population from the coffee and minor-crops subregion of the population from the sugarcane and sugarcane and coffee subregions, which were articulated in this fashion. The population of the mountains served as a marginally articulated source of workers for the sugar industry.

This discussion of demographic history provides an empirical base, which can be interpreted in various ways, and allows me to propose an alternative to the neo-Malthusian theory of population dynamics that is both plausible and testable.

At the turn of the century, most of the relative surplus population was of the seasonal and concealed varieties, owing to the nature of hacienda-style agriculture and the degree to which labor was immobilized by debts and other obligations. In southwestern Puerto Rico, unemployment in 1899 stood at about 40 percent for men, and 90 percent of the women were listed as being "without gainful employment." Of course, these figures do not include underemployment, nor do they permit a direct estimation of the different classes of unemployment. Agriculture provided most of the employment for men, but unemployment actually was highest in those municipalities where agricultural employment was highest! However, unemployment was somewhat lower where cultivation was more intensive. And smallholders existed in the niches at the interstices of the hacienda economy.[16]

The imposition of the plantation system in the first two decades of the twentieth century led to the destruction of the class of rural smallholders and the further transformation of agricultural workers into a genuine proletariat, which no longer was held or could hold onto the personalistic bonds that united *hacendado* and worker. While total farm area was on the increase, land was consolidated into fewer hands and larger units, and over a third of the farms were eliminated. By 1925, less than 2 percent of the population owned almost 80 percent of the land, while under 15 percent of the population owned only about 10 percent of the land, and a large proportion—perhaps 70 percent—was landless. The smallholders reasserted themselves briefly after 1920, but after this time their class dwindled. The owners of intermediate-sized farms held their own until about 1950 but have declined in numbers since them. The class of large landowners has also declined in numbers, but their dominance of regional agriculture has continued in spite of fluctuations in area and number of farms.

With the intensification of capitalist agriculture in the form of the plantations, there was a quick replacement of many landowners with farm managers, especially during the 1920s and the

1930s. Just as quickly, this managerial class began to disappear in the first years of the 1930s. To a certain extent, the managerial farm class was replaced by landowners, whose resurgence should not be ignored, but a newly defined class of tenant farmers also grew during the postwar period, especially in the sugarcane subregion.

The depressed conditions of life for the newly defined proletariat created numerous problems, documented in several earlier studies. The Diffies (1931), for instance, note that in the 1920s people had to work much harder to maintain the standard of living to which they had become accustomed before the turn of the century. In 1897, workers had to labor twenty-five days to get their annual rice supply, but in 1928 they had to spend thirty-three days to get the same (1931:175). Rice importation rose, while the consumption of codfish and the proportion of land in food crops fell (1931:167-68). Food cost about 25 percent more in Puerto Rico in the 1920s than in the continental United States (1931:177-79), much as it does today.

At the same time, wages fell drastically, from about 90 cents per nine- or ten-hour day in 1900 to 50 or 60 cents a day in the mid-1930s (Gayer et al. 1938:221),[17] and the seasonality of labor was greatly aggravated (1938:166). As a sensitive Puerto Rican observer commented in 1935, "Life presses these workers so hard that in order to make ends meet, it becomes necessary to put everyone to work, males, females, and children" (Rodríguez 1935:11). As the century progressed, the seasonal and superannuated forms became intertwined and the transient form began to grow. By the 1930s, the movement of unemployed became so great that overpopulation was considered a threat to economic and political stability. By the beginning of the 1940s, after the collapse of the plantations and the coming to power of the Popular Democratic Party, migration to and from the United States created a recondite form of relative surplus population.

In the 1950s, when many unemployed agricultural workers found more regular work in manufacturing and many others continued to work seasonally in the United States, the transient and recondite forms of relative surplus population became the most important ones. Employment was not decreasing during this time but was becoming a problem for manufacturing rather than for agriculture, thus evoking another wave of alarm concerning overpopulation.

Return migration to Puerto Rico in the 1960s also meant that the transient form reasserted itself in a new guise: the completely proletarianized worker.[18] As this process increased during the 1970s, the capital-intensive development program was unable to keep pace with the need for new sources of employment and precipitated another round in the Puerto Rican population debate.

These changes meant that internal movement from the mountains to the coast and from the coastal plantations to the cities followed various cycles. Because of the large movement of population into the cities of Puerto Rico and to the continental United States, overpopulation in the rural areas took the form of seasonal and recondite relative surplus population. Consequently, the rural population has remained relatively constant in size, and unemployment has not diminished to the extent that island-wide rising incomes would suggest.

Conclusion

This discussion of population dynamics and employment in southwestern Puerto Rico suggests that population growth in the plantation periphery can best be understood in terms of the reproduction of labor power, a process often fraught with contradictions. In the case of Puerto Rico, moreover, the process of proletarianization most adequately accounts for the process of social-structural transformation leading to relative surplus population. This formulation cannot be shown conclusively, but it is plausible and testable, and, unlike neo-Malthusian interpretations, it does not rely on untestable notions of cultural values as causes of changes. Furthermore, the emphasis upon social-structural transformation and proletarianization is consistent with the other recent attempts to rewrite Puerto Rican social history mentioned at the outset.

The question appropriate to this analysis is: Why would the population *not* have grown as it did? The cost of producing a new human being was minimal in terms of such socially necessary resources as education. It cannot be denied that population growth was a contradictory response to difficult circumstances, nor can it be denied that the growth of the proletariat was one of a complex set of factors that effectively coopted its chances of revolutionary or even rapid evolutionary change. Yet how could it have been otherwise?

Obviously, these conditions were altered and the past century has witnessed important demographic changes. The population of Puerto Rico is growing at a rate above that of the continental United States, and it probably will continue to do so well into the future. The contradiction between production and consumption in a colonial capitalist economy was not resolved but simply ameliorated by the industrialization program, which created new problems of its own. The current crisis in Puerto Rico must lead either to further population growth or to a new strategy for dealing with the incompatibilities of its status.

Notes

1. I want to thank those who read the earlier versions of this paper and offered helpful suggestions: Scott Cook, Ben Magubane, Jim Faris, and Bob Bee, of the University of Connecticut; Julia Crane, Jim Peacock, Tony Thomas, Conrad Seipp, Jeff Boyer, and the late John Honigmann, of the University of North Carolina; and Wendell Wessman of Mankato State University. Parts of section two were taken from a paper called "Is There a Plantation Mode of Reproduction? Comparative Evidence from Puerto Rico and Cuba," presented at a conference on exports and change in Third World societies, held at Duke University in January 1978. Henry Landsberger of the University of North Carolina and William Roseberry of the New School for Social Research commented on the latter paper. I have also used part of this argument in Chapter 7 of my book, *Anthropology and Marxism* (1981).

2. I have published a related essay on family structure in three *barrios*

of San Germán, employing the last Spanish censuses of population and agriculture, conducted in 1898 (Wessman 1977). See also my manuscript, "The Dialectics of Class, Ethnicity and Family in the Early Capitalist Transformation of Puerto Rico."

3. Flores (1970:151) defines land reform as a "revolutionary measure which passes power, property and status from one group of the community to another." In Puerto Rico, the *populares* who, according to Quintero Rivera (1972), represent the social heirs of the nineteenth-century planter class, passed power, property, and status *back* to themselves by making the government a principal landowner and by establishing themselves in a position of class hegemony in the political structure, all in the name of agrarian reform.

4. Of course, some *populares* (for example, Muñoz Marín in the 1940s) expressed concern with population growth before the 1950s or the 1970s, but as long as the industrialization program continued without major problems, the issue of population growth was secondary to them and of primary importance only to outsiders, such as those mentioned previously.

5. The statehooders won the 1976 election, and there were some changes in population policy. No analysis, however, has been attempted of the administration headed by Carlos Romero Barceló, who was re-elected in 1980.

6. The quotes presented in this section were taken from the two principal newspapers of Puerto Rico, *El Mundo* and the *San Juan Star*. The translations from *El Mundo* are mine.

7. In Puerto Rico, employment in manufacturing literally *replaced* employment in agriculture. The unemployment rate was not affected significantly.

8. The labor-force participation rate in Puerto Rico is already among the lowest in the world. See History Task Force (1979).

9. On labor migration, see the History Task Force (1979) and the NACLA newsletter on Caribbean migration (1977).

10. Estimates of the proportion of the population that uses federal food stamps range from one-half to two-thirds.

11. Other published work on this region includes Wessman 1977, 1978a, 1978b, 1980a, and 1980b.

12. A *cuerda* is a unit of land roughly equivalent to an acre.

13. The density of the island population in 1970 was just under 800 persons per square mile. Currently the density is over 1,000 persons per square mile.

14. These comparisons are based upon the 1970 census of population, as the detailed results of the 1980 census are not yet available.

15. The dependent population consists of those persons under fifteen years of age and sixty-five years or over.

16. I intentionally do not call smallholders "peasants" because the concept of peasant has been used so misleadingly in Caribbeanist literature (see Mintz 1973, 1974a, 1974b).

17. My research on the economic organization of a Puerto Rican sugarcane hacienda in Sabana Grande for the year 1911 indicates that the standard workday (when there was work to be done) was twelve hours long (Wessman 1978b, 1980a). Wages ranged from $0.50 per day for cane planters and cutters to $1.00 for the sugarmaster and $1.50 for the mason.

18. By this I mean that kinship was no longer a mitigating factor in social class relations, at least compared to earlier in the century.

Country Roads Take Me Home:
The Political Economy of Wage-Labor Migration in an Eastern Kentucky Community

Sari Tudiver

This essay focuses on the movement of close to 4 million persons between 1940 and 1970 from rural Appalachia to major U.S. metropolitan centers outside or on the periphery of the Appalachian region.[1] More specifically, the analysis deals with one sector of this migration, that of people moving from rural eastern Kentucky to such northern and midwestern cities as Detroit, Chicago, Dayton, Cincinnati, and Indianapolis. Nearly every rural area in eastern Kentucky and most parts of rural Appalachia have been touched in some way by this process. Many eastern Kentucky counties have sustained losses of 30 to 40 percent of their population through out-migration, causing major transformations in the economic and social relations within rural communities.[2]

This movement of rural labor to centers of capital is integral to a capitalist mode of production, in which the development of metropolitan centers occurs at the expense of such hinterland regions as rural Appalachia. Out-migration is a part of the political and economic processes maintaining underdevelopment within the region, processes that are reproduced through social structures such as the community and household. Analysis of a single community in rural eastern Kentucky reveals the specific ways in which a rural population serves as a reserve labor pool for metropolitan centers outside the region.

Social relations within the community are thus understood as strategies of coping with and resisting marginal economic conditions. A community represents the conjuncture of the various

The research for this essay was carried out from June 1972 through July 1974 in the Appalachian community of Robin's Branch, in which I resided. I acknowledge with gratitude the aid received from the Canada Council during that time.

macroeconomic and political processes as they have developed historically in interaction with local conditions. In order to fully explain social relations observed at the "micro" levels of community and household, an analysis must first explicate the dynamics of the political economy—the nature of the dominant mode of production and class structure—of the state society within which such local structures are embedded.

Economic Underdevelopment of the Appalachian Region

It has been amply documented that Appalachian out-migration has been, in large part, an involuntary movement. A majority of the persons who leave eastern Kentucky and other parts of Appalachia would prefer to remain there—and have strongly and explicitly stated so in hundreds of interviews (see Schackelford and Weinberg 1977). Of those who leave, many attempt to return, or at least to maintain strong and continuing ties with their areas of origin. To choose only a few characteristic examples, in numerous families the wife and children remain in eastern Kentucky while the husband works in Cincinnati or Dayton, Ohio, returning home perhaps once or twice a month, a pattern which may continue for a number of years; eastern Kentucky families living outside the region return frequently to visit kin and old neighbors, as attested by the heavy streams of traffic heading south on Highway 75 on Friday evenings and north again on Sunday nights.[3] Persons from eastern Kentucky who have worked for thirty years in a Michigan plant maintain property "back home" and retire there, and local funeral parlors derive a steady business from out-migration—eastern Kentuckians returning from various points in the midwest for burial in family graveyards. The nostalgic song, "Country Roads Take Me Home to the Place I Belong," popularized by John Denver, has specific referents and meanings to eastern Kentucky migrants and their kin. It suggests a very real process of dislocation, heightened since the World War II period, and points to the significant allocations of time and resources that migrants make to maintain ties "back home."

The pattern of involuntary out-migration can best be understood as an integral part of a capitalist mode of production, in which the development of metropolitan centers is made possible through the drain of raw materials and labor from peripheral economies. The historical experiences of eastern Kentucky and the nature of its political economy share many common features with underdeveloped regions in other parts of the world (see Amin 1974; Stavenhagen 1968; Rodney 1974; Szentes 1973). In such regions, out-migration constitutes the movement of labor from regions now characterized by high rates of unemployment and underemployment to developed metropolitan centers where capital is concentrated and labor needed. Unemployment and underemployment have consistently been generated through contact between a relatively self-sufficient regional economy and an expanding capitalist system. The maintenance of some degree of unemployment is integral to capitalist development, since reliance on reserve pools of cheap labor ensure high—or at least adequate—profit margins to private industry (Braverman 1974). Out-migration can be seen as the drawing of cheap labor to centers of production; it is also the only viable response on the part of a population to the destruction of its mode of production and to the *lack* of investment, by government or industry, that would create adequate employment opportunities within rural areas.

Eastern Kentucky—indeed, all of central Appalachia—suffers from high rates of unemployment and underemployment, poor social services, and a low standard of living.[4] These conditions result from a long history of extensive contacts with capitalist interests based in northeastern U.S. metropolitan centers.[5] The subsistence-oriented eastern Kentucky economy of the early nineteenth century was radically transformed by the 1880s, when corporations outside the region acquired huge tracts of timber and mineral rights, thus taking control over critical resources. Since that time, the region has served as a major source of raw materials, especially coal, for metropolitan markets. The extraction of raw materials provided meager returns to the region itself, most of the value added and returns to capital occur outside the region, with the result that little capital is available for local reinvestment.

This dominance of extractive industries, divorced from local control, has spawned little diversification of the region's economy. Large sectors of the mountain population, many of whom were uprooted from farming as a result of land sales to corporations, or who experienced diminishing returns in farming because of erosion from mining and timber clear-cutting, have become a rural proletariat, serving as a source of unskilled or semiskilled labor within the extractive industries. Management has consistently been imported from outside the region. The only other major sources of wage labor are those provided through the public sector—the limited but relatively significant numbers of jobs in the school systems and in the various government agencies and departments located within the region.

Out-migration from eastern Kentucky is thus the individual's response to a regional economy that provides few options for employment. The availability of industrial wage labor within central Appalachia has been closely tied to world market prices for coal and to the technological changes within that industry since the early 1900s. Out-migration has occurred with reduced employment opportunities in coal mining or when these conditions have coincided with the needs of capital for labor in other industries outside the region. For example, massive out-migration took place during World War II as people sought employment in northern war industries. Out-migration tapered off, even to the extent of including some return migration, during the height of the Depression and during the more recent economic recession of the mid-1970s.[6]

Mechanization and Changes in the U.S. Labor Force

The movement of people out of the Appalachian region in the post–World War II period must be understood as an integral part of developments occurring on a national, and even an international scale. In the 1950s, U.S. energy markets changed to favor cheaper imported oil. Railroads switched to diesel and homes began to use gas, oil, and electricity for heating and cooking (Ridgeway 1973). During the late 1950s and into the 1960s, the increasing mechanization of the coal mining industry and the expansion of strip mining (with little attention to land reclamation) meant a reduction in the necessary industrial labor force within the region.[7] As Harry Braverman demonstrates, in the period of rapid capital accumulation that has taken place throughout the capitalist world since World War II, there have been two major changes in the structure of the U.S. labor force: (1) a diminishing percentage of workers in mining, manufacturing, transportation, communications, public utilities, and construction industries—areas to which mechanization and automation have been applied, and (2) an increasing percentage in clerical, service, and sales occupations—sectors of high labor intensity. He notes a repeated cycle since the 1940s of the movement of labor from mechanized industries to the less mechanized areas of capital accumulation, with the following result:

> Labor tends to pile up in the industries and occupations which are less susceptible to engineering improvements in labor productivity. Wage rates in these "new" industries and occupations are held down by the continuous availability of the relative surplus population created by the steadily increasing productivity of labor in the machine occupations. This in turn encourages the investment of capital in forms of the labor process which require masses of low-wage hand labor. As a result, we see in capitalist industry a secular trend to accumulate labor in those portions of industry and trade which are least affected by the scientific-technical revolution: service work, sales and other forms of marketing, clerical work insofar as it has not yet been mechanized, etc. (Braverman 1974:383-84)

Regions such as central Appalachia, whose economy is highly dependent on a single extractive industry controlled by multinational oil corporations (Ridgeway 1973) and which is undergoing increasing mechanization, serve increasingly as reserve labor pool areas for metropolitan centers. Large numbers of mountain residents, coming from a region characterized by poor educational services, move into the expanding, low-paid, and highly labor-intensive sectors.[8] With slumps and resulting lay-offs in the national economy, many mountain migrants return to their home areas, where it is possible to maintain a subsistence base and rely on kin for critical support. The continued poverty of the region is ensured through the drain of basic resources—raw materials, labor, and investable surplus—to the metropolis.

Government Policies and Programs

State and federal government legislation, policies, and pro-grams support the drain of resources from the central Appala-chian region. For example, federal tax laws have allowed coal companies to pay only minimal taxes on the surface rights to land and none on the value of the minerals below. This tax structure has resulted in little capital return through taxation to the mountain areas, and thus poor provision of basic services in transportation, water and sewage, health care, and education (Wells 1977; Kirby 1969; Millstone 1972).[9]

Those policies and programs that are specifically addressed to development of the Appalachian region encourage large-scale out-migration of the region's population and support the main-tenance of the region as an energy reserve area. Such policies have been formalized since 1965, when the Appalachian Re-gional Commission (ARC) was created, ostensibly to deal with the region's economic problems. This joint federal-state plan-ning and administrative agency was the first major federally funded organization of its kind in the United States. It has followed the regional planning strategy of designating certain cities, notably those on the periphery of central Appalachia, as "growth centers" and hence major channels for the receipt of federal funds. Commission policies encourage out-migration of the rural population to these growth centers and argue against the development of the many dying mountain communities.[10]

The allocation of funds within the ARC budget reflects the

Table 1
Federal Funds Appropriated Under the
Appalachian Regional Development Act, 1965–1976

Item	Amount (millions)	Percent
Highways	$1,714.7	59.1
Area development programs[a]	1,064.3	36.6
Research and administration	83.7	2.9
Renewable resources	24.7	.9
Housing	9.5	.3
Sewage treatment	6.8	.2
Total	$2,903.7	100.0

Source: ARC 1976 Annual Report, Washington, D.C., March 31, 1977.
[a]   Includes health demonstration, vocational education facilities, mine area restoration, and supplemental grants to other federal grant-in-aid programs.

position of the region as a reserve labor area for large metropolitan centers while revealing the lack of commitment to the economic development of the rural areas of the region (see Table 1). The major portion of the funds has gone to the development of a highway system, linking sections of the rural areas to the designated growth centers and to other major cities beyond the region, while little has been done to upgrade the poor condition of the roads which link communities within the region. Significantly, almost no monies have been allocated for economic development projects within the rural areas of the region. The ARC has funded some additional medical and educational services but has not greatly altered the disaster-level conditions in these sectors. Further, it has had only marginal impact on raising the per capita income of the population relative to that of the United States as a whole.[11] New highways have shortened driving time to metropolitan areas—a convenience for some migrants—but the tolls on some of the roads often force poorer local residents to take the older, longer routes.

Recent pronouncements from the ARC reiterate Appalachia's

critical role as a supplier of the nation's coal and stress the need for the ARC to recognize national energy needs as a priority in regional planning (ARC 1976). Such statements suggest continued government support for the coal industry and hence a lack of commitment to developing a diversified economic base within the rural areas of the region. There continue to be few significant employment opportunities for those who wish to live and work in rural Appalachia.

The above analysis of regional underdevelopment provides the context within which to understand the structure of social relationships in any community within the central Appalachian region. Indeed, the social structure of a community cannot be adequately analyzed without the explanation of such macroprocesses. Class relations at a national level—embedded in a capitalist mode of production—allocate limited resources to the region and set parameters to the subsistence options available to local residents. Within a community, available resources are allocated through the local political structure, as it has developed under particular historical and material conditions. Wage labor is secured by local elites through their control over key networks of political influence. The nature and degree of access which a household has to such jobs determine its various social relations and survival strategies. Availability of wage labor determines whether a household activates certain networks of support, joins with others in cooperative economic activities, or moves temporarily to a large urban center. It thus has significant impact on the personal relations of local residents.

Developments in the coal industry continue to determine the availability of wage labor and the economic future of most communities in the region. While other communities have provided skilled labor for coal mining within the county, Robin's Branch is one of many which serves as a reserve labor pool for industries in metropolitan centers outside the region. Significantly, the mineral rights within the community are currently being purchased by absentee corporations, as other parts of eastern Kentucky are depleted of coal reserves. The dynamics of industrial capitalist development in the nation as a whole have maintained the community as a source of industrial labor, and now may drain its natural resources as well.

Robin's Branch

The community of Robin's Branch is made up of 42 house-holds with a population of about 150. It is located in a rural southeastern Kentucky county on a fork of the Kentucky River— 20 miles on a winding but paved road to the county seat and approximately 100 miles southeast of Lexington. While large sections of the western part of the county have been heavily strip-mined, much of the eastern part, within which the commu-nity is located, has good agricultural bottom land given over to subsistence agriculture, small-scale tobacco farming, and some cattle grazing.[12]

The community comprises three distinct social groups distin-guished by relationship to activities of production.[13] Several sets of families, comprising nineteen households, some of whose members have relatively large landholdings (200 to 700 acres) constitute a local elite, controlling access to the better agricul-tural land and other important resources. These households all claim kinship to one another and to the early settlers in the area. In addition, six households with relatively small landholdings (1 to 100 acres) form a smallholders category and seventeen households owning no land form a tenants category. Ties of consanguinity or affinity link each of these twenty-three house-holds to at least one other. While there are a few kinship ties between these two social groups and the local elites, these are rare and stressed only weakly.

Of the nineteen households in the elite group, six engage in tobacco farming and cattle raising as their primary source of income. A subsistence base is provided by the women who raise large gardens, can produce, and keep chickens. In three of these six cases, the farming household joins with that of either a son or brother to form a joint work unit. In this arrangement, the younger man holds a full-time wage job and engages in tobacco cultiva-tion part-time, receiving some proportion of the income from the tobacco crop when it is sold. Seven of the local elite households draw their primary sources of income from wage labor or as petty entrepreneurs. Significantly, of the seven adult women and six adult men in these households, only one—a woman—is not employed in wage labor outside the home. Men and women of these households hold professional, other white-collar, or skilled blue-collar positions such as postal chief, storekeeper, construction supervisor, oil field worker, strip miner, high school teacher, school athletic coach, school administrator, bookkeeper, social service worker, and cook. Most of the households also raise some tobacco and corn or engage in other entrepreneurial activities as supplementary sources of income. Women who work full-time outside the home all have access to home canning and garden produce from the household of a mother or mother-in-law.

The other six elite households are composed of semi-retirees. Several persons were teachers, and one woman was a nurse. All had been engaged in farming and subsistence activities for most of their lives and continue to do so on a small scale. Currently, their primary sources of income are from social security, small pensions, and the renting out of their tobacco allotment on shares. Remittances and gifts from children contribute to any additional needs.

The six households with small landholdings are dependent for their main source of income on the skilled or unskilled blue-collar jobs secured by one or more of their members. The men hold such jobs as automechanic, school janitor, and strip-miner (one man was retired), while two of the six adult women work outside the home—one as a part-time cook for the local school, the other as a part-time housekeeper for an elderly widower in the community. In several cases, income is supplemented through renting a tobacco allotment of less than a half acre and working it on shares with the owner.

The seventeen tenant households have a variety of less permanent sources of income. Several of the men work intermittently as local school bus drivers. Five have more permanent jobs, such as night watchman and delivery truck driver. Two of the women hold full-time jobs: one works in a shoe factory in a neighboring county and the other as a cashier in the county seat. One woman works part-time as a school cook. In six of the tenant households, the primary source of income is provided by the men doing occasional day labor on the larger farms, usually working for those from whom they rent their houses. These six families each receive no more than several hundred dollars per year cash income.[14] They secure some additional food and clothing from kin or the landlord's family. They are also eligible for food stamps. In five other tenant households, the adult members, most of whom are over sixty years old, do not perform any wage labor. They maintain themselves primarily through food stamps, aid from kin, and in a few cases social security payments.

People from all social groups take on multiple tasks, carving out productive niches to keep themselves supplied with basic goods and services. There are significant differences, however, among social groups. Members of the local elite control the better agricultural land within the community. Through county-wide networks of political influence, they are often able to secure available white-collar and skilled blue-collar jobs for themselves or their children. These monopolies over local resources are particularly evident among those young couples, where both husband and wife hold full-time wage jobs and work part-time as well growing tobacco with one set of their parents.

Smallholders and tenants often depend on the local elites for wage work. While many derive income from multiple sources, these tend to involve activities outside the formal economic structures and yield small returns. Some cash is obtained through trapping, digging ginseng, selling homemade quilts, and collecting scrap metal and soda bottles. Savings are achieved through the purchase of second-hand clothing and other items, and through men trading old cars and car parts and doing their own repair work. Landlord families often provide tenant households with opportunities to secure additional cash. Women are asked to make quilts and receive $20 to $40 per quilt for several weeks of part-time labor. One unemployed man aged thirty stacked several thousand bricks into neat piles for a landlord and received $40 for two weeks' work. Several women perform house-keeping or babysitting chores for the wealthier families. In these jobs, not only is the wage rate low, but people only vaguely calculate their time. Instead, they often mention the specific items for which they are working, such as school clothes and shoes for their children or payment on a new appliance.

A significant number of jobs held by community residents are dependent for their sources of funds on special federal programs directed toward regions of high unemployment. While some of these programs have been maintained for at least a dozen years, they are inherently unstable. Temporary and permanent layoffs of cooks, janitorial personnel, and teacher's aides are common, as are reductions in hours.[15] Job insecurity also applies to the many categories of paraprofessional social service workers, which traditionally proliferate in areas of high unemployment but which are rarely assured of funding for more than one year at a time. Such cutbacks in social service programs at a national level affect household incomes in all social groups.

The degree of unemployment in the community would be much higher without such federal programs. However, the community is characterized by a high degree of unemployment among young men and women recently graduated from high school, among young men returned from the service, and among young women with school age children who would eagerly work if full-time or part-time wage labor were available.[16] There is also a great deal of underemployment, particularly among the young men who perform day wage labor on the larger farms. Despite the large-scale unemployment and underemployment within the community—and the fact that the poorest core of families earn no more than several hundred dollars a year—no household is eligible for welfare payments.[17] The only direct government aid provided to such families is through the food stamp program.

The local economy is dependent on various sources of federal funds, on income derived from relatively small-scale tobacco farming, and on some subsistence agriculture. It is maintained through the exchange of labor, goods, and services that pass among households. There is a certain stability to the community based on the fact that almost all residents have long-term affiliations there. When occupational histories of households are examined, however, a more dynamic analysis of the local economy and social relations emerges. Thus, every household has been touched by some form of wage-labor migration. The following are typical situations:

1. The husband is away working in a metropolitan area such as Cincinnati, Dayton, Covington, Detroit, or the suburbs of these; the wife and children remain within the community. Such an arrangement may persist for several years, or involve only seasonal work. The husband generally comes home on weekends, the frequency depending on the distance and the nature of the work.
2. A nuclear family and perhaps other household members move to a metropolitan center for between a few months and a few years and then returns. Several members of the household may be engaged in wage labor during this time. This pattern may be repeated.
3. A nuclear family leaves eastern Kentucky for perhaps twenty-five years and the parents return to retire.
4. One or more children of a household—usually sons of eighteen years or older, sometimes daughters—are working in urban areas. Some establish their own nuclear families there and remain permanently. Others return periodically—they quit or are laid off—and then go back again.

Sets of related households presently within the community constitute "home-based" segments of extended kin networks, the majority of whose members are located in metropolitan centers outside the region. It is through such networks that people exchange various forms of mutual aid, such as information regarding jobs and housing for potential migrants (Brown 1967; 1970; Maloney et al. 1972).

These patterns of wage labor migration, heightened since the 1940s, have become integral and permanent aspects of the social and economic structure of the community. During this period, poor employment prospects within the region and the loss of a number of jobs within the community as a result of the closing of a large mission school further reduced the economic options available to the community. Out-migration has been the dominant response to the large-scale unemployment and underemployment that characterize the regional and local economies. These migrants now occupy skilled or unskilled jobs outside the region, or have joined the ranks of the urban unemployed. The community also continues to experience the circulation of people between metropolitan areas and the rural home base. Local residents leave the community when they hear that work can be obtained elsewhere and return when they are laid off or have grown tired of urban living.

It is through these patterns of migration that the community functions as a source of reserve labor for metropolitan-based industries. The migrant's position in the local social structure determines the level of skills and training which he or she has when leaving eastern Kentucky to enter an urban job market. Tenants and their children have less formal education and skilled training than members of the local elite. Members of the local elite who have left permanently have for the most part located themselves in white-collar or skilled blue-collar jobs or have accumulated the capital necessary to become petty entrepreneurs. Many become teachers, legal secretaries, mail carriers, fire fighters, bakers, and small shopkeepers. Small landholders and tenants generally have a history of work in unskilled factory jobs in urban areas. The cycle of working for several years in the city and then returning "home" may be repeated several times. Tenants constitute both a source of low-paid farm labor to the larger landowners in the rural areas, and the cheapest category of unskilled labor in the cities.

As a reserve labor pool for metropolitan centers, Robin's Branch is drained of critical labor power after having absorbed the costs of their education, health care, and provision of other services. It does not, in turn, draw many resources from other sectors of the economy. As noted earlier, many local residents maintain themselves through *creating* work in the interstices of a capitalist economy and through providing their own subsistence base. In such ways the community is able to provide for migrants who return when layoffs occur in northern industries. As well, relatively few welfare services are provided to this economically marginal community. While special federal funds and transfer payments provide important sources of income, there is virtually no capital for reinvestment in the development of the community.

Family and Gender Relations

The conditions of underdevelopment and the pressures associated with out-migration have profound effects on family and gender relations. With shortages of wage labor, productive land, and basic social services, kinship relations assume deep significance. For all social groups, nuclear and extended families are the ultimate, obligatory social relationships to which an individual may appeal for aid. It is as family members that people engage in subsistence activities and pool their skills to repair houses, cars, and clothing, performing these necessary services out of love or obligation. Thus men, women, and children are recruited to socially productive activities through the strong ideological bonds of kinship. People of all ages—including teenagers—readily acknowledge the importance of family ties.

Kinship also offers a broad idiom through which all classes may claim extensive ties and so maximize access to strategic and scarce resources. In this political idiom terms such as "cousin," "brother," and "sister" are used widely, particularly by local politicians. The successful politician is someone who claims kinship to persons throughout a county; who attends funerals and memorial meetings; who wouldn't hesitate to "stay all night" or eat at someone's house; who can be called "cousin" and doesn't "talk proud."[18] Expressions such as "we're from the same tribe of people" or "I'm kin to her mommy" or persons with the same surname claiming "we're the same set of Thomases" provide an avenue through which an individual may approach another about securing a job, a government subsidy, or a vote. In any particular situation a person may choose to emphasize one or more bonds from a wide range of often overlapping networks, traced bilaterally. This expansive idiom designating friends and supporters as kin tends to mitigate some of the harsher aspects of class relations that have developed within counties and communities, such as those between patron and client.

The importance of kinship to an individual's economic and political success has tended to enhance the status and power of women in eastern Kentucky society. Most men and women recognize the significance of domestic production to the local economy and acknowledge the central role of women in production and reproduction. It is widely accepted that women work as hard as or harder than men and are as capable and clever. Men will frequently volunteer the opinion that it was the woman in a particular family who kept things going under conditions of adversity, such as when the husband was working away from home or was laid off or ill.[19]

These attitudes are most prevalent among rural elite and small-holder families, where women are the dominant figures in the running of the households as well as active, informed participants in the management of the farm. Their marriages tend to be egalitarian relationships. Most married women in the community own major assets jointly with their husbands and it is not unusual for women to own some land in their own right, usually inherited from their parents. While there is an accepted division of labor by gender—the husband assuming primary responsibility for heavy outdoor farm work and the wife for care of the children, the home, and garden—such couples form interdependent economic units in which both are seen to contribute equally to sustaining the household and farm. Many of these women keep the account books for the farm and decide along with their husbands and grown sons about major and minor expenditures. Where husband and wife are also employed at paying jobs outside the home, *both* work a double day, performing necessary, though usually different tasks.

Women from the landholding families also use their influence as members of extensive kin networks to secure jobs for themselves or for members of their immediate family. Since the largest local employers are the county school system and government social service agencies—employment sectors in the United States that hire large numbers of women—there are few occupational barriers by virtue of gender to women with influence in eastern Kentucky. In Robin's Branch, this is evident in the large proportion of younger and middle-aged women from the landowning families who are currently in the labor force and in the fact that most of the retired women from the rural elite families worked at some time in the past for the local school or the county health department. In the county as a whole, women hold prominent positions as executive directors and senior bureaucrats of government agencies, as school principals, teachers, health professionals and paraprofessionals, editor and staff of the county newspaper, office managers, entrepreneurs, and as elected officers in the county and state Democratic and Republican party organizations. Not only is it accepted that women work outside the home, but it is unquestioned that women can be as politically astute and uncompromising as their male counterparts.

Power and status thus accrue to women from the landholding families who control resources such as land, personal income, and access to influential people. In contrast, tenant women experience severe economic hardship and social subordination to their husbands. Wives whose husbands are day laborers on local farms must deal with the immediate consequences of unemployment and underemployment: they are responsible for the daily care of their families under conditions of abject poverty. In Robin's Branch, many of the younger tenant wives spend their days at the home of their mothers or mothers-in-law where, in addition to companionship, the older woman provides help in the form of food, access to a sewing machine, a wringer washer, a quilting frame, and fuel. These women have few resources to draw upon beyond their own domestic skills, in-kind donations from landlords and kin and some government assistance such as food stamps. Many also bear the brunt of their husbands' frustrations and feelings of inadequacy. Men have drinking bouts, which may be followed by verbal or physical abuse of their wives.[20] They also guard their wives and daughters closely. These women are rarely allowed out alone, even to the local grocery store and post office a mile from their homes, and any efforts at socializing are watched closely. With few opportunities for education, employment, and social contacts, they remain socially and geographically isolated, with little recourse beyond their extended families.

Family relationships vary, therefore, depending on a household's economic position, i.e., its access to critical resources and on the ability of its members to cope with the demands of the larger society. Women and men may control different resources and experience these demands in different ways. For example, the fluctuating needs for male labor in the metropolis result in many poor couples experiencing difficult cycles of adjustment and readjustment when the husband is away working and then returns. Tenant families may live this way for years—men visit their families once or twice a month and remain socially isolated in the city while their wives take on the double responsibilities concerning children, home, and farm. Recently, a number of assembly plants, attracted to eastern Kentucky as a source of cheap labor, have hired women onto shift work, while their husbands remain unemployed.[21] Similarly, among the better-off rural families, marriages are placed under stress when women are offered opportunities for employment or futher education and their interests begin to diverge significantly from those of their farmer husbands. Such shifts cause serious strains on family relationships.

While work-related tensions such as these are endemic to family life, families also provide an arena within which men and women can exert some degree of autonomy and control in their lives, again depending on their economic position. For example, for all but the poorest households, where survival dictates the pace of work, subsistence activities and other household or farm work can be performed at a pace determined by the workers and men and women make daily decisions about the allocation of labor and resources.

Most significantly, people actively shape the process of social reproduction. The economic, political, and social importance of families in eastern Kentucky society is reflected in the great value placed on children and their socialization. Children are almost always welcomed for the joy, pleasure, and entertainment they bring and because they are the very essence of what it means to be a family—a social unit sustained by the productive activities of its members that has deep roots in a community and region. People gain position and pride in their roles as parents and children.[22] In eastern Kentucky, if you can't answer the question, Whose girl or boy are you? to local satisfaction, you are an outsider and must prove your worth.

While children are welcomed, the decision to have more than two is often part of a subtle or not so subtle negotiation process between husband and wife over control of reproduction. Data from Robin's Branch indicate that this involves a number of factors related to gender, each of which varies according to class position. These include:

1. *The wife's status and decision-making role within the marriage:* Where marriages are egalitarian, as among the landholding families, the decision of the woman tends to prevail. Where the wife is subordinate to the husband, she has few options and her reproductive role is a way of securing her status within the nuclear and extended family.

2. *Access to contraception:* Women from the tenant families are least able to travel the twenty miles to attend a family planning clinic, nor can they afford to see a private doctor or pay for pills. Husbands who see their wives' fertility as a resource over which they can exercize control—perhaps one of the few available to them—discourage use of contraceptives.

3. *Availability of paid work for a women:* Women with few options for employment and whose children are almost grown consider the birth of a last child to fill the gap of their middle years. This seems to be less true for women engaged in full-time paid employment outside the home.

4. *Women's support networks:* The availability of babysitters— whether grandmothers, aunts, neighbors, or older daughters at home—obviates the problems of isolation, which many urban women encounter when they have small children. Many women with three or four small children work full-time outside the home.

5. *Migration patterns:* Much more difficult to assess are the specific impacts which cyclical patterns of migration have on fertility patterns for each social class. The birthrate for the eastern Kentucky counties declined dramatically by 1960, owing in part to the permanent loss of reproductively fertile individuals through migration; the increasing availability of contraception; the decline of small farms; the increasing integration of women into the labor force; and changing attitudes which tended to see very large families as socially outdated (DeJong 1968). There are no studies that detail how the changing demands for labor in the metropolis have affected the reproductive decisions of families such as those in Robin's Branch who comprise pools of reserve labor for industries

outside the region. Eastern Kentuckians have a long history of coping with separations; they weigh the social and personal costs of raising children under difficult conditions alongside the emotional gratifications and other benefits of having children. As noted in the beginning of this essay, out-migration is an involuntary decision for a majority of those who leave. People live in separated households because they prefer to raise their children "back home."

Children enable a family to expand its network of social relationships, ultimately through incorporating new sets of kin. At the same time, mountaineers are able to build a defensive bulwark against the outside world through nurturing strong family loyalties; children are taught to close ranks against "outsiders" —whether social workers, missionaries, teachers, or entrepreneurs who attempt to manipulate and undermine their strong cohesion. Mountain children of all social classes learn, more or less successfully, to be bicultural—comfortable with local idioms and "hillbilly" behavior in the supportive context of the family and community and yet able to behave "appropriately" at school or in other nonfamilial settings. (Smathers 1973; Lewis et al. 1972).

Kinship thus provides a potent ideology for organization in eastern Kentucky society. It encompasses closed social groups from whom an individual may claim immediate aid, extensive social and political networks, and an historic attachment to ancestors and place. It is through kinship that class relations are reproduced and resisted.

Conclusions

In a community such as Robin's Branch, families embedded in very different class relations meet each other daily and come to terms. A multiplicity of economic and social ties bind landlords and tenants, political patrons and clients, neighbors and kin into reciprocating networks, which sustain and recreate the social fabric of the community. At the same time, fluctuating demands for cheap labor and resources in the metropolis pull people and resources away.

This essay has stressed some of the ways in which local rural residents cope with marginal economic conditions. There are also indications throughout the region that people are struggling to establish economic options apart from out-migration and the coal industry. In various parts of central Appalachia, people have organized consumer and producer cooperatives and developed some locally owned and controlled small industries.[23] For the most part, these are economically marginal operations but they are important attempts to develop alternate organizational forms for economic development of the region. The formation of welfare rights organizations, black lung associations, anti-strip mine groups, and renewed militancy among miners are all evidence of mobilization against the involuntary movement of people out of a potentially viable region. They encompass a broad-based, politically conscious network of people with strong ties to kin and place, resisting current government planning and corporate strategies for Appalachia. It is evident that a signficant form of class struggle is continuing within the Appalachian region.

Notes

1. The Appalachian region has had various definitions imposed upon it since the early 1900s. The one used here follows the Appalachian Regional Commission, which defines Appalachia as all of West Virginia and parts of twelve other states: Alabama, Georgia, Kentucky, Maryland, Mississippi, New York, North Carolina, Ohio, Pennsylvania, South Carolina, Tennessee, and Virginia. Central Appalachia includes the forty-nine counties of Appalachian Kentucky (i.e., eastern Kentucky), twenty northwestern counties of Tennessee, seven counties in southwestern Virginia, and nine southern counties in West Virginia. Estimated regional population for 1975 is 19,010,485; for central Appalachia, 1,866,504; for eastern Kentucky, 939,440.
2. Eastern Kentucky had a net migration rate of −31.8 percent between

1950–1960, and of −15.9 percent between 1960–1970. The region lost 3.3 million people during that twenty-year period alone, and its growth rate was +2 percent as compared with +18.5 percent for the U.S. as a whole for 1950–1960, and +2.7 percent as compared with a national growth rate of +13.3 percent for 1960–1970 (ARC 1972).

3. Highway 75 is a major north-south artery linking Detroit, Dayton, Cincinnati, Covington, Lexington, and Knoxville.

4. The unemployment rate for eastern Kentucky was officially 10.2 percent in 1970, while the national rate was 4.9 percent. ARC reports suggest that the statistics mask much "hidden unemployment" and that the rate could effectively be more like one-third. In addition, 35 percent of the population of central Appalachia had incomes below the poverty line in that year, as compared with a national average of 14 percent. Eastern Kentucky formed the core of central Appalachian poverty, with 46 percent of its population below the poverty line. For an evaluation of low standards of living in terms of housing, poor medical and educational services, see ARC (1972, 1975).

5. Large sections of the region's land were sold in the 1700s for speculative purposes even prior to settlement. For some of the better historical works on the region, see Campbell (1981), Rice (1970), Verhoef (1919), Caudill (1962); for a good economic analysis, see issues of the *Peoples' Appalachia: A Critical Research Report* (Peoples' Appalachian Research Collective 1970–1975). My own work looks at the political economy of the region's isolation in the first half of the nineteenth century and the emergence of class relations in the late nineteenth and early twentieth centuries (Tudiver, 1978, unpublished).

6. Increases in out-migration took place with slumps in the coal industry in the late 1920s and with mechanization and the increases in strip mining in the early 1950s (Brown and Hillery 1967; Belcher 1967; *Peoples' Appalachia* July, 1972). For recent data on return migration see ARC (1976) and Primack (1973).

7. Between 1947 and 1961, mechanization in the mines and the shift from coal to imported oil resulted in a reduction nationally from 427,600 workers to 144,914—a decline of 65 percent. Even with increased coal production since 1961, the method of strip mining has kept the labor force in mining low (Miernyk 1975).

8. It might be noted that mountain peoples have many skills appropriate to a rural lifestyle but that these count for little in securing wage employment in urban centers, where skilled training through previous work or formal education are the prime hiring criteria.

9. In fact, the wealth of natural resources leaving the region has not been taxed sufficiently to pay for the infrastructure required by the extractive industries. Coal companies create excessive damage to roads, soil erosion, and water pollution—with impunity—and the costs for the repairs of these are borne by local and state governments, thus providing subsidies to private capital (Concerned Citizens for Fair Taxes 1973).

10. ARC planners have argued that through development of growth centers, some economic benefits will trickle down to outlying areas. Much of this argument is spurious. Strong political lobbies by state governors forced the extension of the boundaries of the region, resulting in the addition of ten Major Labor Market Areas and hence fewer funds for rural areas in deep economic distress. Many ARC projects seem determined by political expediency rather than by the critical needs of the region. One example is the recent satellite project in conjunction with NASA, which involved spending over $2 million to beam teacher training courses into several areas of the region. For a summary history of ARC see Rothblatt (1971) and Newman (1972); for current projects, see *Appalachia: A Journal of the Appalachian Regional Commission.*

11. According to ARC figures, in 1965 central Appalachia had a per capita income that was 52 percent of the U.S. average. In 1973, it was 62 percent. The ARC attempts to argue that this change is a result of their development policies in the region. It is most likely attributable to the coal boom of the 1970s and to such factors as increased black lung payments and the attraction of some industries to central Appalachia as a source of cheap, nonunion labor. Note, too, that the regional per capita income has not increased much relative to the wider United States—from 79 percent in 1965 to 81 percent in 1973 (ARC 1976).

12. Since most of the land is hilly, farming takes place in the narrow bottom lands on the banks of the rivers or creeks. A farm of 300 acres might have no more than thirty acres of tillable land in dispersed plots. Tobacco allotments in the county ranged from one-tenth of an acre to six acres.

13. I am refering to these as social groups or social categories rather than local "classes" since, as I will discuss, surplus value is not really being produced by one group for another within the community. Rather, as wage workers, a large proportion of persons in both social groups produce surplus value for employers located outside the community. There are, however, significant differences between the local groups in the access to and control over basic resources.

14. This is calculated on the prevailing rate in 1974 of $5 or $6 per day for no more than eighty days per year. Generally, renters doing agricultural work on the farm on which they lived paid no rent. Rental rates in the community were $20 per month or less for houses without indoor plumbing or running water.

15. For example, several persons in the community whose jobs were funded through Operation Mainstream were cut back to a four-day work week when the minimum wage in the United States rose from $1.60 to $2 per hour. Thus, the low weekly compensation of $64 was maintained despite the legislated intent to raise it to $80.

16. It must be pointed out that it often proved irrational for women in the smallholding and tenant groups to work outside the home. Transportation cost to and from work, added expenses of clothing and childcare absorbed most of the increased income. All available jobs for these women paid the minimum wage or less and were nonunion.

17. All tenant families with small children were nuclear—and hence ineligible for Aid to Families With Dependent Children (AFDC).

18. The importance of kinship to politics is publicly acknowledged at election time. Candidates for county offices unabashedly list in newspapers, radio advertisements, and leaflets all the common family names to whom they claim bonds of kinship and solicit their support.

19. I hazard these generalizations on the basis of three years of field research and a wide range of contacts with persons of all social classes. Review of several hundred taped oral history interviews with elderly mountaineers revealed similar attitudes.

20. This is not to imply that all men who are tenants drink heavily, nor that other men in the community do not drink. However, a number of the tenants would carouse together at night, driving up and down the country roads and frequently running the car off into a field. While other men drink, tenant wives have fewer options with which to deal with the problem.

21. For example, Control Data Corporation has a computer assembly plant in Wolfe County, Kentucky. Over 80 percent of their more than 200 employees are women. The personnel manager justified such hiring practices by claiming that women's fingers were more dextrous than men's and that they were good, fast, quiet workers. "Mountain men," he added "are a bit ornery," and so not very good factory workers. The company provides counseling services to its employees to deal with marital problems resulting from the work situation.

22. Little stigma is attached to unwed mothers and the baby and its mother are usually supported by the grandparents. Mountain families are also known for their acceptance of handicapped children and their integration into the family.
23. For a careful analysis of such groups see N. Tudiver (1973). *Mountain Life and Work*, a monthly publication of the Council of the Southern Mountains, does extensive reporting on grass-roots organizations and their political struggles.

Bibliography

Ad Hoc Women's Studies Committee Against Sterilization Abuse. 1978. *Workbook on Sterilization and Sterilization Abuse.* Bronxville, N.Y.: Sarah Lawrence College.

Althusser, Louis. 1972. Ideology and Ideological State Apparatuses: Notes Towards an Investigation. In *Education, Structure and Society,* ed. B. R. Cosin. New York: Penguin.

Amin, Samir. 1974. *Accumulation on a World Scale.* 2 vols. New York: Monthly Review Press.

————. 1976. *Unequal Development.* New York: Monthly Review Press.

Anderson, Perry. 1962. *Portugal: End of Ultra-Colonialism.* London: New Left Books.

Appalachian Regional Commission (ARC). 1972. *Appalachia—An Economic Report. Trends in Employment, Income and Population.* Washington, D.C.

————. 1975. *Annual Report.* Washington, D.C.

————. 1976. *Annual Report.* Washington, D.C.

Arnold, C. B. 1978. Public Health Aspects of Contraceptive Sterilization. In *Behavioral-Social Aspects of Contraceptive Sterilization,* eds. S. M. Newman and Z. E. Klein. Lexington, Mass.: Lexington Books.

Aswad, Barbara. 1971. *Property Control and Social Strategies: Settlers on a Middle Eastern Plain.* Ann Arbor, Mich.: Museum of Anthropology Anthropological Papers.

Bahr, Stephen J. 1980. *Economics and the Family.* Lexington, Mass.: Lexington Books.

Baird, Peter, and McCaughan, Ed. 1976. *Harvest of Anger: Agroimperialism in Mexico's Northwest.* New York: NACLA Publication.

Balibar, Etienne. 1970. The Basic Concepts of Historical Imperialism. In *Reading Capital,* by Etienne Balibar and Louis Althusser. New York: Pantheon.

Baran, Paul, and Sweezy, Paul M. 1966. *Monopoly Capital.* New York: Monthly Review Press.

Belcher, John C. 1967. Population Growth and Characteristics. In *The*

Southern Appalachian Region: A Survey, ed. Thomas R. Ford. Lexington, Ky.: University Press of Kentucky.

Benhabib, S. 1979. Rightwing Groups Behind Political Violence in Turkey. *Middle East Research and Information Report,* no. 77. Washington, D.C.

Benedict, Burton. 1972. The Social Regulation of Fertility. In *The Structure of Human Populations,* eds. G. A. Harrison and A. J. Boyce. New York: Oxford University Press.

Berger, John, and Mohr, Jean. 1975. *A Seventh Man: Migrant Workers in Europe.* New York: Viking Press.

Bettelheim, Charles. 1968. *India Independent.* New York: Monthly Review Press.

―――. 1971. Appendix to *Unequal Exchange,* by Immanuel Arghiri. New York: Monthly Review Press.

Böhning, W. R. 1972. *The Migration of Workers in the United Kingdom and the European Community.* London: Oxford University Press.

Bopp, J. R., and Hall, D. G. 1970. Indicators for Surgical Sterilization. *Obstetrics and Gynecology* 35(5).

Boserup, Ester. 1965. *The Conditions of Agricultural Growth.* Chicago: Aldine.

Braverman, Harry. 1974. *Labor and Monopoly Capital: The Degradation of Work in the Twentieth Century.* New York: Monthly Review Press.

Breman, Jan. 1974. *Patronage and Exploitation: Changing Agrarian Relations in South Gujarat.* Berkeley: University of California Press.

Brown, James S., and Hillery, George A., Jr. 1967. The Great Migration, 1940–1960. In *The Southern Appalachian Region: A Survey,* ed. Thomas R. Ford. Lexington, Ky.: University Press of Kentucky.

―――. 1970. Population and Migration Changes in Appalachia. In *Change in Rural Appalachia. Implications for Action Programs,* eds. John D. Photiadis and Harry K. Schwarzweller. Philadelphia: University of Pennsylvania Press.

―――. 1972. A Look at the 1970 Census. In *Appalachia in the Sixties,* eds. David S. Walls and John B. Stephenson. Lexington, Ky.: University Press of Kentucky.

Campbell, John C. 1921. *The Southern Highlander and His Homeland.* Russell Sage Foundation. Reprint. Lexington, Ky.: University Press of Kentucky, 1969.

Campos, R. de O. 1962. Case Studies of Employment Problems and Policies: A. Brazil. *Appendix to Employment Objectives in Eco-*

nomic Development, Studies and Reports: New Series, no. 62. Geneva: International Labor Organization.

Carter, Nicholas. 1975. Population, Environment and Natural Resources: A Critical Review of Recent Models. In *The Population Debate,* vol. 2. New York: United Nations.

Castells, Manuel. 1975. Immigrant Workers and Class Struggles in Advanced Capitalism. *Politics and Society* 5:1.

———. 1977. *The Urban Question.* Trans. Alan Sheridan. Cambridge, Mass.: M.I.T. Press.

Castles, Stephen, and Kosack, Godula. 1973. *Immigrant Workers and Class Structure in Western Europe.* London: Oxford University Press.

Caudill, Harry. 1962. *Night Comes to the Cumberlands.* Boston: Little, Brown.

Chavkin, W. 1979. Occupational Hazards to Reproduction—A Review of the Literature. *Feminist Studies* 5:310-25.

Clark, Victor S. et al. 1930. *Porto Rico and Its Problems.* Washington, D.C.: The Brookings Institution.

Clinton, Richard L. 1973. Population Politics and Political Science. In *Population and Politics: New Directions in Political Science Research,* ed. Richard L. Clinton. Lexington, Mass.: Lexington Books.

Cohen, M. R. et al. 1970. Interval Tubal Sterilization via Laparoscopy. *American Journal of Obstetrics and Gynecology* 108(3).

Concerned Citizens for Fair Taxes. 1973. "Coal Taxes in Southwest Virginia: A Report for the Senate Subcommittee on Intergovernmental Relations." Mimeographed. Appalachia, Va.

Cook, R. C. 1951. *Human Fertility: The Modern Dilemma.* London: Victor Gollancz.

Coontz, Sydney. 1957. *Population Theories and Their Economic Interpretation.* Reprint. London: Routledge & Kegan Paul, 1968.

Coryell, Schofield. 1974. The New Grapes of Wrath. *Ramparts* 12.

Courtenay, P. P. 1964. *Plantation Agriculture.* New York: Praeger.

Cowgill, George L. 1975. On Causes and Consequences of Ancient and Modern Population Changes. *American Anthropologist* 77:505-25.

Davenport, William, and Coker, Gullbun. 1967. The Moro Movement of Guadalcanal, British Solomon Islands Protectorate. *Journal of the Polynesian Society* 76:123-75.

Davis, Kingsley. 1953. Puerto Rico: A Crowded Island. *Annals of the American Academy of Political and Social Science* 285:116-22.

DeJong, Gordon F. 1968. *Appalachian Fertility Decline. A Demographic and Sociological Analysis*. Lexington, Ky.: University Press of Kentucky.

deKadt, Emanuel, and Williams, Gavin, eds. 1974. *Sociology and Development*. London: Tavistock.

Demerath, Nicholas J. 1976. *Birth Control and Foreign Policy: The Alternatives to Family Planning*. New York: Harper & Row.

Desai, A. R. 1959. *The Social Background of Indian Nationalism*. Bombay: Popular Book Depot.

Devereux, G. 1967. A Typological Study of Abortion in 350 Primitive, Ancient, and Preindustrial Societies. In *Abortion in America*, ed. Harold Rosen. Boston: Beacon.

Diffie, Bailey W., and Diffie, Justine Whitfield. 1931. *Porto Rico: A Broken Pledge*. New York: Vanguard.

Dow, James. 1973. Models of Middlemen. *Human Organization* 32.

Environmental Fund. 1979. *World Population Estimates*. Washington, D.C.: Environmental Fund.

Epstein, T. S., and Jackson, Darrell, eds. 1977. *The Feasibility of Fertility Planning: Micro Perspectives*. London: Pergamon.

Espenshade, Thomas J. 1977. The Value and Cost of Children. *Population Bulletin* 321(1). Washington, D.C.: Population Reference Bureau.

Faris, James C. 1975. Social Evolution, Population and Production. In *Population, Ecology and Social Evolution*, ed. S. Polgar. The Hague: Mouton. Also published in *Toward a Marxist Anthropology*, ed. S. Diamond. The Hague: Mouton, 1979.

Federal Register. 1978. Rules and Regulations—Provision of Sterilization in Federally Assisted Programs of the Public Health Service. Publication no. 43-217 (Washington, D.C.: U.S. Government Printing Office).

Financial Mail (Johannesburg). July 14, 1967.

————. Feb. 24, 1978.

Firth, Raymond. 1931. A Native Voyage to Rennell. *Oceania* 2:179-90.

————. 1936. *We, the Tikopia*. Reprint. Boston: Beacon, 1963.

————. 1940. *The Work of the Gods in Tikopia*. London: P. Lund, Humphries & Sons.

————. 1954. Anuta and Tikopia: Symbiotic Elements in Social Organization. *Journal of the Polynesian Society* 63:87-131.

————. 1959. *Social Change in Tikopia*. London: Routledge & Kegan Paul.

Fleagle, Fred. 1917. *Social Problems in Porto Rico*. Lexington, Mass.: D. C. Heath.

Flores, Edmundo. 1970. The Economics of Land Reform. In *Agrarian*

Problems and Peasant Movements in Latin America, ed. R. Staven-hagen. Garden City, N.Y.: Doubleday.

Ford, K. 1978a. Contraceptive Use in the United States, 1973-1976. *Family Planning Perspectives* 10:264-69.

————. 1978b. "Recent Changes in Contraceptive Practice Among Couples: Results from the 1976 National Survey of Family Growth." Paper read at the Population Association of America, Atlanta, Ga.

Forrest, J., Tietze, C., and Sullivan, E. 1978. Abortion in the United States, 1976-1977. *Family Planning Perspectives* 10:329-41.

Fox, F. W. 1937. "Infant and Child Mortality in the Ciskei and Trans-kei." Unpublished manuscript. New York: Population Council.

Franke, R. 1974. Miracle Seeds and Shattered Dreams. *Natural History* 83:1.

Frankel, Francine. 1978. *India's Political Economy, 1947-1977.* Prince-ton: Princeton University Press.

Friedman, Julian R. 1977. *Basic Facts on the Republic of South Africa and the Policy of Apartheid.* UN Notes and Documents no. 8/77, April. New York: United Nations.

Fuchs, V. R. 1974. *Who Shall Live? Health, Economics, and Social Choice.* New York: Basic Books.

Gayer, A., Homan, P., and James, E. 1938. *The Sugar Economy of Puerto Rico.* New York: Columbia University Press.

Godelier, Maurice. 1972. *Rationality and Irrationality in Economics.* New York: Monthly Review Press.

Godwin, Kenneth. 1973. Methodology and Policy. In *Population and Politics: New Directions in Political Science Research,* ed. Richard Clinton. Lexington, Mass.: Lexington Books.

Gordon, Linda. 1977. *Woman's Body, Woman's Right: A Social History of Birth Control in America.* New York: Penguin.

Green, Jim, 1978. Holding the Line: Miner's Militancy and the Strike of 1978. *Radical America* 12(3).

Gross, D., and Underwood, B. 1971. Technological Change and Caloric Costs—Sisal Agriculture in Northeastern Brazil. *American Anthro-pologist* 72:725-40.

Guzevaty, Y. 1974. The Socioeconomic Determinants of Demographic Processes. *Population Problems.* Moscow: USSR Academy of Sciences.

Hamer, John Hayward. 1962. "The Cultural Aspects of Infant Mortality in Subsaharan Africa." Ph.D. dissertation, Northwestern University.

Hance, William A. 1970. *Population, Migration and Urbanization.* New York: Columbia University Press.

————. 1975. *The Geography of Modern Africa*. New York: Columbia University Press.

Hancock, G., ed. 1978. *Africa Guide*. Essex: World of Information.

Hansen, Millard. 1952. The Family in Puerto Rico Research Project. In *Approaches to Problems of High Fertility in Agrarian Societies*. New York: Milbank Memorial Fund.

Hardin, Garrett. 1968. The Tragedy of the Commons. *Science* 1(162): 1243-48.

Harvey, David. 1975. *Social Justice and the City*. Baltimore: Johns Hopkins University Press.

Hatt, Paul. 1952. *Background of Human Fertility in Puerto Rico: A Sociological Survey*. Princeton: Princeton University Press.

Hepple, Alex. 1971. *South Africa: Workers Under Apartheid*. 2d ed. London: International Defence and Aid Fund.

Hernandez Alvarez, José. 1964. "The Sociological Implications of Return Migration to Puerto Rico: An Exploratory Study." Ph.D. dissertation, University of Minnesota.

Hillery, G. A., Jr., Brown, James S., and DeJong, Gordon F. 1965. Migration Systems of the Southern Appalachians: Some Demographic Observations. *Rural Sociology* 30(1):33-48.

History Task Force, Centro de Estudios Puertorriqueños. 1979. *Labor Migration Under Capitalism: The Puerto Rican Experience*. New York: Monthly Review Press.

Hoover, Robert et al. 1978. Oral Contraceptive Use: Association with Frequency of Hospitalization and Chronic Disease Risk Indicators. *American Journal of Public Health* 68(4):335-41.

Horrel, M., et al. 1973. *A Survey of Race Relations in South Africa*. Johannesburg: Institute of Race Relations.

Houghton, B. Robert. 1960. Men of Two Worlds: Some Aspects of Migratory Labor in South Africa. *South African Journal of Economics* 28(3):180-81.

Hussein, M. 1973. *Class Conflict in Egypt, 1945-1970*. New York: Monthly Review Press.

International Defence and Aid Fund. 1969. *South Africa: Resettlement, the New Violence to Africans*. London.

International Planned Parenthood Federation. 1979. *People* (London) 6(2).

Jerome, Harry. 1926. *Migration and Business Cycles*. New York: National Bureau of Economic Research.

Joshi, Heather, and Joshi, Vijay. 1976. *Surplus Labor and the City: A Study of Bombay*. London: Oxford University Press.

Kindleberger, C. P. 1967. *Europe's Postwar Growth and the Role of Labour Supply*. London: Oxford University Press.

King, Timothy et al. 1974. *Population Policies and Economic Development*. World Bank Staff Report. Baltimore: Johns Hopkins University Press.

Kirby, Richard M. 1969. Kentucky Coal: Owners, Taxes, Profits. *Appalachian Lookout* 1(6).

Klarman, H. E. 1977. The Financing of Health Care. *Daedalus* 106(1): 218-20.

Kleinman, David S. 1980. *Human Adaptation and Population Growth— a Non-Malthusian Perspective*. Montclair, N.J.: Allanheld, Osmun.

Koening, Nathan. 1953. *A Comprehensive Agricultural Program for Puerto Rico*. Washington, D.C.: U.S. Government Printing Office.

Kritz, Mary, and Gurak, Douglas. 1979. International Migration Trends in Latin America: Research and Data Survey. *International Migration Review* 13(3).

Langschmidt, W. D. 1968/69. Some Characteristics of the Urban Bantu Market. Johannesburg: The National Development and Management Foundation of South Africa. Cited in a special issue of *Africa Today* 17(5):12.

Larson, Eric H. 1966. *Nukufero: A Tikopia Colony in the Russell Islands*. Eugene, Ore: University of Oregon.

————. 1970. Tikopia Plantation Labor and Company Management Relations. *Oceania* 40:195-209.

Levine, David. 1977. *Family Formation in an Age of Nascent Capitalism*. New York: Academic Press.

Lewis, Gordon K. 1974. *Notes on the Puerto Rican Revolution: An Essay on American Dominance and Caribbean Resistance*. New York: Monthly Review Press.

Lewis, Helen, Kobak, Sue Easterling, and Johnson, Linda. 1972. "Family Religion and Colonialism in Central Appalachia." Paper read at the 71st annual meeting of the American Anthropological Association, Toronto, Canada.

Littlejohn, G. 1973. The Peasantry and the Russian Revolution. *Economy and Society* 2:112-25.

Lorimer, Frank. 1961. *Demographic Information on Tropical Africa*. Boston: Boston University Press.

Luxemburg, Rosa. 1951. *The Accumulation of Capital*. London: Routledge & Kegan Paul. Published in paperback by Monthly Review Press, 1968.

Mafeje, Archie. 1973. The Fallacy of Dual Economics Revisited: a Case for East, Central and Southern Africa. In *Dualism and Rural Development in East Africa*, ed. R. Leys. Copenhagen: Institute for Development Research.

Magubane, Bernard. 1976. The Evolution of Class Structure in Africa. In *The Political Economy of Contemporary Africa*, eds. Peter C. W. Gutkind and Immanuel Wallerstein. London: Sage Publications.

————. 1979. *The Political Economy of Race and Class in South Africa*. New York: Monthly Review Press.

Maldonado Denis, Manuel. 1972. *Puerto Rico: A Socio-Historic Interpretation*. New York: Random House.

————. 1978. *Puerto Rico y Estados Unidos: Emigración y Colonialismo*. Mexico: Siglo 21 Editores.

Maloney, Mike, et al. 1972. Urban Migrants. *People's Appalachia*, July.

Mamdani, Mahmood. 1972. *The Myth of Population Control: Family, Caste and Class in an Indian Village*. New York: Monthly Review Press.

————. 1974. *The Ideology of Population Control*. Bucharest: World Population Conference.

————. 1976. *Politics and Class Formation in Uganda*. New York: Monthly Review Press.

Mandel, Ernest. 1973. *Capitalism and Regional Disparities*. Trans. Ted Richmond and Jim Paterson. Toronto: New Hogtown Press.

Mandelbaum, David G. 1974. *Human Fertility in India: Social Components and Policy Perspectives*. Berkeley: University of California Press.

Marshall, Adriana. 1979. Immigrant Workers in the Buenos Aires Labor Market. *International Migration Review* 13(3).

Marshall, John F. 1972. "Culture and Contraception: Response Determinants to a Family Planning Program in a North Indian Village." Ph.D. dissertation, University of North Carolina.

Marx, Karl. 1967. *Capital*, vol. 1. New York: International Publishers.

Mass, Bonnie. 1976. *Population Target: The Political Economy of Population Control in Latin America*. Toronto: Women's Educational Press.

McWilliams, Carey. 1971. *Factories in the Field*. Santa Barbara, Calif.: Peregrine Publishers.

Medick, Hans. 1976. Proto-Industrial Family Economy: Structural Function of Household and Family During the Transition from Peasant Society to Industrial Capitalism. *Social History* 3:291-315.

Meek, Ronald, ed. 1971. *Marx and Engels on the Population Bomb*. Palo Alto, Calif.: Ramparts Press.

Meillassoux, Claude. 1972. From Reproduction to Production: A Marxist

Approach to Economic Anthropology. *Economy and Society* 6: 93-105.

Mencher, Joan. 1970. Family Planning in India: the Role of Class Values. *Family Planning Perspectives* 2(2):53-63.

Michaelson, Karen L. 1972. Caste, Class and Network in an Indian City. *Western Canadian Journal of Anthropology* 3(2).

————. 1976. Patronage, Mediators, and the Historical Context of Social Organization in Bombay. *American Ethnologist* 3(2):281-95.

Miernyk, William. 1975. Coal and the Future of the Appalachian Economy. *Appalachia* 9(2).

Millstone, James. 1972. East Kentucky Coal Makes Profit for Owners, Not Region. In *Appalachia in the Sixties*, eds. D. S. Walls and J. D. Stephenson. Lexington, Ky.: University Press of Kentucky.

Mintz, Sidney W. 1957. The Plantation as a Socio-cultural Type. *Plantation Systems of the New World*. Washington, D.C.: Pan American Union.

————. 1973. A Note on the Definition of Peasantries. *Journal of Peasant Studies* 1(1)91-106.

————. 1974a. *Caribbean Transformation*. Chicago: Aldine.

————. 1974b. The Rural Proletariat and the Problem of Rural Proletarian Consciousness. *Journal of Peasant Studies* 1(3):291-325. Also published in *Peasants and Proletarians*, eds. R. Cohen, et al. New York: Monthly Review Press, 1979.

Mishan, E. J., and Needleman, L. 1966. Immigration: Some Economic Effects. *Lloyds Bank Review* (London), no. 81.

Moore, D. 1981. The Only Child Phenomenon. *New York Times Magazine*, January 18, 1981.

Moore, K. A., and Hofferth, S. L. 1979. Women and Their Children. In *The Subtle Revolution: Women at Work*, ed. Ralph E. Smith. Washington, D.C.: Urban Institute.

Muller, C. 1978. Insurance Coverage of Abortion, Contraception, and Sterilization. *Family Planning Perspectives* 10(2):71-77.

NACLA. 1977. Caribbean Migration: Contract Labor in U.S. Agriculture. *NACLA Report on the Americas* 11(8).

Nag, Moni. 1980. How Modernization Can also Increase Fertility. *Current Anthropology* 21(5).

Nag, Moni, White, B. N. F., and Peet, R. Creighton. 1978. An Anthropological Approach to the Study of the Economic Value of Children in Java and Nepal. *Current Anthropology* 19(2).

Nathanson, C. A., and Becker, M. H. 1977. The Influence of Physicians' Attitudes on Abortion Performance, Patient Management, and Professional Fees. *Family Planning Perspectives* 9:158-63.

————. 1980. Obstetricians' Attitudes and Hospital Abortion Services. *Family Planning Perspectives* 12:26-32.

The New Internationalist. 1979. September, no. 77.

Newman, Monroe. 1972. *The Political Economy of Appalachia: A Case Study in Regional Integration.* Lexington, Mass.: D. C. Heath.

Newman, S. H., and Klein, Z. E. 1978. *Behavioral-Social Aspects of Contraceptive Sterilization.* Lexington, Mass.: Lexington Books.

Nikolinakos, Marios. 1975. Notes Towards a General Theory of Migration in Late Capitalism. *Race and Class* 17(1).

Norbeck, Edward. 1959. *Pineapple Town: Hawaii.* Berkeley: University of California Press.

Oliver, Douglas L. 1961. *The Pacific Islands.* New York: Doubleday.

Overbeek, J. 1974. *History of Population Theories.* Rotterdam: Rotterdam University Press.

————. 1976. The Population Challenge. *Contributions in Sociology* no. 19. Westport, Conn.: Greenwood Press.

Owens, Raymond. 1974. "Disguised Unemployment and Underemployment in Urban India." Paper read at the meetings of the American Anthropological Association, Mexico City.

Paine, Suzanne. 1974. *Exporting Workers: The Turkish Case.* Cambridge: Cambridge University Press.

Pajeska, Josef. 1974. Population and Development in Perspective with Particular Reference to the Second UN Development Decade. *The Population Debate,* vol. 1. New York: United Nations.

Patnaik, Utsa. 1972. On the Mode of Production in Indian Agriculture. *Economic and Political Weekly* (Bombay) 8(40).

People's Appalachian Research Collective. 1975. *Morgantown, West Virginia.*

Petchesky, Rosalind P. 1979a. Workers, Reproductive Hazards, and the Politics of Protection: An Introduction. *Feminist Studies* 5:233-45.

————. 1979b. Reproduction, Ethics and Public Policy: The Federal Sterilization Regulations. *The Hastings Center Report.*

————. 1981. Anti-Abortion, Anti-Feminism, and the Rise of the "New Right." *Feminist Studies* 7(2).

Perloff, Harvey S. 1950. *Porto Rico's Economic Future.* Chicago: University of Chicago Press.

Pico, Rafael. 1974. *Geography of Puerto Rico.* Chicago: Aldine.

Planlama, Kademesinde. 1961. Amik Ovasi Zirai. *Ekonomi Raporu* (Ankara).

Poffenberger, Thomas. 1975. *Fertility and Family Life in an Indian*

Village. Michigan Papers on South and Southeast Asia no. 10. Ann Arbor, Michigan.

Polgar, Steven. 1972. Population History and Population Policies from an Anthropological Perspective. *Current Anthropology* 13:203-11.

————. 1975. Birth Planning: Between Neglect and Coercion. In *Population and Social Organization,* ed. Moni Nag. The Hague: Mouton.

Poma, P. 1980. Tubal Sterilization and Later Hospitalization. *Journal of Reproductive Medicine* 25(5).

Porter, C. W., and Hulka, J. F. 1974. Female Sterilization in Current Clinical Practice. *Family Planning Perspectives* 6:30-38.

Pratt, W. F. 1975. "Sterilization in the United States: Preliminary Findings from the National Survey of Family Growth, 1973." Paper read at the Population Association of America, Seattle, Wash.

Presser, Harriet. 1978. Contraceptive Sterilization as a Grass-roots Response: A Comparative View of the Puerto Rican and United States Experience. In *Behavioral-Social Aspects of Contraceptive Sterilization,* eds. S. M. Newman and Z. E. Klein. Lexington, Mass.: Lexington Books.

————, and Bumpass, L. L. 1972. Demographic and Social Aspects of Contraceptive Sterilization in the United States: 1965-1970. In *Demographic and Social Aspects of Population Growth,* eds. C. F. Westoff and R. Parke, Jr. Washington, D.C.: U.S. Commission on Population and the American Future.

Primack, Phil. 1973. ARC Say Mountaineers Returning. *The Mountain Eagle* (Whiteburg, Ky.), Dec. 13, 1973.

Quintero Rivera, A. G. 1972. El Desarrollo de las Clases Sociales y los Conflictos Politicos en Puerto Rico. In *Problemas de Desigualdad Social en Puerto Rico,* eds. Rafael Ramirez, Carlos Buitrago Ortiz, and Barry Levine. Rio Piedras: Ediciones Libreria Internacional.

Rainwater, Lee. 1960. *And the Poor Get Children.* Chicago: Quadrangle.

Ramos, Carlos, and Henderson, Peta. 1975. Political Ideology and Population Policy in Puerto Rico. In *Topias and Utopias in Health,* eds. Stan Ingman and Anthony C. Thomas. The Hague: Mouton

Rand Daily Mail (Johannesburg). January 15, 1969.

————. April 18, 1970.

Rice, Otis. 1970. *The Allegheny Frontier: West Virginia Beginnings 1730-1830.* Lexington, Ky.: University Press of Kentucky.

Ridgeway, James. 1973. *The Struggle to Monopolize the World's Energy Resources.* New York: Mentor.

Rodinson, M. 1973. *Islam and Capitalism.* New York: Pantheon.

Rodney, Walter, 1972. *How Europe Underdeveloped Africa.* London: Bogle-Louverture Publications.

Rodriguez, Artemio P. 1935. *A Report Dealing with Labor Statistics, Cost of Living, Housing Conditions and Craftsmanship of Workers in Puerto Rico for the Fiscal Year 1933-34.* Government of Puerto Rico, Department of Labor Bulletin no. 6. San Juan: Bureau of Supplies, Printing and Transportation.

Rodriguez-Trias, H. 1978. Sterilization Abuse. *The Women's Center Reid Lectureship.* New York: Barnard College.

Rogers, Barbara. 1972. *South Africa, The Bantu Homelands.* London: International Defence and Aid.

Roseberry, William. 1976. Rent, Differentiation and the Development of Capitalism Among Peasants. *American Anthropologist* 78(1):45-58.

Rosenblum, Gerald. 1973. *Immigrant Workers.* New York: Basic Books.

Rothblatt, Donald. 1971. *Regional Planning: The Appalachian Experience.* Lexington, Mass.: D. C. Heath

Sadie, J. L. 1972. *Projections of the South African Population, 1970-2020.* Industrial Development Corporation, Ltd. Stellenbosch: University of Stellenbosch.

Sanjian, A. 1957. *The Sanjak of Alexandria (Hatay): A Study of Franco-Turco-Syrian Relations.* Ann Arbor, Mich.: University Microfilms.

Scrimshaw, S. C., and Pasquariella, B. 1970. Obstacles to Sterilization in One Community. *Family Planning Perspectives* 2:40-42.

Segal, Aaron. 1973. The Rich, the Poor, and Population. In *Population and Politics,* ed. Richard Clinton. Lexington, Mass.: Lexington Books.

Setai, Butuel. 1975. Recruiting Labor for the South African Mines at the Turn of the Twentieth Century. *Ufahamu* 5(3):144-59.

Shackelford, Laurel, and Weinberg, Bill. 1977. *Our Appalachia: An Oral History.* New York: Hill and Wang.

Silva Recio, L., Moscoso, T., Cruz, R., and Cobas, A. 1973. *Oportunidades de Empleo, Educación y Adiestramiento.* San Juan: Commonwealth of Puerto Rico.

Simkins, Charles, and Clarke, Duncan. 1978. *Structural Unemployment in Southern Africa.* Pietermaritzburg: University of Natal Press.

Simon, Julian L. 1974. *The Effects of Income on Fertility.* Chapel Hill: Carolina Population Center, University of North Carolina.

Smathers, Mike. 1973. Appalachia: Notes of a Native Son on Turning 31. *Mountain Life & Work* 49:19-22.

Spillius, James. 1957. Polynesian Experiment: Tikopia as Plantation Labor. *Progress* 46:91-96.

Stavenhagen, Rudolfo. 1968. Seven Fallacies About Latin America. In

Latin America, Reform or Revolution, eds. James Petras and Maurice Zeitlin. New York: Fawcett.

————. 1975. *Social Classes in Agrarian Societies*. New York: Anchor/Doubleday.

Stevenson, Robert F. 1968. *Population and Political Systems in Tropical Africa*. New York: Columbia University Press.

Stycos, J. M. 1955. *Family and Fertility in Puerto Rico: A Study of the Lower Income Group*. New York: Columbia University Press.

————. 1968. *Human Fertility in Latin America*. Ithaca, N.Y.: Cornell Universty Press.

Sullerot, E. 1971. *Woman, Society and Change*. New York: McGraw-Hill.

Sweezy, Paul M. 1968. *The Theory of Capitalist Development*. New York: Monthly Review Press.

Szentes, Tamas. 1973. *The Political Economy of Underdevelopment*. Budapest: Akademiai Kiado.

Tepperman, Lorne. 1979. *Malthus and a Contemporary Dilemma: The Social Limits to Growth*. Research paper no. 4, Structural Analysis Programme. Toronto: University of Toronto.

Thomas, Brinley. 1959. International Migration. In *The Study of Population*, eds. P. Hauser and O. D. Duncan. Chicago: University of Chicago Press.

————. 1961. *International Migration and Economic Development*. Geneva: UNESCO.

————. 1972. *Migration and Urban Development: A Reappraisal of British and American Long Cycles*. London: Metheun.

Thompson, Leonard, ed. 1960. *African Societies in Southern Africa*. New York: Praeger.

Transkei Study Project. 1976. *Transkei Independence*. National Union of South African Students, Wages and Economic Commission. Johannesburg: University of Witwatersrand.

Trussel, J., Menken, J., Lindheim, B. L., and Vaughan, B. 1980. The Impact of Restricting Medicaid Financing for Abortion. *Family Planning Perspectives* 12:120-30.

Tudiver, Neil. 1973. "Why Aid Doesn't Help: Organizing for Community Economic Development in Central Appalachia." Ph.D. dissertation, University of Michigan.

Tudiver, Sari. 1978a. "Central Appalachia: The Early Years, 1790-1870, The Political Economy of Mountain Isolation." Unpublished manuscript.

————. 1978b. "The Transformation of a Pre-Capitalist Mode of Pro-

duction: The Penetration of Industrial Capitalism into Central Appalachia, 1870-1914." Unpublished manuscript.

Turner, Louis. 1973. *Multinational Companies and the Third World.*
New York: Hill and Wang.

United Nations. 1971. *Basic Facts and Figures on South Africa.* Unit on
Apartheid, Notes and Documents no. 7/71.

——. 1977. *Demographic Yearbook.*

——. 1978. *Demographic Yearbook.*

——, ECA (Economic Commission for Africa). 1975. *Demographic
Handbook for Africa.*

——, ECLA (Economic Commission for Latin America). 1972. *The
Economic Development of Latin America in the Post-War Period.*
CN.12/659.

——, FAO (Food and Agricultural Organization). 1978. *Ideas and
Action for Development.* Apartheid Bulletin 1267/8. Rome.

——, ILO (International Labor Organization). 1960. *Why Labor
Leaves the Land.* Geneva.

——. *Yearbook of Labor Statistics.* Geneva.

——, UNESCO (UN Emergency Services for Children Organization). 1956. *Social Implications of Industrialization and Urbanization in South Africa South of the Sahara.*

U.S. Department of Health, Education and Welfare. 1978. *Health: United
States, 1978.* DHEW publication no. (PHS) 78-1232.

——. 1978. *Surgical Operations in Short-Stay Hospitals, United
States, 1975.* DHEW publication no. (PHS) 78-1785.

——. 1978. *Advancedata from Vital and Health Statistics of the
National Center for Health Statistics.* DHEW publication nos. 36
and 40.

U.S. Department of Health and Human Services. 1979. *Surgical Sterilization Surveillance: Hysterectomy in Women Aged 15-44.* Center
for Disease Control.

U.S. Immigrant Commission. 1911. *Abstract of Statistical Review of
Immigration to the United States, 1820-1911.* U.S. Government
Printing Office.

Unterhaler, Beryl. 1955. "A Study of Fertility and Infant Mortality in an
Urban African Community." M.A. thesis, University of Witwatersrand.

van der Merwe, P. J. 1976. Black Employment Problems in South Africa.
Finance and Trade Review 12(2):50.

van Rensburg, Nic J. 1972. *Population Explosion in Southern Africa.*
Pretoria: J. L. van Schaik.

Vayda, Andrew P., and Rappaport, Roy A. 1970. Island Cultures. In

Cultures of the Pacific, eds. Harding and Wallace. New York: Free Press.

Vázquez Calzada, José. 1964. "The Demographic Evolution of Puerto Rico." Ph.D. dissertation, University of Chicago.

————. 1968. Fertility Decline in Puerto Rico: Extent and Causes. *Demography* 5(2):855-65.

Verhoef, Mary. 1919. *The Kentucky Mountains: Transportation and Commerce, 1750-1911.* Publication 26. Louisville, Ky.: Filson Club.

Villareal, Sofia Mendez. 1973. La Capacidad del Sector Industrial para Generar Ocupación. *Demografia Económica* 7(1):96-105.

Wallerstein, Immanuel. 1974. *The Modern World System.* New York: Academic Press.

Ward, Anthony. 1975a. European Capitalism's Reserve Army. *Monthly Review* 27(6).

————. 1975b. European Migratory Labor: A Myth of Development. *Monthly Review* 27(7).

Wells, John Calhoun, Jr. 1977. "Poverty Amidst Riches: Why People Are Poor in Appalachia." Ph.D. dissertation, Rutgers University.

Westoff, C. F., and Ryder, N. B. 1977. *The Contraceptive Revolution.* Princeton: Princeton University Press.

———— and McCarthy, J. 1979. Sterilization in the United States. *Family Planning Perspectives* 11:147-52.

Wessman, James W. 1976. "Demographic Evolution and Agrarian Structure of a Sugar Cane Region in Puerto Rico." Ph.D. dissertation, University of Connecticut.

————. 1977. Towards a Marxist Demography: A Comparison of Puerto Rican Landowners, Peasants and Rural Proletarians. *Dialectical Anthropology* 2(3):223-33.

————. 1978a. The Sugar Cane Hacienda in the Agrarian Structure of Southwestern Puerto Rico in 1902. *Revista/Review Interamericana* 8(1):99-115.

————. 1978b. Division of Labor, Capital Accumulation and Commodity Exchange on a Puerto Rican Sugar Cane Hacienda. *Social and Economic Studies* 27.

————. 1980a. Theory of Value, Labor Process and Price Formation: A Study of a Puerto Rican Sugarcane Hacienda. *American Ethnologist* 7(3):479-92.

————. 1980b. The Demographic Structure of Slavery in Puerto Rico: Some Aspects of Agrarian Capitalism in the Late Nineteenth Century. *Journal of Latin American Studies* 12(2):271-89.

————. 1980c. The Puerto Rican Circuit. Review of Labor Migration

Under Capitalism: The Puerto Rican Experience, eds. History Task Force, Centro de Estudios Puertorriqueños, City University of New York. *Caribbean Review* 9(3):42-43.

————. 1981. *Anthropology and Marxism*. Cambridge, Mass.: Schenkman.

Wheeless, C. R. 1970. Outpatient Tubal Sterilization. *Obstetrics and Gynecology* 36(2).

White, Benjamin. 1973. Demand for Labor and Population Growth. *Human Ecology* 1:217-44.

Wilson, Charles. 1954. *The History of Unilever*, vol. 1. London: Cassell & Co.

Wright, M. J. 1979. Reproductive Hazards and "Protective" Discrimination. *Feminist Studies* 5:302-9.

Wylie, E. McL. 1977. *All About Voluntary Sterilization: The Revolutionary New Birth Control Method for Men and Women*. New York: Berkley.

Index